Restorative Faith
Christianity for the 21st Century Rationalist

by Alexander Lang

RESTORATIVE FAITH

CHRISTIANITY FOR THE 21ST CENTURY RATIONALIST

by Alexander Lang

Restorative Faith

Dedicated to Courtney

The most brilliant, talented and loving woman
I have ever known.
Without you, none of this would have been possible.

His crime was his belief

the universe does not revolve around

the human being: God is no

fixed point or central government, but rather is

poured in waves through all things. All things

move. "If God is not the soul itself, He is

the soul of the soul of the world."

Such was his heresy.

Excerpt from *What He Thought*
By Heather McHugh

TABLE OF CONTENTS

PART 3: JESUS

INTERPRETATIVE INTERLUDE

READER NOTES

Unless otherwise specified, all scripture references are from the NRSV translation.

Date references are B.C.E. (Before the Common Era) and C.E. (Common Era) in lieu of B.C. (Before Christ) and A.D. (Anno Domini—the year of our Lord).

Academic references have been placed at the end of the book and are organized by section.

The owl icon highlights information or arguments that are critical to the central thesis of the book.

† Provides cross-references for concepts covered in previous sections of the book.

About the cover photo: In Japan, there is an art called kintsugi. The fragments of a broken piece of pottery are mended together with a gold resin. Such is the purpose of this book for those whose faith has been broken.

ACKNOWLEDGMENTS

This book would not have been possible without the support of many colleagues, friends and family. I am greatly indebted to all of them. First and foremost, I want to thank the Rev. Dr. Barbara Gorsky for inspiring me to put pen to paper. If it weren't for her persistent encouragement that I transform the thoughts from my sermons into a book, I never would have endeavored to create such a work.

I would also like to thank my research assistant, Rebekah Anderson, who spent many hours helping me comb through endless volumes of scholarly research. Rebekah is a budding scholar in her own right and I feel privileged that she so willingly offered her time and wisdom to my efforts.

The content of the book was strengthened by the many readers who took time to evaluate various revisions. Perhaps the most important of these readers was my friend Steve McMullen, who spent numerous hours helping me to narrow the focus and purpose of my writing.

I would also like to thank Bryan Ho, Dan Grippo, Liz Peterson, Nancy Pardo, Emily Alford, Doug Hiskes, Mario Alberico, Ken Hockenberry, Francie Taylor, Kristie Cerniglia, Larry Olson and Judi Holmes for providing critical feedback on the logic, substance and order of the book. By reading my book in detail and highlighting different issues within the overall manuscript, they helped to strengthen the language of my arguments.

The streamlined visual layout of the book and the cover were created by Laurie Ruhlin. Her expertise in graphic design has enhanced a number of my sermon series and I feel honored that she contributed her immense talent to this project.

Finally, I would like to thank my family, Courtney, Elijah and Lucas, for giving me the necessary hours outside of church to write this book. Thank you for your kindness and eternal understanding, even when I felt like I was never going to cross the finish line. You mean the world to me and I love you to the ends of the earth!

PREFACE

In 2012, one of my wife's good friends from high school, Melissa, called me and asked if I would be willing to perform her wedding ceremony. I was very happy to do the wedding, but I was a little surprised that she asked me. Melissa grew up attending a very conservative church, the kind that believes everything portrayed in the Bible happened exactly the way it is written. Every person is real. Every story is completely factual. Since this is not my view of the Bible, I assumed that Melissa would ask a pastor from her home church to perform the ceremony.

I soon found out why Melissa was asking me. She no longer attended the church of her youth. Over the last several years, Melissa had come to the conclusion that many of the things she had been taught by the church no longer made sense. She had spent time travelling the world and had been exposed to a variety of different cultures. These cultures adhered to vastly different belief systems than the one she had been taught. Melissa had been told that without faith in Jesus, a human being's soul was damned to hell forever. She had trouble reconciling this belief with the fact that most of the people she encountered were good, honest, loving people. Would God really send them to hell if they didn't believe Jesus was their savior?

When Melissa returned from her journeys, she also returned to her church and posed this question. Not surprisingly, she received the exact same answers that she had been taught as a teenager. The only problem was that those answers, which had made so much sense earlier in her life, were no longer sufficient. Melissa decided that perhaps she needed to switch churches. She began attending another popular church in the area, but again, the answers were always the same. Slowly Melissa came to realize that the institution to which she had dedicated her life was rapidly losing credibility in her mind. Her faith, which had been the center of her life, was falling apart right before her eyes.

Melissa decided that she had to make a choice: she could continue to attend church and pretend that she believed in something that no longer seemed legitimate or she could be honest with how she felt and abandon the church entirely. Like so many people in our modern world, Melissa chose abandonment. I will admit that Melissa's decision left me unsettled. Not because I believed she was going to hell, but because unlike the vast majority of people who label themselves Christians, Melissa actually walked the walk. She was not a hypocrite. If you needed help, she would drop everything to be there for you. She was a true servant to those who needed her. Indeed, she still is. Nothing has changed in that regard. The only difference is that Melissa no longer identifies with the Christian faith.

Melissa's story is not uncommon. The current trend in most North American churches is rapid decline. Countless people who were raised in the Christian religion have abandoned the faith. Somewhere along the way, they came to the realization that the things they were taught in church just didn't add up in the real world. When their faith disintegrated, they were unable to put the pieces back together in a way that made sense, so they simply chose to leave it all behind.

At the time Melissa was transitioning out of the church, I kept wishing I had a resource at my disposal that would answer those questions that seemed unanswerable, but no such resource existed. That is why I have written this book. I want to provide the glue that will allow those whose faith has been shattered by the limitations of conservative Christianity to piece it back together in a way that not only makes sense, but is truly believable. I want to give people a new option; a different way of understanding this great and ancient faith. I want to ensure that Christianity survives beyond the 21st century, which won't happen if we keep alienating amazing people like Melissa.

INTRODUCTION

Hello. My name is Alex and I'm a pastor. Many people I meet quickly lose interest in speaking to me after learning that fact. That's because the word *pastor* has more than one meaning in American culture today. Depending on whom you ask, a pastor can be anything from an agent for positive change in the world to a person who wastes an hour of your time on Sunday morning to a narrow-minded bigot to a child-molesting predator.

By proclaiming that I am a pastor, I take my place next to all of them—the good and the bad. The problem is that the reputation of those who tarnish the profession has become the dominant perception of what it means to be a pastor. Their teachings and their actions have taken such a massive toll on the public consciousness that many people have chosen to simply ignore Christianity and the church in favor of living their lives as they see fit. Personally, I don't blame them. In my experience, the negatives of going to church can often outweigh the positives. Let me give you an example.

Assume for a moment that you wake up one day and you feel a nagging sensation that something is missing from your life. You're not entirely sure *what* is missing, but your mind keeps drifting towards the idea that perhaps you should go to church. However, before you assent to this idea, you start to play out the scenario in your mind. Let's say you go church. Let's say you like what you see. Let's say you discover that church/God/spirituality is the missing piece in your life—how does that realization impact your life?

You happen to be a person who thinks science offers a lot of answers about the mysteries in the world. For instance, you studied evolution in high school. In recent years, you have read some articles here and there about new discoveries and the theory seems pretty sound. But if you go to church, you're going to be listening to the Bible, which says that the Earth was created in six days. Do you have to abandon your belief in evolution in order to embrace this missing piece of your life? Do you have to believe that the earth is 6,000 years old or can you still trust the scientists who study geology and astrophysics and claim the earth is 4.5 billion years old?

Furthermore, you're kind of partial to the idea that all religions contain some truth. But many of the church-going people you know tend to believe that Christianity is the only true faith. They say that you can only go to heaven if you believe in Jesus. In fact, they say that if you don't believe what the Bible says, word for word, then you will spend eternity in hell. If you start going to church, will you be obligated to tell your Jewish, Muslim and atheist friends they have to convert or suffer the consequences?

Thinking about your multi-cultural friends causes your mind to wander to your gay friends. A lot of the Christians you see in the media seem to think that homosexuality is sinful. They claim that God says in the Bible that people who engage in homosexual behavior should be put to death! But you know a number of gay people who are in committed, loving relationships. Come to think of it, your gay friends seem to be faring better than your heterosexual friends in terms of relationship longevity. If church becomes an important part of your life, will you have to tell your gay friends that God wants nothing to do with them? Will you have to encourage them to change their sexual identity so they can go to heaven? You never thought there was anything all that bad about being gay, but will that have to change if you start going to church?

But let's say that the church you attend believes in the science of evolution, accepts that other religious traditions are valid approaches to understanding God and doesn't discriminate against the gay community. You are still faced with a perception issue. When you make church a regular part of your life, you are assuming the label of Christian whether you like it or not. Therefore, even if your Christian community is very accepting of people and views that have been traditionally excluded by the church, do you really want to spend your time explaining to your non-religious friends that your Christianity is different from so many others? Wouldn't it just be easier to remain as you are rather than to assume this new identity that comes with so many challenges and problems?

If it were me—lying in my bed on Sunday morning weighing all the pros and cons of church participation—I would choose to roll over and go back to sleep. It is far easier to simply live with the feeling that something is missing from my life than to go through all the hassle of exploring what it would take to find spiritual fulfillment in the church. But most people don't lie in bed weighing the pros and cons of church participation. Most people don't systematically analyze their reasons for not pursing a religious identity. They just know intuitively that organized religion, it doesn't matter which kind, is not for them. They know that whatever answers religion might provide to existential questions are not worth the cost. Besides, if they require answers to difficult questions about God, morality and the afterlife, there's always Google.

And yet, even though I understand all the reasons why people choose not to engage with Christianity, I am still a pastor. I believe that Christianity is a religion that is full of potential, but to find that potential, we have to work our way through landmines that threaten to shatter our faith: Why should I care about the Bible when it's full of mythology? Why does a good God allow evil to thrive in the world? Do I have to believe in Jesus to go to heaven? Do I have to believe he was born of a virgin? The goal of this book is not to avoid these landmines, but to set them off, one at a time. We're going to break down Christianity into its most basic parts and rebuild it into something actually worth believing.

Our journey will begin with an effort to disassemble the Bible. Through Chapters 1 and 2, we will look at the various ways the Bible is interpreted by Christians in the U.S. and provide an alternative that is compatible with contemporary reality. This new approach to the Bible will allow us to reconfigure our understanding of God in Chapters 3 and 4. With this foundation in place, the remaining six chapters will be dedicated to wrestling Jesus away from the outmoded doctrines of the Christian faith that are strangling his message. Together, we are going to breathe fresh life into this ancient religion that is relevant to our lives in the present and vital for a sustainable future.

— PART ONE —

THE BIBLE

Restorative Faith

— CHAPTER ONE —

HOW DID WE GET HERE?

A STRANGE COINCIDENCE

In June of 1998, I had just graduated from high school and was nervously staring at a thick packet I had recently received in the mail. I had been accepted at Rice University. On paper, I should not have been attending Rice. I was not a valedictorian or salutatorian like many of my peers there. I was not particularly gifted musically, nor had I done anything noteworthy in my extracurricular activities. I was, however, a marginally talented swimmer and thanks to the fact that Rice did not have a well-funded men's swim team, I was a perfect fit. I had done well enough academically to pass their athletic admissions standards and I was just fast enough to warrant their attention. In other words, I snuck in beneath the radar.

When I arrived at Rice, I met my roommates, two people who would significantly alter the course of my life, Ethan and Grant.* All three of us would end up working in the church, albeit, in radically different areas and with radically different views of Christianity. Ethan came to Rice to study music and is presently one of the top improvisational organists in the country. Grant came to Rice to

---

* Names have been changed to protect their identity.

study chemical engineering and is now a missionary teaching students in East Asia. I came to Rice to study electrical engineering and ended up graduating with a degree in religious studies. My transformation began with a conversation I had with Grant during my first week at Rice.

We were hanging out in our room when a senior peeked her head in our door to see how we were getting along. I noticed that she had henna markings on her hands. I asked where the markings had come from and she explained that she had just been to a wedding for a family member. I was curious about her religious background. She explained that her family was Hindu, which led all of us to discuss our religious identities. I had grown up attending a Presbyterian church, but I knew almost nothing about the Bible and did not identify myself as Christian. Grant had grown up Baptist, knew a lot about the Bible and very much identified as a Christian.

Eventually, I took out a piece of paper and drew two dots at opposite ends. One dot represented God; the other dot represented humans. I drew several different lines from one dot to the next. I explained that I believed there were many paths people could take to find God. The important thing to me was that you be on a path

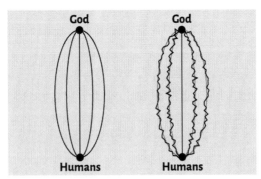

to find God. The senior seemed to agree with me, but Grant did not. Grant took the pen and marked through all the lines except the one in the middle. Then he said, "What if there is only one way to get to God? What does that do to all the other paths? It makes them wrong." I asked him to explain why he believed there was only one path to God. Grant then quoted scripture from the Bible: "I am the way, and the truth, and the life. No one comes to the Father except through me." *(Jn. 14:6)*

If you've ever had someone quote scripture at you, then you know it changes the nature of the discussion. First of all, you can no longer simply talk about abstract ideas of who you feel God to be. We are now dealing with specifics because scriptures tend to define how a religion approaches God. Second, if you are not well versed in the scriptures of the religion being quoted, then it becomes difficult for you to remain in the discussion. Scripture quotation is often used to make a statement—I know something you don't know and, therefore, you need to cede the argument because you are not as well-versed as I am.

Grant knew I had no background in the Bible and, by quoting that verse from the gospel of John, he was hoping to put an end to the discussion. He was using what he considered to be a trump card because, from his perspective, the scripture gave him authority that I did not possess. The scriptures, by supporting Grant's belief, seemed to invalidate my argument in his eyes. This conversation marked my introduction to what is commonly called biblical literalism—the notion that, by taking the words of the Bible at face value, the basic meaning is simple enough to be understood by anyone.

I have always wondered why I was paired up with Grant because I didn't identify myself as Christian at the time I filled out my housing form. It must have been because I stated that I enjoyed religious discussions. I guess that made me the perfect choice to be paired with one of the most conservative Christians on Rice's campus. Little did Grant know that every time he used scripture as a weapon to prove his point, he was only inspiring me to become his opposite. I eventually decided to become a pastor for those who saw the world not as black and white, but in shades of grey.

TURNING BACK THE CLOCK

The beauty of living with Grant was that our close proximity provided plenty of opportunity to challenge one another's religious beliefs. Through these debates, I not only strengthened my own arguments, but I also gained important clarity concerning Grant's perceptions of the world. I came to appreciate that, deep down, Grant had good intentions. He believed he was doing something very important for the world. He believed that God had given him a job. He was trying to save me, and everyone else he encountered, from going to hell.

Think about it from his perspective. What if everywhere you traveled you encountered people who you believed were destined for hell? Every time you ate at a restaurant, every time you sat in a theater, every time you walked down the street, you were crossing paths with people who were going to suffer eternal torment...unless you intervened. If you could just speak to them, talk to them about the scriptures, guide them to understand what you had come to understand—that Jesus was the only way to go to heaven—then perhaps one less person would suffer the agony that awaited them in the afterlife.

That's a really hard way to live, thinking that other people's salvation rests on your shoulders. That's a lot of responsibility. Why do people like Grant think this makes sense? To answer this question, I need to turn back the clock about 500 years because Christianity hasn't always been this way.

Martin Luther was born November 10, 1483 in Germany. Luther originally went to school to study law, but dropped out to study theology and philosophy. Luther's father, who was funding his education, was not particularly happy about this decision, because there was not a lot of money to be made in theology. A few years into his studies, Luther was travelling from his home in Eisleben to the University of Erfurt when a thunderstorm suddenly came upon him. When lightning struck a nearby tree Luther exclaimed, "Help! Saint Anna, I will become a monk!"[1.1] I don't know if a bad thunderstorm would be enough to make me consider becoming a monk, but it was enough for him. Apparently, the storm subsided and Luther kept his word. He dropped out of school again and joined a monastery.

There are many different kinds of monks in the Catholic Church, each with their own traditions, but the kind that Luther joined was an order founded on the teachings of a man named Augustine (354-430 C.E.). Augustine was an incredibly smart man and is responsible for creating much of the thinking that the church uses today. Because Augustine was so focused on propagating the Catholic faith and teachings, Augustinians were known for bringing Catholicism and education to people all around the world. Augustinian Monks were expected to be like their founder—devoted to God and intelligent. This describes Martin Luther to a T.

Martin Luther was a man of deep faith, but he struggled with his worthiness as a human being. He felt himself always to be lacking in his devotion to God. He used to perform excruciating penance for what he perceived to be his inability to lead a godly life. He would walk upstairs on his knees, sleep out in the snow and cloister himself in his room, fasting until he was so weak he would pass out.[1,2] But what Luther found most soothing to his sense of self-loathing was reading the Bible. Luther was unusual in this way.

This might come as a surprise, but most monks in Luther's day were not that interested in the Bible. Catholicism is not built on the Bible so much as on biblical tradition. Catholicism is similar to Judaism in this way. For the Jewish people, the scriptures are important, but equally important are the traditions of rabbinical interpretation that clarify those scriptures. From the Jewish perspective, great rabbis are so connected to God that their insights into the scriptures hold as much merit as the scriptures themselves. Jewish people assume that by learning the traditions of the rabbis, you will eventually learn the scriptures because the foundations of their teachings are in the scriptures.

The same line of thinking is prevalent in the Catholic Church. Catholics tend to believe that the teachings of church fathers like Augustine who have illuminated those scriptures are just as important as the Bible. Augustinian monks, for example, assume that the best way to learn the scriptures is by studying the teachings of Augustine. Put simply, the Bible was thought to be a good starting point for understanding God, but great thinkers had helped us take our understanding of God to the next level. All this to say that Luther's preoccupation with the Bible was considered to be rather odd by his fellow monks.

Luther read the Bible so obsessively that he ended up memorizing large portions of the scriptures. In the midst of this process, he began to realize that a lot of the practices of those in leadership in the Catholic Church had strayed from the core teachings of the Bible. Perhaps the best example was the sale of indulgences. The Catholic Church had developed the idea that when people die, their souls do not go directly to heaven, but first must be purified from sin. This time of purification became known as purgatory, and the Catholic Church promoted the idea that if you paid a certain amount of money, you would receive an indulgence, a reduction of the time your soul would spend in purgatory.

Luther realized that the sale of indulgences was in direct conflict with the teachings of the New Testament. Luther read a passage that said, "For there is no distinction, since all have sinned and fall short of the glory of God; they are now justified by his grace as a gift, through the redemption that is in Christ Jesus..." *(Rm. 3:22-24)* In other words, no one is able to earn forgiveness. If redemption is a gift given to humans by God, then the selling of indulgences makes no sense.[13] One cannot buy their way into heaven.

This one revelation caused Luther to begin to wonder how many other practices in the Catholic Church were not promoted by the scriptures. Quite a few, as he came to find. Luther came up with 95 different points of conflict between the teachings of the Catholic Church and the Bible. Luther's hope was that once they were aware of these discrepancies, church officials would recognize how far they had strayed and mend their ways. Unfortunately, this did not happen.

Upon receiving Luther's document, Pope Leo X became enraged. Leo knew that if these ideas got out, the church could no longer sell indulgences, which was Leo's primary source for funding the rebuilding of St. Peter's Basilica in Rome.[1.4] Leo invited Luther to come to Rome for the purpose of placing him on trial so that he could be excommunicated for heresy. The side benefit of being excommunicated was that Luther could be put to death, adding extra incentive for Luther's followers to distance themselves from his teachings. Luther, not surprisingly, declined the invitation.

The Pope's unwillingness to consider the merits of Luther's statement put Luther in a difficult position. He loved the Catholic Church and wanted to see it changed. However, over time he slowly came to realize this would never happen. Therefore, he decided it was time to break away from the Roman Catholic Church and create something new. This movement became known as Protestantism because those who adhered to this new form of Christianity were actively protesting against the rule of the Holy Roman Empire.[1.5] This era in the church's history became known as the Reformation because Luther was trying to re-form or re-mold the church.

The new church that Luther envisioned was grounded in those 95 criticisms that he had sent to Rome. Luther's movement began to gain steam because the ideas within his paper struck a chord with the public. He was able to tap into and articulate many of the problems that people felt were endemic to Catholicism. Furthermore, Luther was offering an alternative to Catholicism that was attractive—being saved by grace, through faith. In other words, you didn't need to pay for your salvation. All you needed to do to find redemption was believe in Jesus, and God would do the rest.

As Luther's popularity grew, people wanted to know how he had arrived at his conclusions. The answer, of course, is that Luther took the time to read the Bible for himself. Luther began telling people that they should read the Bible for themselves in order to determine whether or not his conclusions were correct. But there were a couple of problems with this idea. First of all, the Bible was not readily available in those days. Even though Gutenberg had started printing the Bible on his printing press almost 70 years before (which reduced the price significantly from the hand-written copies), Bibles were still very expensive. Second, you had to know how to read Latin, and unless you were educated, you probably lacked that ability. Therefore, Luther set out to create a German translation of the Bible that was affordable so the average person could read the scriptures for themselves.[1.6]

Luther's motto became *sola scriptura* or *scripture alone*. By making the Bible accessible to everyone, Luther believed that Christianity could get back to its original roots. This new form of church was no longer bound by the old customs and doctrines. The Bible now took center stage and everything in the church revolved around the scriptures. If it wasn't in the Bible, it wasn't in the church. The Bible was so important to Luther that he believed by simply reading the Bible one could be converted to Christianity. Luther was so focused on having people read the Bible for themselves that he hardly noticed what was happening all around him. People were reading the Bible and coming to their own conclusions—including conclusions that were very different from Luther's.

It's hard to overstate the impact of the read-it-yourself Bible movement during the Reformation. The translation of the Bible into everyday language is what changed the landscape of Christianity in ways that nobody could have predicted. Now that anyone could pick up the Bible and begin reading it for themselves, Christianity started taking on every conceivable shape and form because every person who read the Bible saw something different. Prior to the Reformation, there were two main lines of Christianity—Roman Catholic and Greek Orthodox. Over the next 500 years, after Luther sparked the Reformation, the Protestant movement grew to more than 9,000 different denominations.[1.7] It seems that when you allow people to read the Bible for themselves, they often disagree about what it means.

BUT IT SAYS IN THE BIBLE...

Have you ever been walking down the street and off in the distance you see some guy standing on a wooden crate, a megaphone in one hand and a Bible in another, screaming about how you need to believe in Jesus or you will go to hell? You can thank Luther for that wonderfully uncomfortable moment and for being late to wherever you were going since you probably had to take a detour to avoid being berated. Luther had good intentions when he began his movement, but he could never have anticipated the Pandora's box he was opening.

Even though the Catholic Church had a lot of problems and was abusing its power, it understood something that Luther failed to grasp—the Bible is not an easy book to read. One of the reasons why the Catholic Church never bothered to translate the scriptures into the language of the people is because reading and understanding the Bible requires a good deal of education and interpretive guidance. Since most people lacked that, expressing faith through easy-to-understand rituals made things a lot cleaner for the average person in the pew. Luther changed all that and today, when the average person reads the Bible, they are usually misinterpreting what they are reading.

I often tell the people in my church that one cannot open the Bible and read it like a novel. Anyone who tells you that understanding the Bible is easy is lying. If you've never read the Bible before and try to read it from cover to cover, you will come to the end and think, "Why would anybody in their right mind build their lives around this book?" It makes very little sense. It jumps from one event to another with no explanation. The first part of the book seems very different from the last part of the book. Some of it seems like history, other parts like poetry, and still other parts are reminiscent of mythology. Aside from the benefit of understanding how literature draws inspiration from the biblical stories, any reasonable person would set it aside and move on with life.

But there is one tiny problem—Christians say that the Bible was inspired by God. Some people even believe that God literally wrote the Bible, word for word. You can see how this would make things a little more complicated. If the Bible were just any book, then you could easily toss it aside. But if the Bible was written by God, then all of a sudden the Bible has much greater significance. Indeed, this is why people devote their entire lives to reading the Bible over and over again. They believe that by studying the Bible, they can grow closer to God. Of course, Muslims think this way about the Quran and Hindus of the Vedas. This is why some religious people can seem so arrogant. They believe they have access to something directly from God that provides them with insight into the universe which others do not possess.

This is why the guy on the street corner yelling at you is so sure of himself. He believes what he read in the Bible is the capital 'T' Truth. When something is capital 'T' Truth, it means that it applies universally to every person in the world whether you like it or not. His goal is to wake you up to that Truth so that you do not suffer the consequences. But why is he so convinced he is right? Why does he think he has access to the Truth as compared to other people around the world who hold similar convictions, but for very different reasons?

Well, it comes down to an experience. That guy on the street corner had an experience in his life that convinced him that this whole Bible thing has merit. In fact, it had such a profound impact on his life that he believes that you need to have a similar experience. That's why he is yelling at you. That's why he is willing to disrupt the public. He wants you to understand that everything can change if you are willing to embrace his version of God. But you didn't get that from his ranting and raving, did you? All you could see was that this guy seemed really pissed off—so pissed off that you were eager to cross the street to avoid him. Why is there such a disconnect between people who have genuinely good intentions in their hearts and the vitriolic rhetoric that comes out of their mouths? This disconnect exists because of the *way* these people read the Bible.

CONTEXT IS EVERYTHING

Imagine that you are a consultant with a very prestigious consulting firm. Business owners call you to fix their businesses when things aren't going well. Your job is to assess their situation and advise them how to change their business model so they can become profitable. You are so good at what you do that I have hired you to help me figure out how to become profitable. Below is my situation explained in two different ways. Use your best judgment to help me understand what to do.

EXAMPLE 1: I own two businesses. My original business nets $200,000 in profit every month. I was so successful with the first business that I started a second. Unfortunately, my second business has produced a net loss of $200,000 every month. My second business is eating up all the profit from my first business. What do you think I should do? Well, any reasonable, rational consultant, like yourself, would advise me to eliminate my second business. If it is doing that poorly, then obviously I should throw in the towel and focus on the first business.

EXAMPLE 2: I own two businesses. My original business creates a biological nerve agent that is purchased by governments all over the world as part of their chemical weapons arsenal. This business nets $200,000 in profit every month, but the United Nations is working towards implementing an international weapons treaty that would make the sale of such nerve agents illegal. I was so successful with the first business that I started a second business—a biotech company that is working on a cure for angiosarcoma, a rare type of breast cancer that is often fatal. Unfortunately, my second business has produced a net loss of $200,000 every month, although the scientists working on this cancer are closing in fast on a cure. My second business is eating up all the profit from my first business. What do you think I should do? Well, any reasonable, rational consultant, like yourself, would advise me to use all the profits from my first business to make my second business as successful as possible. If my first business is going to be declared illegal, then it is obvious I should throw in the towel, and focus on the second business.

In example 1, you looked at my situation and made a recommendation based on the available information. It made sense for you to recommend closing the second business because it was destroying all the profit from the first business. But in example 2, your recommendation changed. Why? Because you were working with a lot more information. You understood the larger context of my businesses and realized that the second business was my only viable option for moving forward. This is what having more relevant information does. It allows you make a more educated assessment of the situation in front of you. Conversely, the less information you possess, the more likely you are to interpret the situation incorrectly.

This same principle applies to the Bible. Let's take the verse that was quoted to me by my roommate at Rice University: "I am the way, and the truth, and the life. No one comes to the Father except through me." This verse comes from the Gospel of John 14:6. Many people who pick up the Bible and read this verse assume that Jesus is saying that if you don't believe in him, you can't be with God. That's how the guy on the corner reads this verse and that's why he feels compelled to let you know, in no uncertain terms, that without Jesus you are screwed.

But there's more to this verse than meets the eye. The Gospel of John was written and edited between 90 and 110 C.E. Just to be clear, that is a minimum of 60 years after Jesus' death.[1.8] In other words, this gospel was not written as a firsthand account by one of Jesus' disciples, as many Christians assume (we'll talk more about that later). Rather, this gospel was written by Christians two or three generations removed from Jesus' actual life. They wrote this gospel because of a particular situation that arose within their community of Jewish-Christians. What was this situation? Glad you asked.

It's important to understand that the earliest followers of Jesus were Jews. Although the contemporary Christian church is comprised almost exclusively of non-Jews, the early church was the opposite. The earliest Christians were Jews who worshiped in synagogues and believed Jesus of Nazareth was the messiah. The vast majority of Jews, however, did not believe Jesus was the messiah. In fact, many Jews were still waiting for the messiah to come and believed God would be sending him soon.

You can understand how this would cause a lot of friction. Most Jews who believed in Jesus realized early on that staying in the synagogues simply wasn't going to work. It became clear they were going to have to become a separate entity, existing apart from traditional Judaism. The people who wrote John's gospel were some of the last Jews to try to make the Jesus movement work in the synagogues. When the Jewish leaders finally had enough of hearing about Jesus, they expelled this group of Jesus-believing Jews. Their expulsion inspired them to write the story of Jesus that is known as the Gospel of John.[1.9]

John's community was deeply hurt by being severed from the synagogue. John's is the only gospel where the term "the Jews" is used as a derogatory insult against the leaders in the synagogue. The authors believed in Jesus, but also loved Judaism. They felt betrayed by their own. Some scholars have speculated that John's gospel was written as a last ditch effort to convince fellow Jews from the synagogues that they should follow Jesus. Hence, when we get to the verse, "I am the way, and the truth, and the life. No one comes to the Father except through me," you can see why the authors would want these words coming out of Jesus' mouth. They were writing this verse and many others in John's gospel to say, "Expel us if you want, but we're right and you're wrong. In the end, there's no way for a Jew to get to God without Jesus."

Did Jesus ever say those words? Probably not. Parts of John's gospel seems to be designed to convince those on the fence that coming over to the Jesus side is worth the effort.[1.10] That's why John's gospel is filled with some extreme language. John's gospel is the most quoted gospel by street preachers because the statements are biting and invoke a very clear us vs. them dichotomy. But is this dichotomy real? Did Jesus really believe he was the only way to God? Did Jesus, a Jew, ever intend for his movement to be so divisive that it would cause a schism within Judaism and result in an entirely new religion—a new religion that would reject the very people who started his movement?

Jesus undoubtedly wanted to reform certain aspects of Judaism, but I find it hard to believe Jesus would have wanted his followers to abandon Judaism completely. But that's what ultimately happened as Christianity evolved over the first century. Thanks to John's community, words were placed in Jesus' mouth that I believe Jesus himself would have been shocked to hear. These words caused Christianity to become gradually disconnected from its founder's religious identity.

THE PROBLEM

Having dissected this one verse from the Bible, you can begin to understand why picking up the Bible and simply reading the words on the page poses a major problem. If you know nothing of the history concerning how John's gospel was written, you would have no idea of the context of that passage and everything that went into its creation. Most people who read the Bible have not spent any time studying the history surrounding the Bible's creation. Biblical history is complex and nuanced, and the answers scholars provide often only lead to more questions.

As a result, a number of pastors and churches tend to dissuade their congregants from studying any type of scholarly historical research of the Bible. Some even go so far as to say such research is tantamount to heresy. They believe this because the conclusions that are reached by people who know the historical context of the

Bible tend to be very different from the conclusions of those who simply pick up the Bible and read it for themselves.

Even if you are not Christian, I think you can understand how challenging it would be to have a group of people tell you that your understanding of the book you have built your life around is wrong. What if one day you realized the world was round instead of flat? You would have to reassess everything you ever assumed to be true about the world. This is what biblical historical scholarship is like for many Christians. When they begin learning about this scholarship, it tends to unravel much of what they have assumed to be true about God, Jesus, and the Bible. It may upend their world. Sadly, this fear of historical scholarship is what prevents Christianity from evolving.

If we return to our business examples for a moment, I think it's fair to assume that a person who reads the Bible without any prior historical context could be grouped in Example 1. They are reading the Bible with very limited information and coming to conclusions that are not entirely accurate. Anyone who takes John 14:6 at face value and views Jesus as relegating all other religions—even the one from which he himself came—to the trash dump is misrepresenting Christianity because that's not what Jesus did.

The problem is many churches and pastors within Protestantism promote this way of reading the scriptures. But don't judge them too harshly. They are only doing what they were told to do. Remember the Reformation motto—*sola scriptura*—scripture alone? Protestantism is all about reading the Bible for yourself and coming to your own conclusions. The idea that the average person is somehow ill equipped to interpret the scriptures is a foreign concept to most Protestant Christians.

Thanks to Luther, Protestants believe that God's Spirit gives anyone the ability to interpret the scriptures properly. Herein lies the beauty and the tragedy of Protestantism. The beauty of what Luther did in Christianity is that many people have had their lives changed for the better as a result of being exposed to the Bible. I count myself among those people. Within the pages of the Bible are amazing stories that have the ability to transform and change the world around us for the better. Paradoxically, however, the tragedy of opening the Bible to the whole world is that many people have had their lives changed for the worse. I do not need to tell you that the Bible has been used as a tool to support and justify some of humanity's most egregious evils—slavery, genocide, racism, sexism, and homophobia, to name a few. Indeed, because of this checkered past, the inclination of many in the modern world is to simply do away with the Bible.

My goal through this book is to try to persuade you that the Bible deserves one more shot. What if there was a way of interpreting the Bible where the possibility for good outweighs the possibility for evil? What if you could navigate some of those murky waters within the Christian religion that have always caused you trouble and say, "Maybe there is something worth salvaging here?" In order to do this, we need a new way to approach the Bible, one that will paint a more accurate picture of God and Jesus.

In the following pages, we will be tackling some of the most fundamental Christian teachings and how they impact the Christian faith. Some of these teachings are complicated and there will be times when you might wonder why we are discussing a particular issue. This may feel especially acute if you are not familiar with the Christian faith at all, but I need you to trust me. If we are discussing an idea, it's going to lead somewhere important. If you feel at times confused and lost at sea, I promise to do my best to guide you back to solid land.

CHAPTER 1 RECAP: WHAT YOU NEED TO KNOW

1   Martin Luther changed Christianity dramatically by translating the Bible into everyday language and encouraging Christians to read the Bible for themselves.

2   Contrary to the perspective held by many Christians, the Bible cannot be read like a novel. The Bible is a complicated set of documents that requires the aid of historical context to be properly understood.

3   Christians who read the Bible through the lens of scholarly historical research will often come to very different conclusions about the message of the Bible than those who try to interpret the Bible literally, taking every word at face value.

CHAPTER TWO

GRAINS OF TRUTH

SUNDAY SCHOOL

When I was a kid growing up in Fredericksburg, Virginia, my mother saw to it that I participated in church most every Sunday. My ancestors have attended The Presbyterian Church of Fredericksburg since the mid-1800s. Given my family lineage in this church, regular church attendance was expected of me. I can't say I always enjoyed going to church, but I didn't hate it either. It was just part of our weekly routine.

As a kid, I didn't spend a lot of time in the worship service. Kids were shipped off to Sunday school. In Sunday school, we were taught all the Bible stories that are considered palatable for children. We talked about how Jesus loves us, how David triumphed over Goliath, how God appeared to Moses and gave him the Ten Commandments, and, of course, we learned the classic story that every child knows—Noah and the Ark.

Noah and the Ark is arguably the most familiar biblical story in the entire world. Many people who have never once cracked open a Bible know the basic plotline: God intends to flood the world and tells Noah to place all the animals in the world on a boat so they can be saved from a watery death. This story is so well known because it is one of the few Bible stories that is accessible to children. Children love animals and the idea that God would want to save all the animals in the world from harm helps children understand that God isn't such a bad guy after all. I refer to stories like Noah and the Ark as bridge stories because they create a bridge between a person and their concept of God. For millennia, the bridge created by Noah and the Ark conveyed the idea that God possesses a deep love for all creation. However, in the last century this began to change.

Today, Noah and the Ark is still a bridge story, but for very different reasons. My sense is that, for people on the outside of religion, Noah's story tends to convey the idea that Christians indoctrinate their children with lies. Why? If you learn the story of Noah and the Ark as a child, you don't question the logic behind it. As a child, it makes sense that you could build a boat and place all the animals in the world on it. Children don't understand how big the world is or how many species of animals the world contains.

When I was a young child, I had a book that told me about hundreds of different kinds of animals. From my perspective, that book seemed enormous, as though it contained a picture of every animal in the world. I lacked the comprehension to understand that such a book contained only a tiny fraction of the number of organisms that actually exist. So if you've grown up hearing the story of Noah and the Ark in Sunday school and you learn in high school that the diversity of life on the planet is so vast that 1,000 boats could not contain it all, then you come to the logical conclusion that the story of Noah and the Ark is a fairy tale.

Please don't get me wrong, I have nothing against fairy tales. Fairy tales can be useful tools for helping children navigate the world and understand the moral consequences of their actions. But fairy tales are fiction. Children might believe them, but at a certain point every parent wants a child to understand that these stories are not real. If the misconception continues too far into adolescence, the parent will have to correct the child's understanding because everyone needs to be able to distinguish between fact and fiction to function in the real world.

Oddly, certain religious people apply this way of thinking to every aspect of their lives, but when it comes to the Bible, they check that logic at the door. Why would they knowingly engage in such an obvious double standard? Because many Christians believe that God literally wrote the Bible, word for word, through human hands. If you believe that God gave humans the stories in the Bible to convey exactly what happened to God's people in a factual manner, then you have no choice but to believe them, even if many of the stories seem like fairy tales. From this perspective, to even raise the question of whether or not a biblical story is factually accurate could cause your whole belief system to unravel.

If Noah and the Ark is a fairy tale, then what does that say about the rest of the Bible? How can I trust anything in the Bible if one of the most foundational stories that Christians teach their children is untrue? What does that say about David and Goliath? What does that say about Moses? What does that say about Jesus? How can I trust that any of it is true? So rather than engage the Bible in rigorous examination, many Christians check their thinking cap at the door and shy away from questions.

From here, it's not hard to understand why so many people simply reject the Bible altogether. If you have to swallow the Bible whole and believe it unconditionally as factual truth, then most people in the 21st century who are steeped in the scientific method will find the Bible lacking. Particularly for most people of my generation who are now in the process of raising children, Sunday school is nowhere on their radar. They remember going to church and learning these stories as children, only to abandon the church in adulthood because they realized they don't need the Bible in order to be moral. Besides, why would they want to put their children through the same confusion? If the point of Sunday school is to teach Bible stories, most of which seem to be morality fairy tales, then I'll save my kids the trouble and teach them how to be moral myself.

THE JESUS PROBLEM

In my freshman year at Rice University, I had come to a point where I realized I needed to learn more about Christianity if I was going to be able to engage with my roommate Grant in any kind of intelligent conversation. At the end of the fall semester, Rice released the course catalogue for the spring. I turned to the religious studies section and found a class that caught my eye: Jewish-Christian Dialogue. The idea of the class was to explore the differences and similarities between Judaism and Christianity so as to open a much larger discussion about the nature of religious beliefs. I figured that was a good place to start. Since Grant needed a humanities credit, I was able to convince him to take the class with me.

From the moment we entered the class, I could tell that Grant was agitated. The professor made it clear from the start that you needed to check your religious perspective at the door so you could look at these faiths through fresh eyes. He explained that whether we were Christian, Jewish, Buddhist, agnostic or atheist, we brought our own preconceived notions with us, preventing our worldview from expanding. He encouraged us to be a blank slate so we could learn as much as possible. I was hooked. Grant was not. I realized that through religious studies I had discovered Grant's kryptonite.

About half way through the semester, Grant stopped attending the class. The impetus for him to completely abandon the class was a group of readings where we started talking about the gospels in the New Testament. The word *gospel* in Greek literally means *good news* and was a term used during the first century to describe Jesus' teachings.[2.1] In the New Testament, a gospel is a narrative story that describes Jesus' life. Although dozens of gospels were written, there are only four gospels in the New Testament.

The readings described how the gospels in the New Testament were not first-person accounts of Jesus' life. In fact, the gospels were written, at the earliest, 40 years after Jesus' death. The articles introduced us to the idea that these accounts of Jesus' life were written by people who never met Jesus and who were attempting to portray him in a certain light so as to persuade their audience. The articles also suggested that, once you uncover this authorial spin, you realize the information contained within the gospels is not entirely factually accurate.

Grant was not at all happy about this. I remember after class saying to him, "So it seems that the gospels were not written by people who knew Jesus." He looked at me and said very matter-of-factly, "That's not true. He's wrong. What he's saying in that class is a lie." This approach to the Bible was contradictory to everything Grant had been taught growing up. Grant's entire view of the Bible had been built around the first principle of Christian literalism: the various authors of the books in the Bible had been inspired by God to create inerrant documents. If Grant had let go of this grounding principle, he would have opened the door to biblical error and the core Christian beliefs about Jesus would become vulnerable.

Though this vulnerability was new to Grant and me, this way of thinking has been around for more than 200 years. In the 1800s, some New Testament scholars had begun to question the assumption that all the books in the Bible were first-person historical accounts. These scholars had come to the conclusion that the gospels were compiled from a variety of sources rather than from eyewitness accounts of the events.

For instance, many Christians assume that the names attached to the gospels (Matthew, Mark, Luke and John) are disciples who served alongside Jesus during his ministry. The reality is that none of the gospels came with names attached to them.[2.2] In the ancient world, it was not common for authors to place their name at the beginning of a story like we do today. Rather, most authors would insert themselves into the story at some critical juncture, which would indicate to the audience who was the author. This is not unlike a painter inserting himself into a work of art as opposed to signing his name in the corner. When we refer to the name of a gospel, this is the name that tradition has attached to the text and may not be reflective of the actual author or authors.

The majority consensus among scholars is that, of the four gospels found in the New Testament, Mark was written first.[2,3] Mark is thought to have been written around 70 C.E. because, in Chapter 13 of Mark, Jesus talks about the destruction of the Temple in Jerusalem. It is a matter of historical record that the Temple in Jerusalem was destroyed by the Roman army in 70 C.E. Since Jesus died 40 years before the destruction of the Temple, scholars assume it is highly unlikely that Jesus could have known it would be destroyed. Therefore, the conclusion by many scholars is that Mark, who was writing his gospel around the time of the Temple's destruction, inserted this prophecy into Jesus' mouth.

As you can imagine, this conclusion rubbed a lot of Christians the wrong way. How do scholars know that Jesus didn't predict the destruction of the Temple? The truth is, scholars can't prove Jesus didn't foresee the Temple's destruction and Christians can't prove that he did. If you adhere to conventional Christian thought, then you believe that Jesus had many special abilities, not the least of which was the ability to know the future, and that Mark was simply restating Jesus' own words. This is why conservative Christian scholars will often date the writing of Mark much earlier than 70 C.E. so as to get the prophecy closer to Jesus' actual life. However, if you are a scholar who treats the scriptures like any other historical document, then you are approaching Jesus as though he were a normal human being. If Jesus is a normal guy, then it is obvious that the author is attempting to bolster his case that Jesus was a prophet by portraying Jesus as having insight into the future—a move that reinforces Mark's case that Jesus is the messiah.

Mark's gospel became an important document within the early Christian community. It was copied and passed around among the small community of churches in the Mediterranean. Eventually, two other gospel authors, referred to as Matthew and Luke, used Mark as the basic template for the creation of their gospels.[2.4] Matthew wrote his gospel sometime between 80 and 85 C.E., while Luke wrote his gospel in 85 C.E. How do we know that Matthew and Luke used Mark as the basis for their gospels? We know because if you compare the information, you find that 80 percent of Mark is in Matthew and Luke. In today's world, this would be called plagiarism, but at the time, it was common for an author working towards a similar end to borrow heavily from a well-known and respected work. Therefore, if Mark is the blueprint for Jesus' life in the New Testament, then the next question we need to answer is how Mark went about writing his story of Jesus' life, because his source material will determine how much credence we can lend to its accuracy.

CAN I GET A QUOTE?

From what we can tell, Jesus' time on this earth was pretty short. Depending on whom you read, Jesus was on this planet for anywhere from 25-35 years. But the total time of his life isn't nearly as important as the last two or three years before he was crucified because that's the time when people were really paying attention to what he was saying. Jesus spent most of his time among the peasant population talking about the coming of the kingdom of God. (If you don't know what that means, don't worry, we're going to talk more about God's kingdom in Chapters 7 and 8.) It is clear that Jesus had quite an impact on the people whom he met because his teachings became very popular among the peasants. They would tell each other about the things Jesus said and these sayings became known among scholars as oral tradition.[2.5]

These oral traditions were eventually written down, but not until many decades after Jesus' death. The time between Jesus speaking his words and those words being written down is very important. One of the major problems with people who read the Bible today is they assume that how we record history in our modern world is similar to how the biblical authors recorded history. Nothing could be further from the truth. Our perspective of history has been heavily influenced by the tools we possess to record it. When we want to save something for posterity, we're taking notes, taping audio recordings, snapping photographs and even filming the event as it occurs. As a result, over the last 150 years we have developed a very different way of thinking of history, a way that cannot be applied to the individuals who wrote the gospels.

The gospel authors were not like modern reporters, taking notes at the scene so as to make sure the story is 100 percent accurate. How do we know? For one thing, Jesus recruited his disciples from an area known as Galilee, which had an illiteracy rate of 97 percent, so the likelihood that any of his disciples actually wrote the gospels is very, very low.[2.6] What's more, at the time, none of Jesus' followers had any idea how important the events of Jesus' life would be for future generations.

A good analogy might be to think of your own life. The average person is not particularly concerned with remembering everything that happens in his/her life because, frankly, who really needs to know? Jesus was a special guy, but I don't think any of the people who followed him assumed that people would still be talking about him 2,000 years later. It was only with the benefit of hindsight, when Jesus' movement had survived for more than 40 years following his death, that certain people realized it might be beneficial to write down some of the details of his life story.

When Mark decided to write the story of Jesus' life, he needed to gather some information since he never knew Jesus personally. One of the sources Mark relied upon was the oral tradition of Jesus' teachings which had been passed from one generation to the next. Given how information gets easily distorted when we speak to each other, the first question that comes to mind is: if Mark was writing his gospel 40 years after Jesus' death, how accurate could the oral tradition have been? As I came to find, the answer to that question had a lot to do with how well you could read.

Linguistic researchers have discovered that in societies where literacy is almost non-existent, the brain compensates by creating a much more accurate aural memory. Just as a blind person compensates with a more acute sense of hearing, people in illiterate societies have much better memories for what people say because that's their only way of remembering information. One famous study that proved this point was performed by Milman Parry in Yugoslavia during the 1930s. Parry interviewed Serbo-Croatian bards (poets) who spent their days on street corners entertaining people with their tales.[2.7] It's important to note that none of these storytellers could read or write. The researchers approached the storytellers and asked if they could repeat a story told to them, word for word, after hearing it only once. The storytellers said, "Yes."

The researchers told them a story and then made an audiotape of the retelling. Obviously, their rendition of the story was not a verbatim account, but the storytellers were able to maintain the basic narrative twists and turns of the story. Moreover, they could also reproduce the content of important dialogue. It wasn't always spot on, but the basic gist of what was being said tended to shine through. In other words, these illiterate story tellers had much more accurate aural memories than most of us do because, when we really need to remember something, we can simply write it down.

Even though Mark composed his gospel 40 years after Jesus' death, we can assume the oral tradition of Jesus' teachings that had been passed down from one generation to the next was fairly accurate.[2.8] Since Mark is the earliest gospel in the New Testament, Mark's oral tradition is closest to Jesus' actual words. Mark is the closest we are going to get to understanding who Jesus really was. This is not to say that some of the details haven't been changed along the way. They certainly have. But I want you to appreciate that there is a good deal of truth in the biblical rendition of Jesus' life. What we need to do is see our way through the weeds to figure out what is true and what has been artistically inserted by the author. If you take nothing else away from this book, please understand this one point: even though the Bible cannot be taken at face value, it still possesses many important truths. This applies not only to Jesus' life, but even to fanciful stories like Noah and the Ark.

THE REAL STORY OF NOAH AND THE ARK

We began this chapter by discussing the story of Noah and the Ark and how its fairytale-like quality is a stumbling block that prevents people from embracing the Bible as a source of reliable information. However, if my theory of the Bible holds true, then this story, even though it is obviously embellished, should not be completely devoid of truth. In order to prove this to you, I need to walk you through the story, deconstructing the biblical version of events, and then rehabilitating it into something more reasonable for our modern sentiment.

Whenever I delve into a story within the Bible, the first thing I like to do, before performing a lot of research, is to make sure that I'm familiar with the story as it's portrayed in the scriptures because the little details within the story usually provide us with clues as to what really happened. The biblical version of events goes something like this: God is grieved by all of the evil actions of human beings and determines that the entire creation should be scrapped. The text says:

> The Lord saw that the wickedness of humankind was great in the earth, and that every inclination of the thoughts of their hearts was only evil continually. And the Lord was sorry that he had made humankind on the earth, and it grieved him to his heart. So the Lord said, "I will blot out from the earth the human beings I have created—people together with animals and creeping things and birds of the air, for I am sorry that I have made them." But Noah found favor in the sight of the Lord. *(Gn. 6:5-8)*

It is clear from this text that the author believes God wants to get rid of every human being and the only person God feels is worth saving is Noah. The story continues that God decides to spare Noah and his family from the complete genocide of the human race and instructs Noah to build a boat. This boat will not only save Noah's family, but also many of the animals that live on the earth.

Once we've got a grasp of the biblical story, the next step is to perform some outside research, which is something that most Christians are reluctant to do. Many Christians are taught that the Bible was written by God, so all you need to do is read the Bible and your research ends there. In my opinion, if you don't understand the context in which the story was written, then you don't have a chance of comprehending the true meaning behind the story. It's like reading one of Shakespeare's plays. You can probably get the basic gist of what's going on from reading the play, but without understanding the larger context, a lot of it isn't going to make sense or you're going to interpret it the wrong way. The same logic applies to the Bible, so let's get some context around this story.

First of all, when you begin to dig a little bit, you learn that the story of the flood is not unique to the Bible. This story is found in a variety of other creation myths. One such myth, from Sumer and

Babylon, is the Epic of Atrahasis.[2.9] The story goes that humans are molded out of clay by the goddess Mami. When humans become too noisy for the gods, Enlil, the god of earth and air, decides to destroy humanity with a flood. Atrahasis, the hero of this story, is warned by the god Enki to build a boat, fill it with his possessions and a stable of animals and birds.

Another version of this story is the Epic of Gilgamesh.[2.10] In Gilgamesh, the character Utnapishtim is warned by the god Ea that the gods plan to flood the world because humans were too numerous and raucous. Ea instructs Utnapishtim to build a boat, the dimensions of which are very similar to the dimensions of the boat specified in Genesis. When a myth like this shows up in so many different cultures, it tells us that this story is probably rooted in an actual event. The question is: what could that event have been and how do we differentiate fact from fiction?

We need to start with the context of the people of the time. We often take for granted how detailed an understanding of the world we possess. We've grown up seeing globes of the earth in our classrooms. When we watch the evening news, we see satellite images of the earth from space. We've even seen pictures of our planet from the moon, so we're working with a lot more information than folks had back then. At the time this myth originated, most people never travelled more than a radius of 15 miles from their home during their entire lifetime.[2.11] So, the world, from their point of view, was extremely limited. Therefore, when the scriptures say that God flooded the entire world, what this means is that God flooded the area of the world with which they were familiar and that wasn't a whole lot by our standards. Therefore, it is reasonable to assume this myth originated from a flood that affected an isolated area somewhere in the Middle East.

The second thing we know is that this was no ordinary flood. The Bible states the floods occurred from incessant rain, but what we're talking about is something much larger than a flood caused by rains or a river overflowing its banks. This is a flood that killed tens of thousands of people at once. This event wouldn't have made it into all these creation myths if it hadn't been massively destructive in terms of human life. That's why all of these creation myths interpret this event through the lens of God being upset with humans. The only way the ancients could rationalize the destruction of so much life is if they were being punished by God for being evil.

Therefore, we can assume the scale of this kind of flood is something on par with tsunamis or other earthquake-related disasters. There is a major tectonic fault line that runs through the Mediterranean Sea, but the Mediterranean is too small to produce a tsunami of the scale we often see in Japan or Indonesia. For that you need a body of water like the Pacific Ocean. Even highly destructive hurricanes cannot produce the kind of devastation alluded to in the biblical text. So if it wasn't rains, rivers or tsunamis, the only option left is to look at the bodies of water in the surrounding area and ask, "Have they always been there?"

Two marine geologists at Columbia University, Ryan William and Walter Pitman, attempted to place dates on the various flood stories that appear in creation myths throughout the Middle East.[2.12] As they did, they found a fascinating pattern: the older the story, the closer it gets geographically to the Black Sea. The earliest versions of this story originate from an area around the edge of the Black Sea. This led William and Pitman to speculate that perhaps the Black Sea is not as old as they had formerly believed. The theory goes something like this: around 5600 B.C.E., the Black Sea was a low-lying valley surrounding a massive fresh water lake. A large number of people inhabited this valley because it was good for agriculture. At some point, the Mediterranean began to erode the land that separated these two areas. On a map, this connection is called the Bosphorus Strait and is located right next to modern Istanbul.

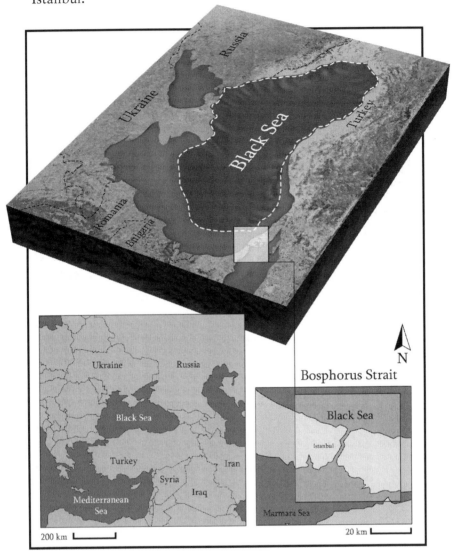

The people who were closest to this erosion point could see what was about to happen. Prior to the major event of water inundating the valley, during the initial stages of flooding, water probably started to pour slowly into the valley. It's not hard to imagine that somebody with foresight built a boat, placed his family and livestock in that boat and then used the boat to float to sea level when the land mass gave way to the pressure of the Marmara Sea. His family and livestock remained safe while everyone else in the valley was killed in a deluge of water. Furthermore, it's not hard to imagine that, from the perspective of the survivors who told this story, the entire world was flooded.

To test this theory, William and Pitman sent research vessels to the bottom of the Black Sea. If you imagine a flood of that scale, it should literally snap the trees like toothpicks, leaving only the stumps. On these dives they found exactly that. Underneath the sediment, there were rows of petrified tree stumps that looked as if they had been ripped in half. Samples from these stumps dated to around the period of time when scholars estimate the story of the flood began to spread. Therefore, even though the biblical version of this story has been highly mythologized and interpreted through the particular lens of God being angry at humans for being evil, the oral tradition from which this story was developed may very well reflect an actual event.

DOES THE END JUSTIFY THE MEANS?

I remember the first time I learned this theory about the events surrounding Noah and the Ark. I was shocked to discover it contained any truth at all because I had dismissed the story as completely false. But then my mind raced through a series of important questions, not the least of which was why should I care? Even if the story of Noah and the Ark had some truth behind it, what difference would it make and why should I waste my time trying to discern fact from fiction? I don't have the time to perform that kind of research every time I read the Bible and, even if I did, is the payoff really worthwhile? How does knowing the truth behind this story enrich my life and help me along my spiritual journey?

In my opinion, how one answers these questions is the litmus test of whether or not the Bible is worth your time. We've already established that Noah's story, as it is presented in the Bible, is not entirely factual. Perhaps there was a flood, but it did not cover the entire earth and the guy who built a boat did not save all the animals on the planet, but, more than likely, just the animals he owned. So if we set aside the details that are factually inaccurate, what is the author trying to convey with this story that is useful for our spiritual journey?

The answer lies in understanding the context of the language in which it was written. Although some American Christians seem to think the Bible was written in King James English, the Bible was written in three different languages: Hebrew, Greek and Aramaic. Without knowledge of these languages, the Bible becomes much more difficult to interpret. The story of Noah and the Ark is found in the Old Testament, which is the portion written in Hebrew.

In the text we read from Genesis, God wished to wipe the slate clean and get rid of humans entirely because "...the wickedness of humankind was great in the earth, and that every inclination of the thoughts of their hearts was only evil continually." *(Gn. 6:5)* The Hebrew words that we translate into English to mean *evil inclination* are יֵצֶר רַע (yetzer hara).[2.13] These two words in Hebrew are very important for interpreting this story. Although an evil inclination could refer to a lot of different things in English, in Hebrew it refers to when humans misuse things that the physical body needs to survive.

For instance, when eating is no longer about simply satiating our hunger, but about overindulging our appetite, then we move from something good, nourishing our bodies, to something bad, gluttony. Here's another example: when sex is no longer an expression of a loving relationship but about serving our sexual desires, we move from something good, sex as a natural consequence of love and intimacy, to something bad, lust. When our minds become preoccupied with a particularly destructive behavior that dictates the way we live our lives, an evil inclination is at work.

One of the most obvious examples of this kind of orientation is drug abuse. For people who are addicted to drugs, their habit becomes the entire focus of their lives. This happens because the drug hijacks their free will. For instance, heroin chemically alters the circuitry of the brain so that the body treats heroin the same way it treats food. Their minds become preoccupied with obtaining heroin in the same way they we are preoccupied with obtaining our next meal.

The difference is that food nourishes our body while drugs destroy it. Perhaps that's what evil is really all about. Evil is not so much the opposite of good, but a perversion of good desires towards a destructive end. The desire for food is a good desire. But take that same desire and make it revolve around heroin and it becomes bad. Another example of this might be strength and fitness. The desire to be strong and in shape is good thing because it helps you live a long, healthy life. But take that same strength and make it revolve around fighting, abuse and power, then all of a sudden it becomes bad.

What these two Hebrew words reveal to us is that evil is primarily about a mindset—a way of thinking and looking at the world. Having dissected this mindset, we can return to the story of Noah and the Ark. We've acknowledged that this story as it is written in the Bible does not reflect the actual event. Therefore, if we set aside the authorial embellishments, it seems clear the author wishes to use this story to make a statement about God. The question we must answer is whether or not this statement is something beneficial to our spiritual development.

The author is making one of two statements about God in this story. The first option is that the author is telling us that God didn't have very much foresight about how much humans could hurt themselves and each other. From this perspective, it's almost as if God were saying, "Obviously this creation thing isn't working out very well. I didn't think through the consequences of what I was trying to do, so let's just scrap it and be done with the whole experiment." Even though you could read the story that way, I don't think the author wanted us to walk away from this story thinking that God is just as ignorant as human beings in predicting the consequences of our actions.

This leads us to the second option. The key to this interpretation is understanding the name Noah. Noah is the one person whom God informs of the coming destruction. God chooses Noah to be the person who will reboot and restart the human race. The word נֹחַ (Noah) in Hebrew means *rest* or *comfort*.[2.14] So in the midst of all this evil, there is a man who brings comfort to God. If we're willing to understand this story as a larger metaphor for the relationship between God and humans, then it tells us something quite profound about God.

I hope we can all agree there isn't a single human that doesn't possess some kind of evil inclination. In our own ways, we all take good desires and pervert them towards a destructive end. We do this in a variety of different ways and some of us are more destructive than others; but let's face it, we're all in the same boat. Now let's assume that instead of being ignorant of this destructive nature, God knows and expects that we're going to have these evil inclinations. Obviously, God doesn't want our evil inclinations to be the dominant force in this world. So what if, inside every single one of us, there's a place where God can start over? What if, inside all of us, there is a Noah, a comfort, a rest?

From this perspective, Noah and the Ark is less about an actual flood and much more about our relationship with each other and the creator. In my opinion, this interpretation changes the story of Noah and the Ark into this beautiful image that speaks deeply to the human condition. If God knows the kind of people you and I will eventually become, then God also knows that one day we will need to wipe the slate clean in our hearts and start over. Therefore, God places a comfort, a rest, a new starting point in our hearts so that, when we're ready, we can become the kind of people God intended us to be. This idea is further expanded upon in the New Testament when we are introduced to the person of Jesus because he teaches that no matter how evil you have been, no matter what you have done, God can remove those evil inclinations and give you a fresh start.

When I read the story of Noah and the Ark now, I no longer see a fairytale. I see a story that contains important spiritual insights that speak to the issues I face in the 21st century. This has not only happened with Noah and the Ark, but with many of the stories in the Bible that I had initially dismissed as irrelevant. What I find to be so striking about the Bible is that, in spite of the haphazard way it was composed over the span of almost 1,000 years, it has a coherence. The authors had no idea their stories would be compiled together into this larger book we call the Bible, and yet, they touched on themes and ideas that would recur over and over again.

There is a larger story that unites the disparate threads from which the Bible was created. The Old Testament lays the foundation for many of the ideas that are expanded upon and refined in the New Testament. The more one understands the original intent of the authors in their historical time and context, the more these universal themes emerge that have deep relevance to our lives. Perhaps this is simply the result of good editing or perhaps there really is a touch of the divine in these texts. Either way, our next endeavor will be to tease out who this God is that is portrayed in the pages of the Bible.

1   The tools we use to record current events (photography, audio, video) have changed the way we think about history and cannot be applied to how the authors of the Bible understood history.

2   The gospels recounting Jesus' life (as well as many other stories in the Bible) are the result of oral tradition that was passed from one generation to the next. These oral traditions are more accurate than we would assume because the people transmitting these stories came from illiterate cultures with strong aural memories.

3   Biblical stories like Noah and the Ark likely have some basis in actual historical events. The events portrayed in the Bible possess grains of factual truth that have been interpreted through a theological lens.

4   These stories, when properly understood in their original context, can provide us with insight into deep spiritual truths that can draw us closer to our creator.

— PART TWO —

GOD

Restorative Faith

— CHAPTER THREE —

THE GOD YOU KNOW

THE GLASS IS HALF FULL

I think it's important to recognize that while the Bible may be divinely inspired, religion is, by its very nature, a man-made invention. Religion is a human interpretation of something well beyond our comprehension. God is something we will never be able to fully understand no matter how many people claim to speak on behalf of God. Therefore, in my mind, no religion is fully representative of God. However, this doesn't mean we should abandon religion entirely. Religion provides us with a good framework through which we can approach God. Let me provide you with an illustration.

On December 14, 2012, in Newtown, Connecticut, a young man named Adam Lanza walked into Sandy Hook Elementary School with a Bushmaster XM15-E2S M4 semi-automatic rifle. Lanza shot his way through Sandy Hook, taking the lives of 20 children and 7 adults, including himself. The nation was devastated by the enormity of the crime, and authorities worked hard to piece together why Lanza decided to unleash his carnage on defenseless children.

As the investigation unfolded, it quickly became clear that Lanza was suffering from mental illness. Though he had been seen by psychiatrists, he was not being treated at the time of the shootings for issues with anxiety, obsessive-compulsive disorder, and undiagnosed anorexia. According to a report produced by Connecticut's Office of the Child Advocate, Lanza's mother, Nancy, who was his first victim before the spree began, was not inclined to seek treatment for her son's psychiatric issues. This in spite of the fact that Yale University's Child Study Center had examined her son when he was in the ninth grade, suggesting he receive "extensive special education supports, ongoing expert consultation and rigorous therapeutic supports."[3.1]

As Lanza became older and was visibly beginning to decompensate (or cease to function normally due to mental illness), his mother still did not seek treatment for her son. Furthermore, she did not limit his access to her large volume of high-capacity firearms. Though we will never know the true motive for the crime, one can make an educated guess based on similar cases where people with severe mental illness have inflicted harm on those around them.

When I was working as a chaplain intern for a psychiatric hospital, one thing I noticed is how frequently anxiety can be a precipitating factor that can cause people to decompensate. We don't often think of anxiety as being associated with mental illness because it is such a common part of our lives, but 40 million people in the United States suffer from some sort of anxiety disorder.[3.2] The only difference between those who are considered mentally ill and those who are not is whether or not their anxiety is debilitating. Most of us would say that our anxiety is not debilitating, but change a few small things here and there and, all of a sudden, what was previously bearable becomes unbearable.

This is not to say that everyone with severe anxiety is in danger of becoming a mass murderer. However, in the right set of circumstances, debilitating anxiety can give way to severe depression. Ninety percent of suicides can be attributed to some diagnosable form of mental illness.[3.3] When you've lost the desire to live and do not value your own life, you stop valuing the lives of others. From there, it's not too much of a leap to understand how certain individuals, like Lanza, despondent about their circumstances, feeling powerless to change the hand they've been dealt, would be willing to hurt themselves and others to make a statement. The statement that we all want to make is, "I matter." Killing those children was Lanza's way of telling the world, in no uncertain terms, that his life mattered. Sadly, his name will always be attached to their deaths.

Please do not think I am trying to make excuses for Lanza's crime. What he did to the children and adults of Sandy Hook is abhorrent and inexcusable, no matter how mentally ill he may have been. So why have I taken all this time to explain what his mental state may have been when he committed these crimes? Because one of the most fundamental aspects of the Christian faith is that all life has inherent value. Indeed, the Christian perspective on humanity is such that no one, even Adam Lanza, can forfeit that value. In the opening chapter of the Bible, there is a verse that says humans are created in God's image and likeness. *(Gn. 1:26)* I take this to mean there is a little bit of God present in all human beings. You could call this the soul or a divine spark, but we all carry a little bit of God's spirit in our hearts.

This means when we hurt ourselves and one another, we are hurting God. Therefore, no matter how badly we hurt each other, Christians are encouraged to view one another as God views us—people with infinite potential for good in spite of our shortcomings. Thus, even though Adam Lanza has been portrayed as a monster by the media, a Christian is not allowed to dismiss him as human garbage and be glad he's dead. A Christian is always supposed to search for the humanity of that person and, in Adam Lanza's case, his mental illness provides us with a window through which we can observe his humanity, however frail it may be.

Again, acknowledging his humanity does not excuse his actions. It simply allows one to see Adam Lanza as a broken human being, but human nevertheless. It is a way of realizing that in a different set of circumstances, you and I have the same potential to do what Adam Lanza did. Likewise, it is a way of realizing that in a different set of circumstances, Adam Lanza could have had the same potential for good as you or I.

I know there are some who might argue that Lanza's actions strip him of the right to be recognized as human. I would assume that many of those people would be Christians. However, if one understands the foundation of the Christian faith, then the premise that all life has intrinsic value is extremely important when it comes to explaining why evil is allowed to exist in the world (a concept we will discuss in the coming chapters) and how God could let a tragedy like this occur. This is what I mean by religion being important for providing us with a framework for understanding the world. The notion that all human life is in some way a reflection of God changes the way one looks at the world. It means that the potential of human beings is so much greater than our individual actions would indicate. The Christian worldview is ultimately one of optimism and the belief that love can truly triumph over evil.

In my opinion, the net impact of a religious framework on society matters a lot more than whether or not it represents absolute truth. If that net impact is positive and helps me decode the most vexing puzzles of life, then I will invest my time and energy into fully comprehending the complexities of that religious tradition. Having spent most of my life studying religions, I feel Christianity represents one of the most useful religious frameworks. Christianity not only offers profound insights into the nature of the universe but, when viewed through the proper lens, has the potential to impact our world in ways that are extremely positive.

WORD PLAY

During my first pastoral internship, I was required to spend a certain number of hours performing pastoral care. Generally, pastoral care is providing counsel for a person who is experiencing a crisis. This crisis could range from a couple experiencing divorce to someone who has been diagnosed with cancer, to a teenager who is acting out against their parents with drugs and alcohol. In the Presbyterian Church, where the median age of the attendees is around 63, much pastoral care revolves around a death in the family.[3,4]

I was instructed to accompany the pastor responsible for providing pastoral care to the congregation so I could learn from him. Our first call of the day was to an elderly woman, Ethel, who had just lost her husband, Don, who had been suffering from Alzheimer's for close to 10 years. The slow degeneration of his mind had been a very painful process for his family to watch because Don had been a brilliant man. He had his Ph.D. in electrical engineering and was responsible for creating a number of important patents for the military during World War II. A kind, affable man, Don had been completely transformed by Alzheimer's. As he became less able to retain information, the disease turned his affability into anger. Ethel was particularly hard hit by this transformation because their marriage had always been a shining example of love and acceptance. However, Don's temper had become so volatile towards the end of his life that Ethel placed him in a nursing home for her own safety.

When we arrived, Don's whole family was sitting around the living room. Ethel looked shell-shocked and answered the pastor's questions in an almost catatonic state. Eventually the pastor started asking about Don's life so he could use some of the details for his funeral sermon. This lightened the atmosphere quite a bit as everyone began recalling the man Don used to be—strong, intelligent, witty and a pleasure to be around. As they worked their way through the timeline of Don's life, they finally got to the years when Alzheimer's began to take its toll. This is the point at which Ethel turned to the pastor and said, "If God is truly all-loving and all-powerful, why did he let this happen to my Donald?"

The pastor didn't have a very good answer and neither did I at that point in my life. Like Ethel, I had always heard that God was supposed to be all-powerful, all-knowing and all-good, but the world certainly didn't seem to reflect those qualities. For years, I struggled to make sense of this notion of a perfect God creating an imperfect world. I asked all the classic questions: If God is so good, why is there so much suffering and evil in the world? Why does God allow tragedies and natural disasters to take the lives of so many people? Why does God allow some people to experience lives free of calamity while others know nothing but pain and anguish? What I came to realize is that when I pitted a perfect God against such tragedy, God always came up short. It wasn't until I went to seminary that I was able to understand why this was the case.

One of the first classes I took at Princeton was from a professor named Diogenes Allen. Dr. Allen was an intimidating presence. As the old saying goes, he didn't suffer fools lightly. He was considered by many at the seminary to be the brightest mind on campus. Dr. Allen taught philosophy and his classes were notorious for being some of the hardest offerings for incoming students. I entered his class with some trepidation, but after the first class I was no longer concerned about my grade. I knew his class was going to be incredibly difficult, but I also knew his wisdom would set the foundation for everything else I learned at seminary.

One of the first things he taught us had to do with how people, particularly Christians, tend to describe God. These descriptions are commonly known as "the omni's"—omnipotent, omniscient, omnibenevolent and omnipresent. These translate into all-powerful, all-knowing, all-good and all-present. Like you, I always assumed these were perfectly reasonable descriptions of God. Not so, according to Dr. Allen. He explained to us that these terms are derived primarily from Greek philosophy.[3.5] People like Socrates, Plato and Aristotle were the ones who used these descriptions when talking about God. Just to be clear, there's nothing wrong with these men. They were brilliant philosophers who have impacted the Western world in enormous ways, not the least of which is the way we employ their terminology when talking about God. The problem is that Socrates, Plato and Aristotle didn't write the Bible. The authors were predominately Hebrew.

"The omni's" should not be applied to the Bible because the authors were not writing about God with those assumptions in mind. This is why, when a person applies these concepts to the Bible, they don't make sense. You might be able to find certain instances where God exhibits qualities of being all-powerful or all-knowing, but those qualities are not consistent throughout the entire Bible. Instead, Dr. Allen encouraged us to apply different terms to the God of the Bible. He provided us with appropriate substitutes that are consistently reflected in the text. Here are the terms that Dr. Allen used in place of the Greek philosophical terms:

Philosophy	Meaning	Hebrew Bible
Omnipresent	All-Present	Transcendent
Omnipotent	All-Powerful	Holy
Omniscient	All-Knowing	Wise
Omnibenevolent	All-Good	Loving

I know replacing one word with another word might seem kind of meaningless in the grand scheme of things, but, I promise you, it makes a huge difference. Most folks spend very little time reflecting on the definition of God. Most of what people think they know about God is what they absorb from the culture around them. American culture tends to promote a God that is represented by "the omni's." People carry these definitions around without ever questioning their validity. When they are faced with a question that relates to God's presence in the world, they fall back on these classical definitions only to find they make no sense.

For instance, the difference between God being omnipresent and God being transcendent is immense. Omnipresence means being everywhere. The result is that we come to think of God as a celestial Santa Claus, always watching whether you have been naughty or nice. But the Hebrew notion of God's presence in the universe is far more elegant than God simply watching your every move.

The God portrayed in the Bible is said to be transcendent, from the Latin word *transcensus*, which literally translates to *climbing over*.[3.6] We often use transcendent to indicate an entity that is able to "climb over" the limitations of the material universe. When a being transcends space and time that being is able to experience a dimension beyond our own. For humans, transcendence means going higher. However, when we talk about God being transcendent in the Bible, the direction of movement is reversed. Transcendence for God is going lower.

The Bible begins with the premise that God exists beyond the fabric of space and time, meaning God resides in a dimension beyond our physical universe. This concept is not unique to the Judeo-Christian God, but can be found in a variety of religious traditions. However, the God of the Bible does not remain beyond our universe. The Bible maintains that God is not only the starting point of the universe, but undergirds the very existence of the universe. *(Gn. 1, Ex. 3:13-14, Ps. 33:6-9, Pr. 8:22-36)* Another way to think about this concept is: if God were to all of a sudden cease to exist, then so would the universe. The biblical God is not simply the creator of the universe, but its reason for continuously existing now and in the future. This aspect of God's transcendence is often referred to as God's immanence, meaning God is present in everything.

This is a very different idea from a God that creates the universe and steps back from creation. If God is simply the cause of the universe's existence, then the universe can exist independent of God. Using this logic, if God were to cease to exist, we could keep on going. This difference may seem slight but it matters a great deal. From the perspective of the Bible, God is simultaneously beyond everything and in everything at the same time. This quality of God being in and beyond everything is why we call God transcendent as opposed to omnipresent. To say that God is everywhere contrasts greatly with the biblical view of God. God is not simply present in all places, observing existence. God is in everything, making existence possible.

When the Bible says God is transcendent, it is not simply suggesting that God is moving lower, climbing over into our dimension. God is not merely entering the fabric of space and time. God *is* the fabric of space and time. Proof of this point of view in the Bible is the word Jesus uses to describe God. Although the New Testament is written in Greek, Jesus spoke in a language known as Aramaic.[3.7] The word *God* in Aramaic is *Alaha*. The best translation of Alaha is *"Sacred Unity"* or *"the All"* or *"oneness."*[3.8] In our modern English, we would say God is everything. Therefore, when Christians say that God is transcendent, we are saying that God is everything. You, me, all existence is God because God is what makes existence possible.

Whether you realize it or not, this slight adjustment has huge consequences for how we envision God working in the world. An omnipresent God is always observing the world, choosing when to intervene and when to remain distant. By contrast, a transcendent God is always in the middle of the action. Indeed, a transcendent God is the reason why the action takes place at all. Such a distinction lays the foundation that will allow us to begin the process of fully answering Ethel's heartfelt question, "Why did God let this happen to my Donald?"

THE GOD PROBLEM

As a pastor in the Presbyterian Church, I have spent a great deal of time with families planning funerals for loved ones. In the vast majority of cases, the members of my congregation who pass away have lived to a ripe old age and their departure from this earth is expected. However, there are times when death afflicts those who have not had the opportunity to live a long, fulfilling life. In those instances, it is not uncommon for people to come to the conclusion that if God exists at all, then God certainly doesn't care about us and our suffering.

For example, I once ministered to a family whose 26-year-old niece, Kayla Mueller, had been captured and killed by ISIS (Islamic State In Syria). Kayla was an aid worker for *Support to Life*, working on the Turkish border with Syria, helping Syrian refugees fleeing the civil war. At some point during her time serving the refugees, she was captured by a militia group in Syria and eventually turned over to ISIS. Her parents were e-mailed by ISIS and told that if they released her name to the press they would kill her. Needless to say, her parents were absolutely frantic. They flew to Qatar and, by using diplomatic channels, discovered that ISIS didn't know what to do with her. They couldn't kill her because she was a woman and an aid worker. They knew that her death would galvanize public opinion against them. On the other hand, they couldn't let her go either because that would demonstrate weakness. Unsure of their next move, ISIS held her in captivity for 18 months.

During that time, no one was aware what was happening except for Kayla's family and the United States government. Her family worked with the FBI, the White House, and foreign diplomats—anyone who would listen. Did I mention that they prayed and prayed and prayed for her release? They prayed all the time that somehow they might be able to secure her release or that she could be rescued. In February of 2015, there was a Jordanian airstrike on an ISIS compound in Syria. Although no members of ISIS were killed in the airstrike, ISIS released a statement that Kayla had been killed by the missile strike. Officials believe that, in fact, ISIS had killed Kayla sometime prior to the Jordanian airstrike and used the destruction of the building as a pretext.

This tragic story raises some important questions about God and how God interacts with the universe. Kayla was in a situation where she needed saving. Why didn't God intervene? Why didn't God listen to the prayers of her family and do something to change the outcome of that situation? If God can part the waters of the Red Sea and save thousands of enslaved Hebrews fleeing from the Egyptians, then why can't God save one young aid worker who was in a similarly desperate situation? Isn't God in the business of answering prayers and performing miracles? Doesn't the Bible say that God cares about the afflicted, the oppressed and the downtrodden? Indeed, Kayla had dedicated her life to helping the very people God purports to care about, so why did God let her slip through the cracks? All of these are valid questions that deserve answers. Unfortunately, the typical answers provided by the religious establishment for why God didn't intervene in a situation like Kayla's are exactly why people are fleeing the church in record numbers.

The conventional Christian perspective starts with a fundamental precept: with God, anything is possible. What this means in the minds of most Christians is that, if God chooses to do so, then God can alter the trajectory of negative events toward a positive outcome. This belief is derived from the Bible, which portrays God as intervening in human history to aid the Hebrew people in a variety of different circumstances. These interventions are usually referred to as miracles. The definition of a miracle is: a positive occurrence that cannot be explained by natural or scientific laws and is attributed to divine agency. I think it is safe to assume that most Christians believe the miracles portrayed in the Bible are reflective of real events and that miracles are still a possibility today.

On the surface, this concept seems reasonable. If the miracles in the Bible are real, then it stands to reason that miracles are possible. Where this equation breaks down is in the real world. For instance, let's say a person is diagnosed with terminal cancer. The doctors do everything in their power to heal this person, but no amount of radiation or chemotherapy will do any good. However, this person prays for God to take away the cancer. Against all odds, this person goes into remission and the cancer disappears. Indeed, the doctors have no explanation for how it could have happened. It is not uncommon in situations like these, where medical justification is absent, for Christians to credit the recovery to God's intervention and categorize an event like this as a miracle. From their perspective, God acted completely in accordance with the way God is portrayed in the Bible—the person prayed and God altered the trajectory of negative events towards a positive outcome.

Great! Except for when that doesn't happen. Now let's use this same example, but with a different outcome. A person is diagnosed with terminal cancer. The doctors do everything in their power to heal this person, but no amount of radiation or chemotherapy will do any good. This person prays for God to take away the cancer, but unfortunately, the cancer is too aggressive and the person dies. In this instance, God did not intervene to change the trajectory of negative events. The question the Christian is left to answer is, "Why? Why did God heal the one person and allow the other person to die?" Well, the most common answer to this question is that God hears all prayers, but sometimes the answer to those prayers is, "No." But that raises the obvious issue of why God says yes to some prayers and no to others?

Here we have stumbled into one of the most challenging problems for the Christian faith. In my mind, Christianity's credibility hinges on how you approach this issue and, generally speaking, pastors are notoriously bad at answering this question. Let's consider some of the most common responses. One is that we didn't pray hard enough or we didn't have enough faith. There is a verse in the New Testament where Jesus says that God will answer the prayers of the faithful: "Whatever you ask for in prayer with faith, you will receive." *(Mt. 21:22)* In essence, what this verse is saying is that if you pray with true faith then God will heed your prayer and intervene. So if you didn't get the outcome you expected, then obviously you didn't ask with enough faith.

Another common answer is to relieve God of responsibility by saying that Satan was victorious in this particular circumstance. For instance, some Christians looking at Kayla's situation would say that because Satan has a strong grip on the members of ISIS, God was unable to change the outcome of the situation for the better. Of course, this explanation assumes two things: 1) that Satan is real and 2) that the members of ISIS are not responsible for their own actions. What many of these Christians fail to recognize is how the existence of a being like Satan reflects on God. If God is really all-powerful and all-good, then what does it say about God that God allows a being like Satan to "win" in situations like these? If God is able to change the outcome of our world as Christians claim, then it seems ridiculous and callous on God's part to allow Satan to ruin so many good lives.

However, in my experience, the most common response for why a prayer was or was not answered has to do with God's plan. God didn't save Kayla because it wasn't part of God's plan. I cannot tell you how often I have heard pastors and other Christians say, "Though we may not understand it, God has a plan." Really? God has a plan? So it was God's plan for Kayla, an aid worker who had dedicated her life to helping those in need, to be captured by ISIS, to be held captive for 18 months and then to be murdered by them? That's a horrible plan if you ask me. I mean, can't God, the creator of the universe, do a little better than that?

I refer to this way of thinking as the theology of convenience because, regardless of how it personally works out for you, it always works out for God. When things go well for you, then God gets all the credit and you become living proof of how God intervenes in the world; but if you end up on the losing end of things, then you're collateral damage for God's plan. The truth is that the logic of God intervening in the world doesn't work the way Christians want it to work and I think most people are intuitively aware that this is the case. Obviously most Christians don't know how to balance the notion that God is all-good with the evil that exists in the world. Therefore, if we are going to shed some light on God's interaction with Kayla's tragedy, then we need to understand how God interacts with evil in the world.

BATTLE OF THE WILLS

Through my time working in the church, I have become acutely aware of how my inclination to question, doubt and deconstruct every aspect of the Christian faith is rare. I have found that most Christians simply trust that the beliefs promoted by the church are true. This trust often means they have not spent the time delving into the intricacies that undergird those beliefs. I understand this perspective. Wading into details of complex material can feel over-whelming. However, if our goal is to progress into new ways of thinking about God and Christianity, I think it is necessary for us to drill down into those intricacies and ask, "Do they make sense?" To begin dissecting these beliefs, I want to tell you a story of one of the most vivid memories from my childhood.

I was in sixth grade and my mother was putting my sisters to bed. I was still up doing my homework in the kitchen when my father called out to me to join him in the den. When I entered he said, "I want to show you something." My father picked up a videotape, slid it into the VCR and sat down in a chair. Then he said, "Have you ever heard of the Holocaust?" I had not. When my father played the video, I saw black and white images of men and women who were starving to death. It was like I was watching animated skeletons. Many of the survivors in these camps had such hollow expressions in their eyes that it seemed as though they had been robbed of their souls.

Who were these people and why were there dead bodies strewn all over the ground and inside pits? I looked over at my dad and asked, "Is this real?" He said, "Yes, very much so." I sat quiet for another few minutes staring at the screen and then I said, "Why did this happen to them?" That's when my father explained to me that a man named Adolf Hitler had a vision of the world where Jews no longer existed. In order to set about making that vision a reality, he created camps where Jews were sent to be exterminated. What I was watching was footage from the British soldiers who had liberated the concentration camps at the end of World War II.

That was the first time in my life I asked myself, "Why didn't God save them?" Like so many people raised in the church, I had grown up being taught that God is all-powerful (omnipotent) and that for God, anything is possible. At age 11, I already knew that God does not give us everything we want, but I felt as though God was watching over me, trying to keep me safe from harm. If God can keep me safe, why didn't God do that for them? Shouldn't God have done something to stop Hitler and his soldiers from murdering six million Jews? Something didn't add up. If God is truly all-powerful, then the Holocaust seems like one of the most important times when God should have exerted that power. The fact that God didn't intervene to prevent the Holocaust was a direct contradiction to the Christian claim that God is all-powerful.

I know from many conversations that this contradiction is a big reason why so many people eventually turn their backs on Christianity. We have inherited this conviction from centuries of Christians teaching that God can do anything if God so chooses. The problem is that the world around us does not demonstrate this reality to be true. For every "miracle" you show me where you believe God interceded on behalf of humans, I can highlight hundreds of other instances where God should have interceded but didn't. Therefore, even if we agree that God possesses the power to do whatever God wants to do, it is clear that God rarely, if ever, exercises that power. This lack of intercession on God's part leaves us in a difficult position if we cling to the notion that God is omnipotent. We are forced to conclude that either God created the universe and totally abandoned it or that God is present and totally apathetic about our plight.

I don't know which is worse—a God who creates and chooses to be absent or a God who is present and doesn't care to help us. Either way, such a God cannot be said to be particularly loving. I think most Christians, including myself, would reject both of these conceptions of God. Therefore, we are forced to conclude that characterizing God as omnipotent is inconsistent with the Christian belief in a God of love. Since the evidence suggests that God's intervention in the world is extremely limited, we must reimagine how we think of God's power and influence over the world. We must limit God's role enough to make it consistent with the truth of our day-to-day lives, while giving God enough latitude to have some influence over the outcome of our choices. These parameters are hugely important for our understanding of Christianity because it changes how we think of the battle between our will and God's will.

Generally speaking, Christians understand there to be a constant tension between the human ability to make decisions and God's ability to influence those decisions. Imagine that there are two glasses. One glass represents our ability to make decisions (human free will) and the other glass represents God's ability to make decisions (God's will). There is only enough liquid to fill one

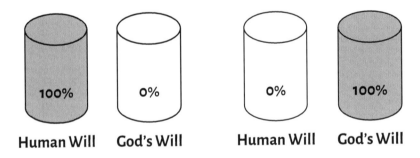

| 100% | 0% | 0% | 100% |
| Human Will | God's Will | Human Will | God's Will |

of the glasses completely. If we fill the human glass to the brim, giving humans complete free reign to do whatever they want, then we end up making God impotent and it becomes impossible for God to have any power over the world God created. Likewise, if we fill God's glass, giving God total control over the universe, then we become like puppets who have no say over our own lives. Therefore, we tend to split the difference, giving both God and humans some control.

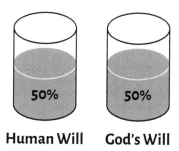

Human Will   God's Will

Unfortunately, this leads to a very messy way of thinking about the world. What Christians want to claim is that the world is designed so that humans are free to make decisions while also allowing God the latitude to intervene in our lives when necessary to guide our paths. The problem is determining who is responsible for what action. If I get drunk, drive my car, and kill an innocent pedestrian, was that my decision or God's decision? Most people would say that because the outcome was negative, obviously God had nothing to do with it. It was my choice to drink and drive, not God's choice. But let's say the person I hit with my car was a serial rapist. Don't you think some people might say that God was guiding my actions so the world would be rid of this horrible human being? If God is in control of the world, couldn't that be part of God's plan? This whole concept of giving both humans and God some control gets tricky fast because nobody knows whom to credit for which action.

Therefore, it's clear to me that we need to reset the parameters of our thinking in order to make sense of how our will and God's will actually function in the world. First of all, let's assume the tension between God's will and human will does not exist. In other words, let's assume that both glasses can be full and mutually coexist. In this world, human free will and God's will are not in conflict with one another, but can be combined in a perfect unity. If we allow for this option, then, all of a sudden, we have moved into a very different realm of possibility—one that lacks all the common contradictions that make us scratch our heads. Let me lay out for you what this type of thinking looks like, using the drunk-driving example.

First of all, we have to remember in this new scenario that God's will is happening 100 percent of the time. This means that if God is not intervening in the world, then God is *choosing* not to intervene in the world. This also means if you are allowed to make your own decisions that God is *choosing* to allow you to make those decisions. In other words, even if God could stop you from making

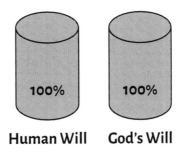

Human Will   God's Will

bad decisions, God *chooses* not to do so. So if you decide to get drunk and drive your car, God is allowing you to make that decision, which demonstrates to us that a major part of God's will is choosing not to intervene in the universe.

If we accept this as a principle about God's will, then all of a sudden the world starts to make a lot more sense. Why didn't God stop you from getting in that car inebriated and running over an innocent pedestrian? Because God allows us to make our own decisions and is not going to try to stop us. However, just because God *allows* you to get drunk and kill a pedestrian doesn't mean that God *wants* you to get drunk and kill a pedestrian. God would prefer that you not cause harm and malice to yourself or your fellow human beings, but God chooses to allow it because God's will is for you to be able to make your own decisions without hindrance.

A lot of Christians don't like this way of thinking about God because it means that God bears ultimate responsibility for the evil in the world. I want to go on the record right now saying that I believe God does bear ultimate responsibility for all the evil in the world. In fact, what most people fail to realize is that Christianity is a religion that revolves around the notion that God is the one who takes responsibility for the evil in the world.

There is a wonderful set of verses in Isaiah that supports this idea: "I am the Lord, and there is no other. I form the light and create darkness, I bring prosperity and create disaster; I, the Lord, do all these things." *(Is. 45:6-7 NIV)* As you can see from these verses, God is clearly taking responsibility for the presence of evil in the world. One of the most harmful aberrations of the Christian faith has been the introduction of the idea that God is all-good and cannot have anything to do with evil. The Hebrew God has always been associated with evil. Indeed, this is part of what it means when we say that God is holy. The word *holy* in our common vernacular is often thought to mean pious or spiritually pure. However, such associations are impositions that we place on the text. The original meaning of the word *holy* in Hebrew is *to be set apart for a special purpose.*[3.9]

For example, the verse surrounding keeping the Sabbath (the day of rest in the Jewish faith) says: "You shall keep the Sabbath, because it is holy for you; everyone who profanes it shall be put to death; whoever does any work on it shall be cut off from among the people." *(Ex. 31:14)* If we insert the meaning above, then this verse makes a lot more sense: "You shall keep the Sabbath, because it *has been set apart for a special purpose.*" The special purpose in this instance is that God wants the Hebrew people to rest for a day from work to allow time for worshiping God. Similarly, when the Bible describes the Hebrew people as being holy, ("For you are a people holy to the Lord your God, the Lord your God has chosen you out of all the peoples on earth to be his people, his treasured possession." *Dt. 6:7*) it is clear that they are set apart for a special purpose by God. Likewise, when God is said to be holy, it means God has been set aside for a special purpose. In Judaism and Christianity, I think one could argue quite convincingly that God's special purpose is that God's being contains both good and evil.

This notion that God can contain and take responsibility for both good and evil is critical to understanding the God of the Bible. Indeed, without this premise, it is impossible to correct the fallacies that have entered into Christian doctrine. Let's review: the conventional way of understanding God's omnipotence is to say that God can do anything. However, reality does not bear this out, so we must come to the conclusion that either God is absent or is present, but does not care. Either way, such a God is not a truly loving God. However, if we characterize God as being holy instead of being omnipotent, then the world makes a lot more sense. The reason why evil exists in the world is because God chooses not to interfere with our decisions. We are given free will by God to do as we wish, which means that God must allow for the existence of evil. Indeed, what the Bible makes clear is that God not only allows evil to exist, but God also takes full responsibility for the presence of that evil. Evil is a part of who God is, just as good is part of who God is.

This way of thinking about God is not only consistent with our real world experience, but it also sets us up to answer the question of how a God that allows evil in the world could still be considered a loving God. The fact that God is holy, taking responsibility for both good and evil, means we must dispose of the notion that God is omnibenevolent (all-good). If you remember from our chart, the descriptor we use in place of an all-good God is a God who is loving. On the surface, this might seem a bit paradoxical. How can a God that contains both good and evil be a God of love? Suffice it to say that unwinding this paradox is not only going to take us the whole next chapter, but also the rest of this book. Not only will this discussion help us come to terms with Kayla's predicament, but also with the issue of how God's love interacts with a universe that contains evil. In my opinion, perhaps the best way to approach this paradox is by dissecting one of the most important stories in the Old Testament—the story of Joseph.

1 Christians often define God by the omni's—omnipotent, omniscient, omnibenevolent and omnipresent—which are derived from Greek philosophy. These terms are not original to the thinking of the Hebrews who wrote the Old Testament. Indeed, these words are inaccurate when describing the God of the Hebrews.

2 God is not omnipresent, observing existence from afar. God is transcendent and immanent, meaning God is in everything, making existence possible. The Hebrews conceived of God undergirding the very fabric of the universe.

3 If God is the reason why everything exists, then God is ultimately responsible for the presence of both good and evil in the universe. Thus, the descriptor of God as being omnibenevolent (all-good) is no longer accurate.

4 God's interaction with evil in the universe is grounded in the principle that God always allows us to make our own decisions, whether they be good or evil. God may not *want* us to make evil decisions, but empirical evidence of the world around us suggests that God will not intervene to stop those decisions.

5 God is not omnipotent (all-powerful), changing the course of the natural order. Rather, the Hebrews thought of God as holy, set apart for the special purpose of taking responsibility for the good and evil brought into the world through our choices.

CHAPTER FOUR

THE GOD OF REDEMPTION

SUFFERING FOR SALVATION

If you are not familiar with the story of Joseph, you should know his tale lays the foundation for many of the themes touched on throughout the Bible. *(Gn. 37, 39-50)* Therefore, I believe it is worth our time to recap his story because it will provide us with some concrete examples of how God does and does not interact in the world.

Joseph was the most cherished of twelve sons of a man named Jacob. To show how much he loved Joseph, Jacob gave Joseph a long robe with sleeves. The Hebrew literally says a *garment of strips* and these strips were made of a fine linen. I know this will come as quite a shock to those who have seen Andrew Lloyd Webber's Broadway musical, *Joseph and the Amazing Technicolor Dreamcoat*, but there was nothing multicolored about it. Joseph was a shepherd and, generally, shepherds wore sleeveless flax tunics and covered themselves with rough wool coats. What made Joseph's coat special was that "it was long and hemmed, a garment usually worn by persons of wealth and authority."[4.1]

Jacob's favoritism towards Joseph led to resentment by his older brothers. To make matters worse, Joseph was somewhat arrogant. He was a good-looking guy who was blessed with many talents, not the least of which was the ability to interpret dreams. The biblical authors believed that God placed certain dreams in our minds at night and that the images in those dreams were communications sent to tell humans about the future.[4.2] Most people lacked the ability to interpret dreams and it was thought that only certain gifted people, like Joseph, could parse out the meaning.

Joseph's brothers went over the edge when Joseph told them about a dream in which he predicted that he would rule over his father and his brothers. Initially, the brothers decided to kill Joseph, but then, at the last minute, they changed their minds and sold him to some slave traders who transported Joseph to Egypt. After arriving in Egypt, Joseph was sold into the house of Potiphar, the captain of the guard, a position likely dedicated to overseeing Pharaoh's personal security detail.

Once inside Potiphar's house, Joseph quickly rose to manager of the household, which meant he would have supervised his fellow slaves. Joseph had gone from a very bad situation to one that was much improved, but his troubles were not over. Joseph was such a good-looking fellow that he attracted the attention of Potiphar's wife who wanted to have an affair with him. Day after day she pursued Joseph until eventually she cornered him. When she grabbed for Joseph's clothes he was forced to run away, tearing the tunic from his body. Unable to explain how Joseph's clothes came into her possession, she accused Joseph of attempting to rape her. When Potiphar was told the story, he sent Joseph to the royal prison, where he would be incarcerated with other political dissidents.

While in prison, Joseph became friendly with the chief jailor who put him in charge of all the prisoners because everything Joseph put his hands on seemed to prosper. Eventually, two prisoners from Pharaoh's court ended up in prison with Joseph: Pharaoh's chief baker and his cup bearer. They each had a dream, but neither of them knew anyone who could interpret it for them. Of course, dream interpretation just happened to be Joseph's area of expertise and he was able to predict the future for the two men. Pharaoh would restore the cup bearer to his position and hang the chief baker. Even though Joseph's predictions came true, the cup bearer forgot about Joseph until two years later when Pharaoh had several dreams that none of his advisors were able to interpret. Pharaoh's cupbearer remembered Joseph from their time together in prison, which resulted in Pharaoh bringing Joseph out of prison to interpret the dreams. Joseph famously predicted there would be seven years of plenty and seven years of famine.

Joseph then advised Pharaoh to appoint someone to store up grain during the years of plenty so that the population would be able to survive during the years of famine. Pharaoh appointed Joseph to the position, commonly known as Grand Vizier, which was second in command to Pharaoh. When Joseph rose from slave to savior in one fell swoop, we realize that Joseph had a larger purpose—Joseph needed to be enslaved so he would eventually have the opportunity to save the Egyptians and his own family from starvation. Joseph suffered so that, in the end, people could be saved.

Similar to the story of Noah, the biblical story of Joseph is largely fictitious with only a few details reflected in the archaeological record.[4.3] However, in the same way that the story of Noah provides insight into how the authors conceived of God, Joseph's story does the same in terms of how the Hebrews understood God's interactions with the world. This idea that God wants to save humans from destruction is commonly expressed among Christians using the term *salvation*. The experience of salvation is the experience of being delivered from harm, ruin or loss. Christians often say that God desires salvation for all humanity.

I'll tell you that I do agree with this idea, however, my understanding of salvation is very different from what Christians commonly promote as salvation. The word *salvation* is a loaded word because it is commonly associated, in modern Christianity, with heaven and hell. Most Christians understand salvation to mean your soul will be allowed into heaven, whereas those who have not attained salvation will go to hell. This is not the original Hebrew conception of salvation. For the Hebrews, salvation had nothing to do with the afterlife.

INDIVIDUAL VS. COMMUNITY

If you pay close attention to the Old Testament, you realize the Hebrews (the ancestors of the Jewish people) had a very limited understanding of the afterlife. In fact, the Old Testament says almost nothing about what happens after we die. The Hebrews were far more concerned with this life. The Bible is often written from the perspective of how God desires to save us from the suffering that defines human existence. Salvation has its roots in the notion that God creates opportunities in human history for redemption.

The easiest way to understand redemption is the idea of taking something bad and using it for good. In Joseph's story, God takes a bad situation (Joseph being sold into slavery) and uses it for something good (Joseph rising to power to store up grain so people do not starve to death). This concept is even spoken by Joseph when his brothers come to him, begging forgiveness for selling him into slavery. Joseph says, "Do not be afraid! Am I in the place of God? Even though you intended to do harm to me, God intended it for good, in order to preserve a numerous people, as he is doing today." *(Gn. 50:19-20)*

The only thing I am certain of when it comes to God's will is redemption. I say this because redemption is the only thread that exists from the beginning of the Bible to the end. Even when we discard all of the preposterous ways that God is portrayed in the Bible, redemption is the one characteristic that remains constant in the scriptures.

Our problem when trying to understand the biblical concept of redemption is that we are interpreting redemption through our cultural lens. The biblical concept of redemption is grounded in a culture that is extremely communal, whereas Western culture is highly individualistic. Although this difference might seem trivial, your cultural perspective makes a big difference in how you interpret the Biblical stories. Let's use Joseph's story to explore this difference.

I would assume that when most Westerners read Joseph's story, the primary person on whom they focus is Joseph. And that makes sense, right? It's Joseph's story and if he doesn't succeed, then everyone will suffer. Unfortunately, our natural inclination to focus solely on the main character results in two interpretive flaws: 1) we come to believe that God has an individual plan for every person's life and 2) we tend to ignore the other people who are merely supporting characters in Joseph's rise to power.

For instance, when Joseph is sold into slavery, he was most certainly sold alongside other slaves. What happened to them? Well, most of those slaves didn't end up as a servant in somebody's home like Joseph. The majority of slaves in Egypt were worked to death in fields or on building projects. So if you're Joseph, God has a plan and God is looking out for you, but if you're just some random slave, you're out of luck.

Another example of this is when the chief baker is hanged by Pharaoh. Sure, this incident provides Joseph with an opportunity to showcase his skill of dream interpretation before Pharaoh, but does no one care that this guy got his neck snapped in half? What if you happened to be in his shoes? No matter how many people Joseph saves, if I were the chief baker, I don't think I would appreciate being collateral damage for God's plan. This is why the concept of God having a plan for every human life is so problematic. If you're Joseph and things work out for you, then God having a plan is a wonderful idea. However, if you're someone else who is not as important, someone who is disposable, then God having a plan would not be that great because things might not work out well for you.

What Christians have a tough time admitting is that not everybody can be a Joseph; not everybody comes out better on the other side of difficult circumstances. In fact, most people are the supporting characters, not the lead. But because Western culture has taught us to love stories where people triumph in the face of adversity, we tend to ignore the harsh reality that things don't work out well for everyone in the end. We try to explain away the examples of children dying from cancer, families murdered in genocide, and the unimaginable hardships faced by people living in abject poverty with the phrase, "We may not understand it, but God has a plan."

No! What kind of God "plans" for all those terrible tragedies? In my opinion, such an answer is a way for those who have been fortunate in their lives to makes themselves feel better about the fact that others suffer horribly. If God has a plan for me and I've been successful, then it makes me feel better imagining that God has a plan for others too, even if it's not immediately apparent what that plan is. Thankfully, this misguided Western interpretation of Christianity has no bearing on how the authors intended for us to interpret Joseph's story. The authors of the stories in the Bible lived at a time when the individual wasn't nearly as important as the community. When the ancients heard the story of Joseph, the pay-off was not the individual accomplishments of Joseph, but rather how his accomplishments impacted the community he was serving.

In other words, we're putting the emphasis in the wrong place. When Joseph saved everyone by storing up grain, the point of the story wasn't to emphasize how great Joseph was as an individual, but how Joseph saved his family and the Egyptians from starvation. It was the effects of the individual on the community that mattered far more than that individual's achievements. Therefore, when the community is more important than the individual, the concern of the person listening to the story is whether the community benefited from or was hurt by that individual's actions. Furthermore, when your focus is on the community, this changes the way you think about individual success and tragedy.

THE REDEMPTIVE ARC

On April 30, 1967, Martin Luther King, Jr. preached his famous sermon in opposition to the Vietnam War. One of the most memorable lines from that sermon is when King says, "The arc of the moral universe is long, but it bends towards justice." These sentiments are not original to King, but were written by Theodore Parker, a famous 19th century abolitionist.[4.4] King made use of Parker's writings because King believed God's primary movement in the universe is righting the wrongs that have been committed. King believed this to be true because he had experienced this type of redemption during the Civil Rights Movement of the 1950s and 1960s.

The fight for civil rights was a tediously long battle. Every step forward inevitably produced several steps backward. Indeed, there were many points along the way where progress had all but come to a halt. By the early 1960s some who had dedicated themselves to the cause felt so fatigued and hopeless that others feared the movement might fail. Racism in the South was entrenched to such a degree that steps towards changing the status quo were often met with violence. It was one thing to protest against racist segregation laws, but it was an entirely different thing to become the target of groups like the Klu Klux Klan who reveled in the opportunity to kill African Americans.

Since the end of the Civil War, countless minorities had been the victims of KKK violence. Often there would be no justice for the victims as the legal system was rigged to favor whites over blacks.

In jury trials it was typical for the entire jury to be comprised of whites who were quick to acquit the guilty party in the name of racial solidarity. Nowhere was this situation more prevalent in the 1960s than in Birmingham, Alabama. Birmingham was infamously known as the most segregated city in America and the commissioner of public safety for Birmingham, Eugene "Bull" Connor, epitomized this mentality. Connor was so outspokenly racist that it was widely acknowledged that the KKK was responsible for helping him get elected to office.

When King arrived in Birmingham, he used the Sixteenth Street Baptist Church as the epicenter of his movement. Knowing that all bets were off with Connor at the helm, King famously anointed each of his deputies in the church, believing they might be killed during the protests. From April 3 through May 10, 1963, King, who had very few willing adult volunteers, rallied support from the black youth in Birmingham. Students ranging from elementary school to college filled the streets, producing the most successful series of protests seen within the Civil Rights Movement. When Connor reacted to the demonstrations with violence, people across the country were outraged that he would allow his officers to harm young children with police dogs and water cannons. In fact, this series of marches was so successful in changing the tide of national public opinion that it became the blueprint for how future protests would be conducted.

The KKK was enraged that King's efforts threatened to undermine the principles of segregation. They wanted to make a bold statement to the black community that whites would ultimately be victorious and so they targeted the center of the Civil Rights Movement in Birmingham. On September 15, 1963, a bomb exploded at the Sixteenth Street Baptist Church, destroying the entire building. Though they had eradicated a very important symbol of the Civil Rights Movement, they had also done something unexpected. Unbeknownst to the KKK, five girls (Addie Mae Collins, Denise McNair, Carole Robertson, Cynthia Wesley and Carolyn

McKinstry) were in the building preparing for worship services to be held later that morning. The blast killed all of the girls with the exception of Carolyn McKinstry, who was badly wounded. Four of the girls were 14 years old and one, Denise McNair, was 11.

When word spread that the KKK had killed four young girls, the public outcry was passionate. The unjust nature of their deaths struck a chord with everyone around the country, even among those who lived in the South and harbored racist sentiment. The deaths of these girls galvanized the Civil Rights Movement and is a big reason why civil rights legislation was successful in Congress in February of 1964.

The story of these five girls begs the question: if the arc of the moral universe bends towards justice, does that mean it was God's plan for these girls to be in that church at that time? For me, the answer to that question is a resounding, "No!" The God who would "plan" someone's death, even if it benefits the greater good, is no God with whom I want to be associated. Think about it for a second: if that were true, it would mean that God caused those Klansmen to bomb that church, anticipating how the girls' deaths would contribute to the success of the Civil Rights Movement. This would suggest that God is willing to use humans like pawns on a chessboard, that we are expendable if it benefits God's larger cause. And this brings us back to the issue we faced in Joseph's story. If you're a Joseph, then you reap all the benefits of those that God sacrificed so you could succeed.

I don't believe that's the way God works. I don't believe God sacrifices some so others can survive. I believe God gives humans freedom of choice to do what we please. Those men in the KKK made a decision. They decided to destroy the Sixteenth Street Baptist Church because, to them, it represented a threat. As a result, those young girls, who had done no harm to anyone, were killed simply because they happened to be there at that time. God did not "plan" for them to be there. So if God isn't intervening in our decisions, then what exactly is God doing to assure that the moral arc of the universe bends towards justice and redemption? To answer that question, we have to shift the emphasis from the individual to the community.

When you attempt to extract justice from the world on a case-by-case basis, you quickly realize that such a task is impossible. The girls who perished in the Sixteenth Street Baptist Church did not deserve to die. Indeed, the tragedy of such a loss is practically incomprehensible. Those girls had their entire lives ahead of them and, due to the decisions of the KKK, they were deprived of that future. Even if you arrest the men who set the bomb, sentence them to death or have them rot in jail for the rest of their lives, that's not righting the wrong that they committed. Prison or execution only prevents those men from hurting more people, which is no doubt important, but that's not true justice. True justice would be to bring those girls back to life, but that is not possible. In truth, nothing can make it right because those girls are gone and nothing can bring them back. Therefore, as much as we might want there to be justice, it doesn't exist on an individual level.

On the other hand, if we shift our focus to the community, taking a much longer view of how God rights the wrongs committed in the world, then justice, salvation and redemption become a possibility. Let's begin again with our basic premise: God didn't plan for those girls to die in that explosion. Every person had the opportunity to make their own decisions. The KKK made their decision to set the bomb and those girls made their decision to be at the church to prepare for worship services. The bomb goes off. The girls die. Now what? If Joseph's story is to be believed, God's role is to take the outcome of those various decisions and attempt to use them for good.

How does God achieve this without directly intervening in the world? Through God's spirit of redemption. God's spirit of redemption resides within every human heart. It's our choice whether or not we want to allow God's redemptive force to influence our actions. In this particular case, individuals throughout the United

States, whose hearts were in touch with God's spirit of redemption, were so moved by the deaths of those young girls that they felt compelled to support the Civil Rights Movement so others might not have to suffer the same fate.

Was it guaranteed to work? No. Did God know this was going to win the battle no matter what? No. God is not omniscient (all-knowing). We are free to make our own choices and, if we choose, we don't have to be moved by tragedies. The Southern white population could have ignored this tragedy like so many others before it. God's spirit of redemption could have remained dormant inside their hearts. Thankfully, enough people were moved by this tragedy that it set off a chain reaction. With every person who expressed outrage, it opened the door a little wider to make redemption a possibility. Eventually, enough people embraced God's spirit of redemption to allow God to bring some justice to the wrong imposed upon those girls.

I want to be crystal clear that God didn't *anticipate* how their deaths would contribute to the success of the Civil Rights Movement. God couldn't have planned for it because God didn't know it was going to happen until those Klansmen conjured the plan in their minds. That's the problem with true free will. God can't control it. But when those girls died, God wept alongside everyone else and did what only God can do—God brought light and redemption to a place of unimaginable darkness.

THE RIPPLE EFFECT

Whenever I hear stories of horrible tragedies, my deepest hope is that the aftermath of the event might create an opening for good in the world. My hope comes from the belief that God's spirit of redemption is inside all of our hearts. Indeed, I believe that spirit of redemption is inside everything in the universe. In the same way that the very basis of all matter is energy, I believe the spiritual essence of that energy is redemption. In this way, not just human beings, but the entire universe is on a trajectory towards redemption. However, what is clear from the human experience is that redemption is not a foregone conclusion. Not everything bad that happens to human beings is used for good and this is, in part, due to freedom of choice. We must choose to utilize God's spirit of redemption that exists inside us. One way of accessing God's spirit of redemption is through prayer.

Most Christians assume that prayer is a way to get God's attention. Prayer lets God know that your situation needs special consideration. Unfortunately, the underlying assumption behind this approach to prayer is that God lacks the ability to keep tabs on everyone in need of help. It's almost as if the popular conception of prayer is like a pop-up calendar reminder for God. If we take this to its logical end, then, when God hears a prayer, God is thinking, "Thanks so much for saying that prayer because I was totally not paying any attention. If you hadn't taken the time to let me know about this, then I would have definitely missed it and that person would have died. Alright, let's see what I can do…"

The idea that God is like an air traffic controller, sitting in heaven making decisions about who's going to crash and who's going to land, is the exact opposite of God's role in our lives. The notion that our prayers have any impact on God whatsoever is very shortsighted. To think that our words have the ability to influence and change God, the being that is responsible for the creation of the entire universe, is misguided. We don't possess that kind of power. Believe me, I wish we did. When I'm watching somebody die in the hospital, I cannot tell you how badly I want to be able to say some special combination of words that will cause God to change the outcome of that situation. There are times when I wish that God was like a celestial Santa Claus who fulfilled our requests because we've been good people. But as we've discussed, that's not how God works and that's not how prayer works. Instead, the purpose of prayer is to change us and, by consequence, the people around us.

Let's take a moment and look at prayer for what it actually does in the world. When I pray, I often feel a closer connection to God. My prayers haven't changed God, they've changed me. That prayer has opened my heart and allowed me to be more conscious of and connected to the love that God has for me. Does feeling God's love in my heart more closely have an effect on the world? Of course it does. Through my connection with God I'm kinder to other people; I'm looking for more opportunities to serve my fellow human beings and, as a result, I'm spreading God's spirit of redemption throughout the world.[4,5]

When we embrace redemption on an individual level, it can have a crucial impact on the health of the relationships around us. If you think of these redemptive decisions as having a ripple effect that moves beyond us and impacts others, then you can understand how a single decision promoting redemption can affect numerous people in positive ways. I have noticed that a single redemptive act by an individual has the potential to neutralize the impact of numerous negative ripples.

When I was growing up, I had a very combative relationship with my mother who suffered from addiction issues. Her addictions were symptomatic of deeper problems from her past, but the substances in her bloodstream were often at the root of her behavior toward my sisters and me. Though I cannot claim any physical abuse, my mother had no compunction about telling me that I was a failure. When that's all you hear day in and day out, you come to have a very low opinion of yourself.

I can say with all honesty that during my adolescence I had grown to hate my mother. I did everything in my power to avoid being around her. I could not understand why someone would intentionally bring so much pain to a child she supposedly loved. I carried that hurt with me everywhere. Her words had made me angry, bitter and miserable. I carried this huge burden in my heart that weighed heavily on my soul. The negative ripples from her actions had left me a hollow shell of a person. But then, when I was 21, there was one positive redemptive ripple that changed everything for me.

I was studying theology at Oxford University in England, when, for the first time, I read the words of Jesus from Matthew's gospel: "You have heard that it was said, 'You shall love your neighbor and hate your enemy.' But I say to you, Love your enemies and pray for those who persecute you." *(Mt. 5:43-44)* This idea of loving your enemy was entirely new to me. Why would anyone ever want to love their enemy? What good could that possibly achieve? Wouldn't loving your enemy just make you more vulnerable, giving them the chance to walk all over you? I posed these questions to some of the monks with whom I was studying and they explained that, while the logic is counter-intuitive, some of the greatest social changes in history have come about as a result of this philosophy.

As I was in England, not surprisingly they cited Gandhi's campaign to free India from British colonial rule as a prime example of how the methods of love and pacifism can transform the world. Gandhi used peaceful protest to force Britain's hand. When the British cracked down on the protests, it only bolstered support for Gandhi's movement. With large numbers of Indians from all levels of society beginning to rally in full support of Gandhi, the British knew it was only a matter of time before they lost their grip on the power structure. Following World War II the British made it known that they planned to exit India and allow for self-rule. This enormous change came about not because the citizens of India fought their oppressors with violence, but because they showed them love. Indeed, Gandhi's success in India inspired Martin Luther King, Jr.'s approach to bringing the Civil Rights Movement to the states.

The monks with whom I studied explained that if the power of love can transform entire nations, think of what it can do for each of us personally. I decided I would give it a chance. Since my greatest enemy was my mother, I decided I would love her without condition. I would accept her for who she was, addictions and all. When she assaulted me with her words, I did not fight back. I listened in silence, waited for her tirade to end and then said, "I'm sorry you feel that way." I soon realized that by not responding to her with anger, I had stripped her of her power. Eventually she stopped criticizing me altogether because she knew it wouldn't achieve the desired result. As time passed and my love towards my mother grew, I was able to forgive her for her actions toward me during my youth. One redemptive ripple based on a verse about loving my enemy was able to heal 21 years of negative assaults on my character.

I know it might not seem possible, but God's spirit of redemption is far more powerful than the evil we bring into the world. Although our redemptive reach as an individual is often limited to our immediate sphere of influence, it can be the spark that starts an entire movement of redemption in our communities. For every person who creates a redemptive ripple, there is an ever-expanding swath of individuals who benefit directly and indirectly by healing the evil they have encountered and created in the world. This is the beauty of God's wisdom. By giving us the free will to choose our own path rather than planning it out for us, God enables us to become a tool for redeeming the brokenness of the world.

My dream is to see entire communities engage in redemption because the possibilities multiply exponentially. The more people who embrace God's spirit of redemption, the more God can create redemptive movements and bring about far-reaching change for the better. In this way, entire social structures of evil can be uprooted and overturned to create what Jesus commonly referred to as God's kingdom. Every redemptive ripple brings us one step closer to the creation of God's kingdom, the culmination of which will be when God's spirit of redemption has finally taken hold of every human heart.

THE IMPURITIES IN THE CLAY

Perhaps one of the most important realizations I have had about God is that God can only work with the decisions we make. The human material with which God works determines a lot about the quality of the outcome God can produce in the world. There is a beautiful verse in Jeremiah where God sends him to a potter's house. Jeremiah sits outside the door of the potter and watches as the potter works with the clay on the wheel. God speaks to Jeremiah: "Can I not do with you, O house of Israel, just as this potter has done? says the Lord. Just like the clay in the potter's hand, so are you in my hand, O house of Israel." *(Je. 18:6)*

I always assumed that the point of this story was to promote God's ultimate authority over the universe. God can do whatever God wants to Israel just like the potter manipulating the clay. But then it occurred to me—not all clay is of the same quality. God can change and reform the people of Israel as long as they are willing to be reformed, but the outcome of that reformation depends greatly on their decisions.

In this analogy, when the people of Israel make poor decisions, it is like giving a potter bad clay with which to work. The potter will do the best that he can, but because the raw material is so bad, the end product will be flawed. On the other hand, when the potter is working with high quality clay, then the final product can be molded into something much better. Thus, when our decisions are more in line with God's spirit of redemption, then God can create a product of high quality. My point is that our decisions determine the outcome of God's redemptive force in the world.

This is a hard concept to grasp, but I really do believe that God is limited by our choices. This is not to say that God is not great, but the world demonstrates to us time and time again that God chooses to allow our decisions to take precedence in shaping God's activity in the world. For some people, the notion that God chooses to limit God's activity in the world is tantamount to abandonment. However, I personally believe that this choice by God is at the core of God's wisdom for our world because it means that God believes in us enough to know we all possess the potential to make the right decisions for love, truth, justice and redemption.

There is one problem with this argument: if so much of God's ability to change the world is based on our decisions, then why didn't God create us to be more inclined to make redemptive decisions? Looking at the world around us, it would seem our decisions too often trend away from the redemptive and towards the selfish. To examine why this is the case, I want to tell you a story about the Milwaukee police department.

Police work is one of the most important and difficult occupations in our society. These men and women have dedicated themselves to keeping our society from devolving into chaos. Ed Flynn, chief of police for the Milwaukee police department from 2008-2018, once said that almost every single officer in training in the academy comes in with the mindset that they want to help people and make the world a better place. His point is that all officers begin with a desire to bring redemption to their own communities. However, Flynn also described how, over time, even the most idealistic officers can become jaded as a result of what they deal with day-to-day.[4.6]

This is partly because officers are constantly encountering people in crisis situations. Whereas most people's first instinct is to run away from chaos, a police officer's job is to enter into chaos and bring peace. A police officer accomplishes this by protecting the victims and arresting the culprits. That might sound simple on the surface, but the reality is far more complicated. When a police officer intervenes in a situation, it is not always easy to tell the victim from the culprit because most people guilty of committing a crime are going to lie to protect themselves. Nor is it unusual for victims to lie. For instance, when an officer responds to a domestic abuse call, the person suffering the abuse may downplay the situation in order to keep their partner from being arrested. Likewise, victims of minor altercations can exaggerate the seriousness of the conflict in order to prompt the officer to make an arrest. The police officer, working with incomplete information, may make wrong decisions through no fault of her own.

Another example of people lying to police officers is when they have been arrested and are being transported to jail. It is very common for people in this situation to claim that they have a medical condition and that they need to be taken to the hospital. The vast majority of people who claim this are faking. They hope that being at the hospital might give them a chance to escape. At the very least, it will delay incarceration. Occasionally, however, such a person is not faking. One such incident occurred in the Milwaukee police department when a man named Derek Williams was arrested for robbery and was being transported to a holding cell. He told the arresting officers that he could not breathe and that he needed medical attention. For eight minutes he begged the officers for help, until he passed out in the back of the police car. Derek Williams died before medical help could arrive.

When the footage of Derek Williams became public, people were appalled that the officers had disregarded his pleas for help. How could they be so heartless and indifferent to this man's condition? What most people don't realize is that these particular officers are not heartless or horrible people. The problem is that police officers are used to having people lie to them. No matter how much they care or how much good they want to do in the world, their environment is teaching them that people lie all the time. Let me be clear, this reality doesn't excuse the fact that they let Derek Williams die in the back of their vehicle. They should have listened to his pleas for help and called an ambulance. Sadly, what a situation like this proves to us is that, in spite of their best intentions to keep the community safe, their environment is changing the way they see people. And this is true of everyone. The more time you spend in a particular environment, the more that environment trains your brain to see the world through a particular lens.

This lens in our brain is more commonly known as prejudice and it affects everyone because our environments shape our prejudices. This is something we don't often like to admit because I think many of us would like to believe that we have no prejudices. But prejudice is part of the human condition because prejudice is part of what keeps us safe. If you're walking down the street and a guy in tattered clothes asks you to walk into a dark alley with him, it's in your best interest to say, "No, thank you." Is that decision prejudiced? Of course it is. You're assuming, based on his looks, that going into a dark alley with him could cause you personal harm. However, for all you know, he wants to show you his rare coin collection.

The problem with prejudice is that, because it is so connected with safety in our brains, it is very common for us to label whole groups of people as being dangerous. This labelling is directly connected to our genetic programming. As creatures who evolved over billions of years, we have inherited a natural inclination for survival. This inclination is the result of our ancestors being concerned about threats in their environment. The fact that you are alive to read this book means that your predecessors were more discerning about their safety than some of their peers. We are members of a long genetic line of worriers. We might be relatively calm, but place us in an environment where our safety is in danger and it is extremely difficult for us to overcome the internal mechanisms in our brains that cause us to make prejudicial decisions.

These prejudices, which explain why our ancestors survived, are also the reason why we shy away from redemptive decisions. If you want to understand why there are so many impurities in the clay of humanity, then all you have to do is look at the environments in which people live. If a person lives in a positive environment with love and support, then the genetics of prejudice are going to be far less active than when someone is in a negative environment where there is a constant threat to their safety. If you change the environment, then you change the probability that God's spirit of redemption can be active in your life.

When I was in high school, I was continually bullied by a group of people who called themselves "rednecks." Due to the fact that this group continually threatened my safety, I developed an intense prejudice against any person who fit their particular profile. Eight years after I had graduated from high school, my environment had changed significantly. During the intervening years, I had graduated from college and was studying at Princeton Theological Seminary. I had not been around the types of people who threatened my safety for nearly a decade.

During my second year of seminary, I took a job as the youth pastor of a Methodist church in the area. This church was highly invested in a mission project called ASP or Appalachia Service Project, a mission project designed to help families who live in the Appalachian Mountains. The type of people we were going to help reminded me of those against whom I had developed my prejudice. I wish I could tell you that it was easy for me to set my prejudice aside, but it wasn't.

Many of the people we went to help only reinforced many of the stereotypes that were already prevalent in my mind. I found that many of the families could afford to perform work on their homes, but they chose to spend their money in other ways. So even though their house was in total disarray and their kids were malnourished, they had a sports car in the driveway. It was really upsetting to me that our time was being used to make up for their poor financial decisions.

What changed my perspective was a conversation with a child on one of my last ASP trips. This young boy lived in the house we were rehabilitating. He told me how on cold nights, because the walls were so thin, he couldn't feel his feet. He alluded to the fact that they had no heat because his father had a drinking problem.

And then it hit me like ton of bricks—this is how many of those kids who used to torture me back in high school probably lived. They had no heat. They had no food. They had no support. Like this little child, they called out to God at night hoping that God would hear them and provide some relief. That's when God's spirit moved inside me and I realized that redemption for this boy was giving him the chance that those other kids in my high school never had.

Honestly, I don't know if I could have come to that realization if I was still living in the same kind of environment I had experienced in high school. However, because I was living in a far more positive environment, God's spirit of redemption was able to help me see the errors in my thinking and the prejudices I had built up in the name of safety. God was able to overturn years of negative reinforcement in a single conversation with a young boy who helped me see the humanity in the people who had treated me with such inhumanity.

Not everyone is so fortunate. Many people remain in the same environment for all their lives, which makes it hard to see past the prejudicial barriers that have been erected in their minds. This is why God's redemption is not a guarantee for every person on the planet. The raw material of humanity is shaped by so many genetic and environmental variables that God can only work with situations we have created for ourselves.[4.7] This helps us to understand why Kayla Mueller's story ended with tragedy. The members of ISIS who executed Kayla did so because their understanding of the world is horribly skewed by the prejudicial barriers erected in their minds toward the United States and the West. Indeed, their perspective of the world is so distorted that God's spirit of redemption is essentially snuffed out of their hearts. If her captors had been more in touch with God's spirit of redemption, then Kayla's fate might have been different.

This point is perhaps the most important key to understanding God's work in the universe from the Christian perspective. God has given *us* the tools that enable us to change our environments, to fight the selfish inclination of our genetics and to bring redemption to the world. We are not supposed to sit around and wait for God to fix everything. God has entrusted us with that responsibility. Therefore, the next question we must ask is how do we make the best decisions to help humanity create an environment where love and redemption can thrive? To answer this question, we must now turn to Jesus of Nazareth.

1   The authors of the stories in the Bible lived at a time when the individual wasn't nearly as important as the community.

2   It is impossible to extract justice from the world on an individual, case-by-case basis. On the other hand, if we shift our focus to the community, taking a longer view of how God rights the wrongs committed in the world, then justice, salvation and redemption become possible.

3   God's spirit of redemption is far more powerful than the evil we bring into the world. Although our individual redemptive reach is often limited to our immediate sphere of influence, it can spark an entire movement of redemption in our communities.

4   God's wisdom for our world is not to interfere with our choices. The downside of this position is that God can only work with situations we have created for ourselves, which are often negative and hurtful. The benefit of this position is that God believes we all possess the potential to make the right decisions for love, truth, justice and redemption.

PART THREE

JESUS

Restorative Faith

WILL THE REAL JESUS PLEASE STAND UP?

One of the problems with being a pastor is that you encounter a lot of people who believe that they can do your job better than you can. It's challenging to stand up in front of an audience every week and have them scrutinize every word you say. The problem is that the people in your congregation are already familiar with the material. Unlike an interaction with a doctor or a lawyer where the average person knows very little about medicine or the law, there are people sitting in the pews who have been studying this material for decades. Furthermore, everyone in your congregation has formed their own conclusions about what Christianity does and does not mean. Therefore, what most people are looking for when they come to church is confirmation of what they already believe to be true.

This reality creates a dynamic where most pastors are very careful about what they say. The average pastor will not give an honest opinion because they don't want to cause church members to become upset and leave. If people leave, contributions decline and there will not be enough money to pay the pastor's salary and keep the lights on. Therefore, most pastors are beholden to the people in the pews. I have seen situations where the person who writes the biggest check gets the most say. In a very real sense, the people with the most money define the type of Jesus you hear from the pulpit.

For instance, let's say the pastor comes to a passage in the Bible where Jesus speaks negatively of wealth: "How hard it will be for those who have wealth to enter the kingdom of God." *(Mk. 10:43)* The pastor will either skip the passage entirely or try to explain away Jesus' criticism of wealth as being related to people who are not generous with their money. Never would the pastor blatantly say that Jesus sees the accumulation of wealth as contradictory to loving God. Indeed, the pastor will make sure that the wealthiest members know that their wealth in no way compromises their relationship with God.

As you can imagine, this means Jesus is portrayed differently in every church you enter. Depending on the people who hold the power and the issues that are important to them, Jesus is going to sound very different. In some churches, Jesus hates homosexuals, while in others Jesus is very concerned about gay rights. In some churches, Jesus wants you to be rich, while in others Jesus only wants you to care for the poor. In some churches, Jesus is black, while in others he's Swedish with blonde hair and blue eyes. In some churches, Jesus is a radical liberal trying to overturn systems of injustice, while in others he's a staunch conservative trying to maintain traditional family values. In other words, Jesus is a reflection of the people sitting in the pews. Therefore, when everyone thinks that Jesus embodies their values and their opinions, how do we ever find the real Jesus?

Honestly, I don't think we can ever truly know the real Jesus. The closest we can get to him is based on two sources: 1) the documents compiled in the New Testament of the Bible and 2) the historical records outside of the Bible that tell us about the period in which Jesus lived. Sometimes these two sources align with each other and sometimes they diverge. The issue is which source material takes precedence when a disagreement arises? Most people raised in the Christian faith have been taught to trust the biblical record of Jesus' life as being more accurate than the history surrounding his life. They are taught this because the church promotes the Bible as being inspired by God, so why would God lie to you?

Indeed, this used to be my default mode of interpretation. However, the more I studied the history surrounding the Bible, the more I came to realize that the biblical writers had agendas. These agendas influenced the way they portrayed certain events in Jesus' life. A good example of this is when Jesus comes before the Roman governor, Pontius Pilate, to be tried for treason. Pilate is portrayed in the gospels as being very sympathetic to Jesus' cause. However, we know from historical evidence outside of the Bible that this is unlikely.

For instance, in 36 C.E. the Samaritans lodged grievances with Vitellius, legate of Syria, complaining that Pilate was putting his subjects to death without even holding a trial.[A.1] Indeed, Pilate was a very cruel man who greatly disliked the Jewish people.[A.2] Therefore, the likelihood that Pilate even held a trial for Jesus is extraordinarily low. If Jesus did go to trial, you can be sure that Pilate never took the time to defend Jesus as is commonly portrayed in the gospels.

When the biblical portrayal of the events surrounding Jesus' life conflict with non-biblical historical sources, one has to question why such a discrepancy exists. Usually this inconsistency has to do with the audience for whom the biblical author is writing. Let's take Mark's gospel as an example. Mark was sensitive to the fact that his community was comprised of Roman citizens. Mark goes to great lengths to portray Rome in a positive light, which is why Pontius Pilate is represented as being sympathetic to Jesus' cause. Mark wants to make sure that the people in his church do not feel responsible for Jesus' death. Thus, even though Rome is in charge of overseeing all death penalty cases, by portraying Pontius Pilate as attempting to defend Jesus, Mark sees to it that Rome does not bear full responsibility for Jesus' execution.

This is not to say that everything the biblical authors wrote about Jesus is untrustworthy. All it means is that they want to portray Jesus in a certain light that may or may not be accurate to who Jesus was in real life. Therefore, when anyone claims to be constructing an "accurate" portrayal of Jesus' life, it is going to be derived from information that is based on the bias of their sources. So let me say up front, I am in no way claiming to be providing a definitive portrait of Jesus' life. Rather, like everyone else who speaks of Jesus' life, I am building a picture of his life based on the information that I believe is most accurate to who he actually was during his time on this earth. Could I be wrong? Absolutely! I have biases just like everyone else, so let's get them out on the table.

As you just read above, one of my biases is that, when there is a discrepancy between the Bible and non-biblical historical documents, I tend to favor the non-biblical documents. Another bias is that I believe the historical Jesus is different from the way Jesus is often portrayed in the Christian religion. In other words, the Jesus who Christians worship in church is not a complete reflection of the Jesus of history. Based on my study of the scriptures, I have come to the conclusion that the Bible contains a mixture of the historical Jesus and the Jesus of religion. Disentangling the real historical Jesus from the Jesus of religion is challenging because one has to make decisions as to what to include as authentic and what to exclude as additions that have no basis in reality. Let me give you an example.

In Mark's gospel, the first and earliest of the gospels in the New Testament, Jesus is portrayed as an itinerate preacher with no real education in the Torah. Mark seems to believe that Jesus gained all of his knowledge of the Bible when he is baptized by John the Baptist around the age of 30. Indeed, Mark portrays everyone who knew Jesus from a young age as being astounded that Jesus knows as much as he does about the Old Testament: "On the Sabbath [Jesus] began to teach in the synagogue, and many who heard him were astounded. They said, 'Where did this man get all this? What is this wisdom that has been given to him?'" *(Mk. 6:2)*

However, by the time Luke writes his gospel, some 20 years later, Jesus is portrayed as a 12 year old boy in the Jerusalem Temple whose knowledge of the Torah rivals the most learned rabbis in Israel: "When the festival was ended and they started to return, the boy Jesus stayed behind in Jerusalem, but his parents did not know it....After three days they found him in the temple, sitting among the teachers, listening to them and asking them questions. And all who heard him were amazed at his understanding and his answers." *(Lk. 2:43, 46-47)*

Clearly, one of these portrayals is inaccurate. Jesus can't be both a poor itinerate preacher of no education who surprises everyone by his knowledge at 30 years of age and a boy genius who knows everything about the Torah. Therefore, knowing that Mark is the earliest portrayal, we can see an evolution in thinking about the person of Jesus. When Mark wrote about Jesus, he portrayed Jesus as he likely was—a poor, uneducated peasant. Over time, the Christian religion began to inflate Jesus into something more than an itinerate preacher. Thus, when Luke writes his gospel, Jesus becomes a fully trained rabbi who knows the teachings of Judaism better than anyone who has ever lived.

When these discrepancies arise, I have to make a decision as to which one is more accurate. Usually, the earlier the information is written in the New Testament, the more likely I am to give it credence. I will admit that these are judgment calls on my part. I could very well be wrong in my assumption that one piece of information is more valid than another. However, I always do my best to weigh the material and provide an interpretation based on what seems most likely. Through this process my hope is that we will be able to dissect and tell the difference between the Jesus of history and the Jesus of religion. Thus, our goal over the next six chapters is to encounter Jesus through these two separate lenses and discover why Jesus' message and movement are still relevant to us in the 21st century.

— CHAPTER FIVE —

FINDING OUR WAY BACK TO EDEN

THE CHERRY TREE

Growing up in Fredericksburg, Virginia, I was constantly reminded that our town was where America's first president, George Washington, grew up. It was hard to walk around town without bumping into some monument or house that was connected to Washington. From where I lived, if you walked two blocks in one direction, you could visit Washington's mother's house. If you walked two blocks in the other direction, you would find Washington's sister's house. There's even a miniature version of the Washington Monument dedicated to Washington's mother called the Mary Washington Monument.

During my elementary school years, we talked a lot about George Washington's childhood. Did you know that, as a young boy, Washington took a silver dollar and threw it all the way across the Potomac River? Never mind the fact that silver dollars didn't exist when Washington was a boy or that the average distance across the Potomac is 1,300 feet. If Washington hadn't become president, he would have made a great baseball player, since the farthest anyone has ever thrown a baseball is 445 feet, a feat presently held by Glen Gorbous.[5.1]

We were also told about how, as a six-year-old boy, Washington received a hatchet as a gift. Why anyone would give a hatchet to a six-year-old boy is beyond me, but apparently, upon receiving the gift, Washington started hacking away at one of his father's cherry trees. When Washington's father discovered the mutilated tree, he confronted George. Rather than deny the offense, Washington owned his mistake saying, "I cannot tell a lie....I did cut it with my hatchet."[5.2] Washington's father, overjoyed at his son's honesty, gave George a big hug and told him that honesty was worth more than a thousand trees.

Clearly, these stories are mythologies that formed around the man who would become one of the most iconic figures in American history. These stories reflect our fascination with a man who helped form the United States of America. We know the source of these mythologies. They were invented by a pastor named Mason Locke Weems. After Washington's death in 1799, Weems wanted to capitalize on the public's interest in all things Washington. When Weems pitched his book to publishers, he said "Washington you know is gone! Millions are gaping to read something about him.... My plan! I give his history, sufficiently minute....I then go on to show that his unparalleled rise and elevation were due to his Great Virtues."[5.3] It is within this "biography" that we find these two stories from Washington's childhood. After the book was published, both of these stories became lodged in the public consciousness and persist to this day.

Although many Christians do not want to admit it, the cherry tree phenomenon is part of Jesus' story in the New Testament. Indeed, if you know the order in which the documents from the New Testament were written, then you can see how the mythologies began to creep into the story of Jesus' life. Below is a list of the documents in the New Testament according to the order they appear in the Bible. Next to that list are the same books in the order that scholars believe they were written, with the estimated dates of their authorship:[5.4]

Order in the New Testament	Order according to the date of composition
1) The Gospel of Matthew	1) 1 Thessalonians – 51 C.E.
2) The Gospel of Mark	2) Galatians – 55 C.E.
3) The Gospel of Luke	3) 1 Corinthians – 56 C.E.
4) The Gospel of John	4) Philemon – 56 C.E.
5) The Acts of the Apostles	5) 2 Corinthians – 57 C.E.
6) Romans	6) Romans – 58 C.E.
7) 1 Corinthians	7) Philippians – 60 C.E.
8) 2 Corinthians	8) The Gospel of Mark – 70 C.E.
9) Galatians	9) James – 80 C.E.
10) Ephesians	10) Colossians – 80 C.E.
11) Philippians	11) The Gospel of Matthew – 80 C.E.
12) Colossians	12) The Gospel of Luke – 85 C.E.
13) 1 Thessalonians	13) The Acts of the Apostles – 85 C.E.
14) 2 Thessalonians	14) Hebrews – 85 C.E.
15) 1 Timothy	15) 1 Peter – 90 C.E.
16) 2 Timothy	16) The Gospel of John – 90 C.E.
17) Titus	17) Revelation – 90 C.E.
18) Philemon	18) Ephesians – 95 C.E.
19) Hebrews	19) 2 Thessalonians – 95 C.E.
20) James	20) 1 John – 95 C.E.
21) 1 Peter	21) 2 John – 95 C.E.
22) 2 Peter	22) Titus – 100 C.E.
23) 1 John	23) 1 Timothy – 100 C.E.
24) 2 John	24) 2 Timothy – 100 C.E.
25) 3 John	25) 3 John – 100 C.E.
26) Jude	26) Jude – 115 C.E.
27) Revelation	27) 2 Peter – 120 C.E.

I know this might not seem that important, but notice how different the order of the column on the right is compared to the column on the left. Many Christians assume that the order of the documents in the New Testament is the order in which they were written, with Matthew composed first and Revelation composed last. However, if you look at the list on right, you can see that the order of the documents in the New Testament has nothing to do with their date of authorship. The earliest documents were written by the Apostle Paul who is the primary person responsible for keeping Jesus' movement alive after Jesus' death. Paul never knew Jesus during his lifetime, but claimed to have met and interacted with Jesus after his execution (an event commonly referred to as the resurrection, which we will discuss at length in Chapter 9). This experience inspired Paul to go out and begin preaching about Jesus, forming churches all over the Mediterranean.

The first letter we have from Paul was written to a church he founded in an area known as Thessalonica. Within this letter, known today as 1 Thessalonians, Paul makes a statement during his closing remarks, "Now may <u>our God and Father</u> himself and <u>our Lord Jesus</u> direct our way to you." *(1 Th. 3:11 – emphasis added)* What I want you to notice about this verse is that Paul believes that Jesus and God are two separate entities.[5.5] Paul refers to God as Father and to Jesus as Lord. I think we can all understand why Paul refers to God as Father, but why does Paul call Jesus "our Lord"? The word *Lord* is Paul's way of saying that Jesus is the messiah. Whatever your understanding of the term messiah from popular culture, a messiah had very specific connotations during Jesus' time.

The word *messiah* in Hebrew simply means *anointed one* and it refers to a Middle Eastern custom of kings having oil poured on their heads during their coronation ceremony.[5.6] The oil was a symbol that this new king had assumed power. During the first century when Jesus was alive, the Jews were waiting for God to send them a messiah. This messiah would be a king who would free the Jewish people from oppression and become the ruler over every nation. However, the Jewish messiah was not a supernatural being. He was a normal human, like Moses or Elijah, whom God chose to lead God's people. Paul believed that Jesus was the messiah the Jews were expecting. Paul was waiting for God to send Jesus back from heaven to have him rule over all the nations of the earth. Jesus' kingship would subsume every nation into one large kingdom known as the kingdom of God.

Therefore, I think it is pretty clear that for Paul, God and Jesus serve two very separate functions. God's role is to be God, the creator and ruler of the universe. Jesus' role is to be the messiah, a king who will rule on behalf of God when God's kingdom is established. 1 Thessalonians was written about 51 C.E. Since Jesus was executed around 30 C.E. that means 1 Thessalonians was composed 20 years after Jesus' death. 1 Thessalonians is the closest document we have in the Bible to Jesus' actual life. Why does that matter? Well, the closer we get to Jesus' life, the more accurate the information should be in terms of how the earliest Christians thought about Jesus. As far as the earliest Christians were concerned, Jesus wasn't God, he was the messiah.

However, if we jump to the last document on our list, 2 Peter, a letter written some 70 years after 1 Thessalonians, we see a dramatic difference in how Christians are speaking about Jesus: "Simeon Peter, a servant and apostle of Jesus Christ, to those who have received a faith as precious as ours through the righteousness of <u>our God and Savior Jesus Christ</u>." *(2 Pt. 1:1 – emphasis added)* Notice that Jesus is no longer only referred to as Lord. In Paul's letters Jesus is called Lord, the messiah, a person who is acting on behalf of God. However, in 2 Peter, Jesus and God are now combined into a single unit. From the perspective of the author of 2 Peter, Jesus and God are one and the same.[5.7]

Clearly, something dramatic has occurred between the writing of 1 Thessalonians and the writing of 2 Peter. In 70 years, Jesus has undergone a transformation from a traditional Jewish messiah to God in the flesh. How did this happen? Well, if you read the books of the New Testament in the order in which they were written, you can see how Jesus is increasingly identified with God. For example, notice that the first gospel written after Paul's letters is the gospel of Mark.[†] In Mark's gospel, the people in Jesus' hometown of Nazareth refer to Jesus as the "son of Mary." *(Mk. 6:3)* This is highly unusual. Normally a Jewish male is identified by his paternal lineage. Therefore, Jesus should be called, "the son of Joseph." The fact that Jesus is called the "son of Mary" is an enormous insult in Jewish culture. Calling someone by their mother's name insinuates that Jesus was an illegitimate child born out of wedlock.

Furthermore, in Mark's gospel, we find out that Jesus has all these brothers and sisters: James, Joses, Judas and Simon to name a few. We don't know if Jesus was the first-born or if he's in the middle. For all we know, he could be the last. Mark never tells us. What's more, it seems in Mark's gospel that Jesus' family doesn't understand what Jesus is doing. They think Jesus has lost his mind and try to restrain him. *(Mk. 3:19b-21)* Mary, Jesus' mother, has no real concept of Jesus being the messiah, so it's clear that Mark knows nothing of the virgin birth.

However, within fifteen years of the writing of Mark's gospel, Christians will attempt to distance themselves from Jesus' sordid past. Both Matthew's and Luke's gospels explain that Jesus is the first child born to Mary. Moreover, God is the one who impregnates Mary, sending angels to explain that God intends for Jesus to be the messiah. *(Mt. 1:18-25, Lk. 1:26-38)* By the time you get to John's gospel, Jesus is said to be present with God at the creation of the universe. *(Jn. 1:1-4)*

Like George Washington, we see that Jesus' followers were eager to know about Jesus' life. As the gospel authors attempted to write biographies of Jesus, the cherry tree stories started to creep into the narrative. In the same way that we ask the question, "Did George Washington really cut down the cherry tree?" we also need

---

†   Review p.29-30 for previous discussion of Mark's gospel.

to ask the question, "Was Jesus really born of a virgin who was impregnated by God?"

Many Christians have argued that if we remove the virgin birth from Jesus' story, then Jesus' movement and message become invalid. To strip Jesus of his divinity is akin to declawing a lion—Jesus' movement cannot survive without the virgin birth because you remove all the meaning and power from Jesus' story. I couldn't disagree more. In my opinion, separating Jesus from the mythology surrounding his birth actually makes Jesus' movement more potent. In order to explain why, we need to talk about that most basic human impulse—sex.

THE LOOP

One of my favorite classes in college was Greek mythology. I had a seemingly insatiable appetite for the stories of the various gods and goddesses. I loved how they would bicker and fight, using humans as pawns in their plots and schemes. Each week we would examine a different myth and my professor would always ask the same question, "What does this story say about us as people?" Many of these conversations were rich and revealing because, as she peeled back the layers of the story, you could always find a part of yourself buried in the mythology. However, of all the conversations we had, the one that really changed my understanding of human nature was the myth of Narcissus.

There are several different versions of the story, but the most well-known begins with Narcissus walking through the woods. A mountain nymph named Echo sees Narcissus, who was regarded by many as a gorgeous man, and falls deeply in love with him. Narcissus, sensing he was being followed, calls out, "Who's there?" Echo calls back, "Who's there?" Eventually, Echo reveals herself to Narcissus, who spurns her advances. Echo is so heartbroken that she spends the rest of her life in lonely glens until nothing but her echo sound remained.

When Nemesis, the goddess of revenge, hears of this story, she lures Narcissus to a pool. When he reaches down to drink, Narcissus sees his own reflection in the water and immediately falls in love, not understanding that it was only an image. Unwilling to leave the pool, Narcissus dies trying to convince his own reflection to come away with him. This story is where we derive the word *narcissistic* or one who is in love with him or herself.[5.8]

My professor explained that it is rare for someone to be narcissistic in the most classical sense of the word. Americans have such low self-esteem that we are far from being in love with ourselves. But where many of us do exhibit narcissistic tendencies is in how we think of other people. We have a propensity to project many of our own insecurities onto the people around us. When we judge another person's appearance (e.g. too fat, too ugly, too skinny, etc.), our comments about that person are usually a reflection of how we feel about our own appearance. Like Narcissus, when we look at that person, we are seeing a reflection of ourselves.

At the end of our conversation about Narcissus, she said something that really stuck with me: "I love reading the term papers in this class because the myth you choose to write about is usually a reflection of who you are as a person. The content of those papers reveals to me your inner thoughts, struggles, anxieties and dreams. But don't be afraid, the same is true for me. As hard as I might try to be objective, my work is always a reflection of my own issues. If you know what to look for, you can always find the Narcissus in a person's writing."

Not long after taking that class I began studying Christianity. It didn't take me long to notice that my mythology professor's insights applied to many of the great thinkers in the Christian faith. This was particularly true for one of the most influential Christian writers of all time—Augustine of Hippo, who lived from 354-430 C.E.[†] Augustine was a genius who shaped the church in dramatic ways.

---

†   Review p.7-8 for previous discussion of Augustine.

Perhaps Augustine's best known work is called *Confessions*, an autobiography. This is required reading in most Humanities 101 classes because it set the standard for how autobiographies would be written. *Confessions* is a fascinating portrait of Augustine's life. Within the first few chapters, it becomes increasingly clear that Augustine has one thing on his mind—sex. Augustine likes sex...a lot.[5.9] He talks extensively about his sexual sins in *Confessions* and, as a result of all of this lust, he fathers a son out of wedlock with his mistress, an act for which he carries great guilt.

Given Augustine's obsession with the subject, I don't think it would be too much of a stretch to say that Augustine could have been classified as a sex addict. Interestingly, Augustine is very similar to many people who struggle with addiction issues. There is no middle ground. It's either all or nothing. When Augustine eventually converts to Christianity, he adopts a very different attitude towards sexuality by becoming celibate. Since Augustine feels incapable of managing his sexual appetite, he determines that he must completely abstain from all sexual relationships.

This decision was not necessarily a bad thing for Augustine. I can't fault the man for trying to find a way to cope with his issues. However, the negative consequence of his decision is that, like Narcissus looking at himself in the pool, Augustine projects his own issues with sexuality onto his understanding of Christianity.[5.10] Throughout his writings on Christianity, he treats sex as an inherently evil action, and this has had major ripple effects on how Christians have approached the topic of sex for the last 1,500 years. Perhaps the greatest impact Augustine's preoccupation with sex had on the Christian faith can be felt through the formation of a doctrine known as Original Sin.

The Doctrine of Original Sin revolves around the first three chapters of Genesis. If you are not familiar with those chapters, let me give you a brief summary. After creating Adam and Eve, God places them in the Garden of Eden. They are given one rule by God that states they are allowed eat the fruit from any of the trees in the garden, but they are not allowed to eat from the fruit of the tree of knowledge of good and evil. One day, Eve is walking in the garden and is approached by a serpent. This serpent convinces Eve that there will be no repercussions if they eat of the forbidden fruit. After eating the fruit, Eve convinces Adam to partake. This action is considered to be the first sin ever committed by humans against God.

When God finds out that Adam and Eve broke the single rule governing their existence, God gets super angry. Not only does God expel the couple from the garden, but God also punishes Adam and Eve with curses. From this point forward, women will experience pain during childbirth; men will have to work to provide food for their families; and humans will live a finite existence. The implication of these curses is that, prior to eating the fruit, childbirth was painless, men didn't have to work hard to gain access to food and humans lived forever.

Augustine was intrigued by these three curses because it was clear to him that they didn't just affect Adam and Eve. Every person since Adam and Eve has had to deal with the consequences of those curses, particularly the curse of death. Therefore, Augustine came to the conclusion that Adam and Eve's sin had permanently corrupted human beings. Indeed, this corruption seemed to be passed from one generation to the next. Not only did every human being inevitably face death, but Augustine felt that every human being was prone to be sinful. Therefore, it made sense to Augustine that every subsequent human born after Adam and Eve was inheriting their original sin.

At the time Augustine developed this doctrine, he knew nothing of how genetics functioned. Augustine believed that the soul was passed from the parent to the child through the act of sexual intercourse. He believed that the semen was transferring the soul of the man into the woman to create the new child.[5.11] Thus, the reason humans are so evil is because each person is inheriting Adam's corrupted soul.

Augustine used this line of thinking to justify why the sexual act should be considered inherently evil. Every human that is born as a result of sexual intercourse will inherit Adam's original sin, meaning that they are destined to live a totally evil and depraved life until they eventually succumb to death. Given this reality, all of us, from the moment we are born, are destined for hell. If only there was some way to escape this endless cycle of bad behavior? Thankfully, God devised a way. His name is Jesus of Nazareth and he was born outside of the loop of original sin.

There are two places in the New Testament where the virgin birth appears—the gospels according to Matthew and Luke. Essentially, these two stories convey the idea that Jesus' mother, Mary, was not impregnated by a human being. Rather, God impregnates Mary through the Holy Spirit. This means that Jesus will not inherit Adam's soul and has the possibility to live a life free of corruption. Indeed, the New Testament tells us that Jesus lived a life completely free of sin from birth until his death on the cross.

So even though the rest of humanity was born inside the loop of Adam's original sin, we can be freed thanks to Jesus' perfect life and sacrifice. All we need to do is believe in Jesus, and this will cause God to overlook the sin we have inherited from our birth. This is why the virgin birth is so critical to Augustine. If sex is the way that Adam's original sin perpetuates itself, then having someone like Mary, who conceives a child without sexual intercourse, is indispensable for Augustine's understanding of Christianity.

Not only is Augustine's Doctrine of Original Sin one of the primary reasons why modern Christians persist in their belief that the virgin birth is non-negotiable, but this doctrine is also the reason why Christians tend to have such a negative view of sex.[5.12] If sex is inherently evil because it produces children inside the loop of Adam's sin, then sex is clearly not a good thing. However, because faith in Jesus frees us from the punishment of Adam's sin, Augustine is willing to admit that sex, within the confines of Christian marriage, is appropriate and necessary. Thus, Augustine is the reason why so many Christian denominations promote the idea that sex prior to marriage is sinful (even though this concept is found nowhere in the Bible). However, once you are within the confines of Christian marriage, then you are free to act on your sexual desires.

If you think all of this seems overly complicated and unnecessary, you're not alone. I cannot help but think that if Augustine could have found a middle ground with his sexual appetite, then Christianity would have been a very different religion. Instead, Augustine shaped Christianity into a religion with a very low opinion of human potential. He promoted the idea that humans can do nothing of worth apart from Jesus. This is why so many conservative Christians refuse to believe that non-Christians can truly perform good deeds. Thanks to Augustine, generations of Christians have been saddled with the conviction that they themselves, and human beings in general, are inherently evil.

And yet, if you study the dominant Christian thinking prior to Augustine, you realize that Augustine very much distorted the original Christian message. Not only are his views of Jesus' purpose inaccurate, but his characterizations of human potential are entirely wrong. Therefore, our next objective is to rediscover what Christianity was intended to be, apart from Augustine.

THE FLAW IN THE DESIGN

I have spent most of my adult life studying the Bible and I am always amazed at how I am able to find little details I missed even though I have read a story dozens of times. Often these details are minor and do not have a major impact on how I interpret the story. However, sometimes these details completely upend an interpretation I've held for years or even decades. One example of this is the story of Adam and Eve. For a long time I interpreted the story of Adam and Eve the way Augustine taught Christians to interpret it. Adam and Eve are prototypes of what we all become when we eventually succumb to our evil predilections. But this interpretation quickly collapsed when I started learning Hebrew (a language that Augustine never knew—Augustine read Latin and some Greek). The Hebrew language revealed details about the story that were hidden by the English translation.

For example, the text says that God forms Man, or in Hebrew, Adam, literally from the dust of the earth. *(Gn. 2:7)* The word אדם (adam) in Hebrew is what is known as a collective noun, best translated as *humanity*.[5.13] This means that Adam is not so much the first human being to walk the earth, but, in this particular story, Adam is representative of all human beings. If the word *adam* represents all people, then it seems unlikely to me that the authors of this story ever intended it to be a historical treatise on the first human being to roam the earth. Indeed, the more we delve into the context and language behind these verses, the more the literal meaning of this story falls apart.

According to Genesis, Adam and Eve have a direct relationship with God. The story portrays them as engaging in a verbal dialogue with God. They speak with God and God speaks back. If we stray away from reading the story as a factual account of history, then the larger point emerges that Adam and Eve are aware of God's presence in the world. Indeed, this is what seems to make Adam unique. It's not that he's the first human being ever created. Rather, Adam is the first human being to exhibit consciousness of God's existence. I would argue that Adam represents the first human being to evolve God consciousness. Although, to be fair, the ancient Jews wouldn't have said it that way. They would have viewed Adam as the first human being to have a direct relationship with the Jewish God. In other words, Adam is the first member of the Jewish faith.

We know the authors of Genesis believed this to be true because of what happens after Adam and Eve are expelled from the Garden of Eden. Adam and Eve have two sons, Cain and Abel. Genesis Chapter 4 tells us that after Cain has killed his brother Abel, God banishes Cain as a wanderer on the earth. Cain becomes concerned that he may not survive and says, "...<u>anyone</u> who meets me may kill me." *(Gn. 4:14 – emphasis added)* If we read this story literally, then at this point there are technically only three people alive on the planet. With Abel's death, the only people left are Adam, Eve and Cain. Who exactly is Cain afraid of out in the world? Well, clearly the authors assume there are a lot more people in the world besides the three to whom we've been introduced in Genesis 1-4. Furthermore, after settling down in the east of Eden, Cain marries a woman. Where did *she* come from? She wasn't anyone he'd met in the Garden of Eden.

There are a lot of little details like this in the early chapters of Genesis that tell us the authors never intended for us to read the Adam and Eve story as reflective of an actual event. In my opinion, the best way to read the story is as though we are looking at the human race through a microscope. We are zooming in on two people who are coming into consciousness of the difference between good and evil. Let's recap the details: Adam and Eve have been given one rule—they can eat of the fruit of any of the trees in the garden with one exception: they are not allowed to eat the fruit of the tree of knowledge of good and evil. It's at this point that the serpent enters the story.

The serpent is described as being craftier than all the other animals. Christians have often interpreted the serpent in this story as the devil or Satan, but that was not the original intent of the authors. First of all, at the time when this story was formulated, the concept of an evil angel Satan didn't exist in Judaism, so let's just set that idea aside.[5.14] However, snakes were considered to be evil creatures. In the Middle East, snakes are everywhere. They are essentially silent as they move and, unlike other predators, they have the ability to sneak up on you without your knowledge. This is why the authors use a snake as a metaphor for temptation. Temptation can sneak up on you without you being aware of it and, like a snake, temptation can kill you.

In the story, the serpent can speak and tells Eve that God was not being truthful about the consequences for eating the fruit from the tree of knowledge of good and evil. The serpent says, "You will not die; for God knows that when you eat of it your eyes will be opened, and you will be like God, knowing good and evil." *(Gn. 3:5)* I think the best way to understand this interaction with the serpent is to read it as though she is having a conversation with herself in her head, which is something we've all done. There's something that we're told we shouldn't do, but we nevertheless rationalize to ourselves why we should do it. So much evil in the world results from humans convincing themselves that their actions are inconsequential or worth the risk.

The second key aspect of Eve's interaction with the serpent is what the serpent says at the end of its statement: "...when you eat of [the fruit], your eyes will be opened, and you will be like God, knowing good and evil." This statement indicates something interesting to us—Eve doesn't know the difference between good and evil unless she eats from the tree. So this begs the question: how is Eve supposed make an informed decision about whether it is good or bad to eat from the tree of knowledge of good and evil, if she doesn't know the difference between good and evil? Kind of a paradox, don't you think? She has to eat from the tree to figure out that she shouldn't have eaten from the tree.

This might seem trivial since the story is fictional, but this paradox tells us a lot about how the authors understood Adam and Eve's relationship with God. There is a commonly held interpretation of this story that God had an expectation that Adam and Eve were going to remain perfect forever. But in order to remain perfect, you have to know the difference between right and wrong, and, as we just discovered, Adam and Eve don't know the difference between right and wrong because they haven't eaten from the tree of knowledge of good and evil, the one thing they are not allowed to do. So does it make any sense that God had no expectation that Adam and Eve would eat the fruit? As far as I'm concerned, God never had an expectation that Adam and Eve would be perfect forever and God never had an expectation that you would be perfect forever.

Why? Because life is a matter of contrast. You cannot know what is truly good unless you have experienced evil. Some of the best people I've met are people who have made many mistakes and endured much evil. I'm not trying to say that God *wants* us to sin. Rather, I'm saying that God *expects* that we are going to make mistakes. My entire life I have heard preachers saying that God can have nothing to do with us because we are sinful. The implied message being that if we were perfect, God would love us. But if I'm reading this story correctly, then that line of thinking makes no sense. If God created us knowing that we would make mistakes, why would God abandon us for doing what we were designed to do?

Even Jesus seems to affirm this understanding that God created humans to be flawed. Jesus says that "occasions for stumbling are bound to come." *(Mt. 18:7)* In other words, it's inevitable that you will make mistakes. Obviously, Jesus would prefer that you didn't, but he knows that it's going to happen because without mistakes we never learn and, ironically, it is our mistakes that bring the most meaning to our lives. Mistakes make life both amazingly beautiful and stunningly sad. So many Christians live under the false assumption that they can never live up to God's expectations for them. Thankfully, the beauty of the Adam and Eve story is how it relays the message that God never expected you to be perfect. God loves you for who you are and that includes all of your imperfections.

All of this leads to an important question: why are we taking all of this time to discuss the story of Adam and Eve? Because how you interpret this story has a huge impact on how you interpret Jesus. If you read the story of Adam and Eve the way that Augustine told us to read it, then Jesus' purpose becomes locked into that old conventional pattern of thinking—God needed to send us Jesus to save us from the sins of Adam and Eve. However, if you read the Adam and Eve story the way I have just laid out for you, then it becomes possible to see Jesus in an entirely different light, one that I believe is much closer to Jesus' original movement and message when he walked the earth.

THE NEW ADAM

At the beginning of this chapter, I demonstrated how when we order the documents in the New Testament according to the dates of their authorship, we see an interesting progression—the further away we get from Jesus' death, the more Jesus becomes a divine being. There are a lot of reasons why this happens, but I think one of the most compelling has to do with the composition of the early church. Within about two generations the church had become separated from its Jewish roots. By the third generation, almost everyone associated with the church was Gentile (non-Jew), many of whom were more familiar with the Greco-Roman gods and goddesses than the traditions of Judaism. Therefore, in order to convince these people that they should follow Jesus, Christians started to reframe Jesus in ways that were more accessible to people unfamiliar with Judaism.

One of the most important ways they achieved this was by defining Jesus in terms of the Greco-Roman thinking about kings. For those who were citizens of the Roman Empire, it was common to view the emperor as a god. In fact, once a year all Roman citizens were expected to worship an image of the emperor, declaring the emperor to be their Lord.[5.15] Therefore, in the minds of the Romans, one cannot be considered a king without being viewed as a divine being. Since Jesus referred to himself as the messiah, he was certainly kingly material. But Jewish kings were not gods. For Jews, the idea that God could be reduced to a human being was an absurd and heretical proposition. The messiah was God's chosen one, a regular human being with a special connection to God who would be responsible for ruling over God's kingdom. This is why in Paul's letters he makes a clear distinction between Jesus and God. They are two separate entities, not one and the same.

Unfortunately, this important nuance is lost as Christianity becomes dominated by people who are unfamiliar with Judaism. Furthermore, this new generation of Christians is faced with a difficult problem: how are you going to convince Romans to follow Jesus if he is not divine? It's a losing proposition to try to argue that Jesus is the greatest king who ever lived. Even the most depraved emperors who ran the Roman Empire were considered divine. Jesus is supposed to be greater and more powerful than they are, which means that to make a compelling case for Jesus' lordship, he must be God. Thus, the association with Jesus as God becomes a necessity, resulting in the mythology surrounding Jesus' birth. All this to say, if you struggle with the Christian assertion that Jesus is God in the flesh, realize that you are in good company. First of all, this belief was not original to the Christian faith and, second, it actually distorts the real importance of Jesus' life.

When Christians make the claim that Jesus is God, their reasoning is often grounded in Augustine's interpretation of the story of Adam and Eve. God sent Jesus in order to make up for Adam's imperfection. Jesus lived the perfect life that Adam could never live. Indeed, one of the earliest ways that Christians thought about Jesus was as the new Adam. *(Rm. 5:12-21)* Jesus is Adam 2.0, the newest version of humanity. From the moment he was born, until the moment he died, Jesus never made a single mistake. Jesus lived the life that Adam was supposed to live, but couldn't.

This line of thinking is based on two huge assumptions. First, it assumes that God expected Adam (and us) to be perfect forever and, as we've already discussed, that doesn't make any sense in the context of the story. Second, it assumes that Jesus' Jewish heritage means nothing in terms of his upbringing. In Judaism, a person is not accountable for their sins until the age of 12 or 13 when they become bar or bat mitzvahed. Until that point, all the sins they commit are ascribed to their parents.[5.16] So technically, according to traditional Judaism, Jesus could sin all he wanted until the age of 12 or 13 and then be considered perfect from that moment onward. That little fact complicates things, doesn't it?

The most challenging problem with the Christian assertion that Jesus lived a perfect life, free of sin, is the fact that humans need to make mistakes in order to learn right from wrong. Apparently, Jesus' moral compass was so finely honed from his birth that he never experienced this important facet of human existence. Many Christians fail to realize that Jesus' state of perfection creates a contradiction. One cannot claim that Jesus truly understands the human condition when he has never endured the most basic human experience of making a mistake. This belief significantly diminishes the beauty of Jesus' movement and message because it means that Jesus never truly understood what it meant to live like one of us.

This perspective is supported by Jesus himself. At one point in the gospels, Jesus is approached by a man who asks him, "Good Teacher, what must I do to inherit eternal life?" Jesus responds to the man by saying, "Why do you call me good? No one is good but God alone." *(Mk. 10:18, Lk. 18:19)* Although many Christians dismiss Jesus' response as simple humility, I think it's pretty clear Jesus is rejecting any association with the word *good*. Furthermore, Jesus is differentiating between God and himself. God is good. Jesus is not. Therefore, if Jesus does not even consider himself worthy of being labeled a good person, then obviously perfection is out of the question.[†]

So if Jesus is not God in the flesh, why should we pay him any kind of special attention? Earlier, we discussed the idea that Adam represents the first human to exhibit consciousness of God's existence. Adam was, for all intents and purposes, the first Jew. However, what the story from the Garden of Eden makes clear is that Adam's God consciousness was imperfect. As much as Adam was able to recognize God's presence, his actions clouded his ability to stay connected with God. In this way, Adam is truly representative of how most of us live. We are conscious of God's existence, but staying actively connected to God is not easy.

This is where Jesus rises far above the average person. Based on his life and teachings, the scriptures convey that Jesus was able to establish a connection with God that greatly surpassed what any human until that point had been able to achieve. In this way, I agree that Jesus is the new Adam. I believe that Jesus is the newest version of humanity. Jesus is Adam 2.0—the best version of who we are supposed to be. What I mean by this is that if Adam is the first human being to evolve God consciousness, then Jesus is the first human being to achieve full God consciousness.[5.17] Jesus is the first person to achieve a direct, fully formed connection with God. As much as is humanly possible, Jesus' spirit and God's spirit are one. To be clear, Jesus' God consciousness does not make him God nor does it mean that he possessed this full God consciousness from his birth. Rather, as we will discuss in Chapter 8, the New Testament conveys that Jesus achieved this God consciousness following his baptism.[5.18]

---

†   Review p.48-49 for previous discussion of God's imperfection.

There are three major implications to take away from this way of thinking about Jesus. The first is that Jesus' connection with God does not imbue Jesus with special insight into the future. Like everyone else, Jesus has free will and God's spirit of redemption works the same inside Jesus as it does inside everyone else.[†] Clearly, Jesus' actions will be more reflective of God's spirit of redemption than the average person because Jesus and God are so closely connected. That said, the same rules apply to Jesus as to everyone else. God can only work with the decisions that Jesus makes (and, as we will discuss, sometimes those decisions turn out to be mistakes).

The second implication is that Jesus represents a state of being that you and I can achieve if we so desire. I'm not saying this is particularly easy, but I believe it is possible if we follow Jesus' example and teachings. Jesus lays out the path to achieve this same connection with God in his teachings (something we will explore further in Chapter 10), which leads me to the third implication of this way of thinking about Jesus. If Jesus has achieved a direct, fully formed connection with God, then his example and teachings are going to truly reflect God's being. This is why I feel that we should pay special attention to Jesus' understanding of God. Not only are his teachings going to give us insight into God's true nature, but because Jesus was a normal human, his achievements can become our achievements if we follow his path.

This way of thinking contrasts greatly with the way Christians have classically portrayed Jesus. Christian doctrine states that, because Jesus is God in the flesh, he lived a life so perfect that it is impossible for people like you and me to attain the same standard. Therefore, his teachings are reflective of standards that are beyond the possibility for a normal human to achieve. From this vantage point, the bar is so high that most people shrug their shoulders and say, "Why should I try?" Indeed, we shouldn't because we can never measure up to perfection. But the message of living a perfect life from birth to death is not Jesus' original message. That's the

---

†   Review p.74-80 for previous discussion of God's spirit of redemption.

message of the people who came after him; people who distorted and obscured the purpose of Jesus' movement.

The original message of Christianity is not about how disappointed God is in God's creation. In fact, quite the opposite is true. God created us with everything we need to live up to our potential. Furthermore, we can never lose that potential regardless of who we are or the mistakes we have made. We just needed someone to show us how to access that potential so that we can become the people God intended us to be. Thankfully, Jesus laid the path before us so that we could follow in his footsteps. Our next task is to peel back the layers of dogma that have enshrouded Jesus' life for the better part of 2,000 years, so we can see those footsteps clearly.

CHAPTER 5 RECAP: WHAT YOU NEED TO KNOW

1. The original Christians did not believe Jesus was born of a virgin. They understood Jesus and God to be two separate entities.

2. Traditional Christian thinking about Jesus can be traced back to Augustine of Hippo. Augustine believed that sexual intercourse is how humans pass Adam and Eve's original sin from one generation to the next. Augustine believed that Jesus was able to live a perfect life because the virgin birth prevented him from inheriting Adam and Eve's original sin.

3. Augustine's interpretation of the Adam and Eve story is greatly flawed. The story is not about God's expectation that humans should be perfect. Rather, the story conveys God's expectation that mistakes are part of human existence because mistakes are how we learn the difference between good and evil.

4. Jesus is not God in the flesh, but the new Adam. Jesus is what all humans should aspire to become because Jesus possessed the first fully formed God consciousness. As Adam 2.0, Jesus lays out the path to achieve this same connection with God through his teachings.

CHAPTER SIX

BREAKING DOWN THE JESUS OF RELIGION

THE FORMULA

When Harvey Samuel Firestone founded the Firestone Tire and Rubber Company in 1900, he began by creating pneumatic tires for wagons and buggies, the most common forms of transportation at the turn of the 20th century. However, as the primary mode of transportation transitioned from horses to automobiles, his company began to focus exclusively on producing tires for cars. Firestone was not the first tire maker to capitalize on America's newfound love for cars, but he was the first person to form an exclusive relationship with an automobile manufacturer.

Firestone was good friends with Henry Ford, who agreed to outfit all of his models with Firestone tires. Furthermore, Firestone had borrowed the assembly line process from Ford, allowing his company to produce tires at a much higher rate than any of his competitors. By the late 1920s, the name Firestone was synonymous with the best tires on the planet. Firestone's reputation for quality combined with the fact that his tires were found attached to the most popular brand of car in America assured his company's position as the top tire manufacturer in the United States for the next five decades.[6.1]

However, Firestone's dominance would crumble in the early 1970s. A new type of tire known as radials had come onto the European market during the 1960s, created by the French tire company Michelin. Radials were much more sturdy and reliable than traditional bias tires produced by Firestone and other American tire manufacturers. The Firestone Corporation was well aware that radials were a threat to their market share in the United States because they had watched as the Michelin radials destroyed their market share in European countries. In fact, Firestone knew that Michelin had every intention of introducing their radial tires to the U.S. in the early 70s.

In anticipation of this superior product, Firestone intended to introduce their own radials to the US market, investing close to $400 million in their new radial tires. This included the creation of a brand new plant and the conversion of several older bias tire plants. The stage was set for Firestone to continue their dominance. All they needed to do was create a radial tire that could compete with Michelin. This might seem like a simple task for a company that had almost single-handedly created the automobile tire market. All they needed to do was rely on the practices that had made them such a great company in the first place. Unfortunately that's exactly what they did. They relied on their time-tested wisdom.[6.2]

Firestone had come to dominate the American car market under a very specific set of conditions. One of those conditions was that of planned obsolescence. Firestone assumed that tires had a very limited lifespan and would need to be frequently replaced. In fact, the short lifespan of tires was a big part of Firestone's formula for success. The more frequently people replaced their tires, the better for the bottom line of the company. This meant that the people in the labs designing the tires and the people in the factories creating the tires were not very concerned with quality control. As long as people trusted the Firestone brand, then the consumer would always come back for more. This factor proved to be a huge disadvantage when Firestone began designing and producing their own radials.

When Michelin produced their radials, they were obsessive about creating a tire that would last for a long time. Michelin's factories for the production of radials had such stringent quality controls that even tires with minor imperfections were not allowed off the assembly line. Firestone plants were not nearly as concerned with the quality of their product. When designing their radials, they simply made minor changes to older models of bias tires. The Firestone radial tire, known as the Firestone 500, was so poorly designed and produced that the tread on the tire began to separate from the tire carcass at high speeds.

After a slew of accidents that could be definitively traced to the Firestone 500s, the U.S. National Highway Traffic Safety Administration announced in 1978 that they were conducting a formal investigation into defects of the Firestone 500. By 1979, the public trust that Harvey Samuel Firestone had worked so hard to establish had been completely destroyed. The Firestone Corporation had more than a billion dollars of debt and was losing almost $250 million a year. The company was eventually restructured and sold to the Japanese company Bridgestone for pennies on the dollar compared to what Firestone had been worth a decade earlier.

The story of Firestone is very much like the story of Christianity in the U.S. In the early 1900s, Christianity was a dominant force in American life. Conservative Christians had developed a formula trusted by the public at large. The formula went something like this: humans are evil, sinful creatures that cannot have a relationship with God. Therefore, God impregnated a young virgin named Mary who gave birth to Jesus. This baby was no ordinary human, but, in fact, God in the flesh. His purpose in being born was to live a perfect life and be sacrificed on our behalf. Because of Jesus, humans no longer have to suffer the consequences of their sins. Through Jesus, humans have been granted access to heaven, preventing them from suffering an eternity in hell. Amazingly, all one has to do to gain this eternal salvation is confess that Jesus is their Lord and savior.

I am sure you have heard this formula spoken at some point in your life. You may have even used it yourself on occasion. This formula is thought to be based on longstanding beliefs that date back to the founding of the Christian church. Not only is it simple, but it's a pretty compelling argument that has inspired Christians all over the world to believe in Jesus. God became a human and suffered a horrible death so you could go to heaven. All you need to do to benefit from God's generosity is believe. Simple enough, except for the fact that by the middle of the 20th century, the formula was no longer functioning as it once did.

In the 1960s, European churches saw a significant decline in attendance. At the time, many people assumed the trend was the result of the younger generation rejecting the values of their parents. Common wisdom held that they would be back in the pews as they married and had children—but that didn't happen. As the 60s became the 70s, 80s and 90s, church attendance continued to decline to the point where many European churches had to close. The reason that almost the entire continent abandoned the church is actually quite simple—they didn't believe in the formula anymore. The idea that they should believe in Jesus to avoid going to hell simply didn't resonate with them. And honestly, why would it?

Europe had just seen the most devastating war in the history of humanity. The entire continent had experienced human death and suffering on such a large scale that no one was immune from the consequences of the bloodshed. In countries like Belarus, the war had decimated a quarter of the population.[6.3] If you were lucky enough not to lose a family member or close friend in the war, you were the exception. When the war ended in 1945 and the soldiers came home, they tried to establish some sense of normalcy in their lives. They returned to their communities (or what was left of them), found jobs, started families and returned to their churches.

These churches were preaching the exact same kinds of messages that were heard before the war had begun. However, this time something didn't ring true for them.

Imagine for a moment that you were one of the soldiers who freed the prisoners of the concentration camps scattered throughout Europe. The people who you had met in these camps were merely skin and bones. You learn that, at the height of the war, the Germans were killing more than 2,000 people per hour in the gas chambers. There were mountains of dead bodies piled up in various locations around the camps. When you questioned the survivors about who they are and how they got there, you realized the vast majority of prisoners have one thing in common—Judaism.

When you return home, you do what you have always done. You go to church on Sunday morning. As you sit in the church pews, you hear the old formula spoken again and again: without Jesus, humans will suffer an eternity in hell. But you just saw hell. You know exactly what hell looks like. You start thinking back on all the Jews you encountered in these camps and you start applying the formula to them. Supposedly, Jews who were murdered by the Nazis are suffering in hell right now because they didn't believe in Jesus. Furthermore, those who were lucky enough to survive the camps have hell to look forward to when they die because they don't believe in Jesus.

Then you start thinking about the Nazi soldiers who carried out all of these heinous atrocities. Most of them claim to be Christian. So as long as they believe in Jesus and ask for forgiveness, their sins will be forgiven. According to the formula, those Nazi soldiers will be granted access to heaven in spite of the fact that they are personally responsible for the deaths of tens of thousands of innocent people. As your thoughts float from the camps back to the pastor's sermon, you keep hearing the pastor talk about how the God of Christianity is a loving God. But how can that be true? What kind of loving God would allow these people, who already suffered so much, to suffer an eternity in hell? After a while, you realize that the formula you had trusted for so long simply doesn't add up. So rather than make a fuss, you decide to stop going to church.

This scenario played itself out again and again among thousands of Europeans following the war, draining the church of its members. Christians in the United States watched this trend as it was occurring and believed they were immune. They believed the formula that had served them so well would continue to work as it had in the past. However, like Firestone, as the trend from Europe made its way to the United States, Christians were caught unprepared. Many churches believed the decline had to do with the old traditional styles of worship so they invested in new styles of contemporary worship. Churches spent millions of dollars on projectors, lighting, and sound equipment. They changed the packaging, but the message remained the same and the end result is that the trend in Europe has become the trend in the United States—the church is rapidly dying.

If Christianity is going to survive, we need to admit that the formula is faulty. The time-tested way of promoting the Christian faith no longer makes sense in our modern world. Therefore, our goal is to break down this formula into its most basic parts. We are going to examine each piece of the formula, discuss its history and whether it is based in fact or fiction. Through this examination my hope is that you will have a clear understanding of the flaws within this formula so that we can begin revising it into something that truly reflects what Christianity was intended to be—a love story.

BATHED IN BLOOD

Likely you are familiar with one of the most pervasive taglines repeated by modern Christians: "Jesus died for your sins!" Whenever I see that tagline written on a sign or spouted by some street corner preacher, I often think, "I bet you have no idea what that actually means." Let's take a moment and try to define the word *sin* because it's not as easy as it sounds.

In popular culture, sin refers to any action or behavior that is deemed socially irresponsible. But sin is much more than doing something wrong in the eyes of society. In religion, sin is any action that *God* finds unacceptable. Therefore, in order to define sin, we need some way of determining which actions are on God's list of dos and don'ts. When it comes to Christians, their list is derived from the Bible.

In the Bible, the list of approved and disapproved actions comes in the form of laws, the vast majority of which are found in the Old Testament. Indeed, within the first five books of the Old Testament, more commonly known as the Torah, there are 613 laws or commandments. These laws regulate everything from food, to the types of fibers in clothes, to the compensation required for sleeping with another man's slave. Indeed, these laws even specify the types of animals we are supposed to sacrifice in order to be forgiven of our sin when we break one of God's laws. Therefore, if we were to attempt to formulate a very basic definition of sin from the Old Testament, we might say any thought, word or deed that contradicts God's laws as expressed in the Torah.

Of course, Christians intentionally ignore the majority of those Old Testament laws. They tend to focus on the first 10 commandments and skip the rest. I just want to make sure you caught the math on that one. Christians say that out of 613 commandments, 603 are basically irrelevant. Why do Christians feel those extra laws can be tossed aside? They think Jesus' teachings in the New Testament are more important. So the Christian definition of sin is any thought, word or deed that directly opposes Jesus' teachings in the New Testament. But simply stating that Jesus' teachings take precedence over the Old Testament laws is not entirely clear cut.

For instance, there is a point in Matthew's gospel where Jesus expressly says, "Do not think that I have come to abolish the law or the prophets; I have come not to abolish but to fulfill…Therefore, whoever breaks one of the least of these commandments, and teaches others to do the same, will be called least in the kingdom of heaven; but whoever does them and teaches them will be called great in the kingdom of heaven." *(Mt. 5:17, 19)* Based on these verses, I think it's evident that Jesus has no intention of overturning those laws. Indeed, Jesus expects his disciples to follow all 613 commandments and implies that if we influence others to break them, then we are sinning.

This leaves Christians in a difficult position. How can Christians claim that Jesus died for our sins when the vast majority of Christians seem to disagree with Jesus about what constitutes a sin? So perhaps we need to rethink this question and approach it from a different angle. Let's take a look at when Jesus uses the word *sin* in the New Testament. Jesus' most famous reference to sin is when he uses it in what Christians call the Lord's Prayer, a short prayer taught by Jesus that most Christians around the world repeat every Sunday during the worship service. The prayer goes like this:

> Our Father who art in heaven, hallowed be thy name. Thy kingdom come. Thy will be done on earth as it is in heaven. Give us this day our daily bread, and forgive us our <u>sins</u>, as we forgive those who <u>sin</u> against us, and lead us not into temptation, but deliver us from evil. *(Mt. 6:9-23, Lk. 11:2-4 – emphasis added)*

There are three basic variations of the lines that include sin: forgive us our trespasses as we forgive those who have trespassed against us; forgive us our debts as we forgive our debtors; and forgive us our sins as we forgive those who have sinned against us. Which translation you use depends on which Lord's Prayer you like better—the one from Matthew or the one from Luke. Debts and debtors is the version from Matthew. This translation is based on the word ὀφείλημα (opheilema) in Greek and refers to debt in the sense of financial debt.[6.4] The Lord's Prayer in Luke is where we get the translation of trespasses and sins. This is based on the Greek word ἁμαρτία (hamartia), which is a term derived from archery that literally means *to miss the mark* and might be better translated in English as *mistakes*.[6.5] So which one is it? Is it debts or is it mistakes and does it matter?

What you need to appreciate about this translation problem is that Jesus never spoke Greek. Jesus spoke Aramaic and the word he would have used was *l-haibenan*, which can be translated as either debts or sins, which explains why it's done one way in Matthew and another way in Luke. I don't think it's too much of a stretch to assume that Jesus wanted us to think of both concepts: financial debts and the mistakes we have made in our lives.

First, let's discuss the idea of financial debts. In order to appreciate why Jesus wants us to forgive financial debts, one has to understand the society that Jesus is trying to create. Jesus refers to this society as the kingdom of God and it looks something like this: a world where nobody suffers; everyone has enough to eat; everyone has clothes to wear and a roof over their heads; everyone is treated for their illnesses; nobody is forgotten. In Jesus' world, people don't have a lot of possessions or money. Everyone is basically on equal footing.

The reason why Jesus looks at the world this way is because he lived in an agrarian society. The majority of people he knew were farmers. The disparity between the wealthy and the poor was staggering. At the time Jesus began his ministry, many Jewish farmers were struggling so much that they had to borrow money from the wealthy in order to feed themselves and their families. These loans often came with hefty interest rates that could range anywhere from 12 to 50 percent, which made them nearly impossible to pay off.[6.6]

These debts would stay with families for generations and would often result in families having to forfeit their land in order remediate the debt. Frequently, the land would not be enough to pay back the loan, so families would then work as indentured servants to the landowner, never making enough to break even. Jesus knew that if God's kingdom was going to become a reality, then these financial debts would need to be forgiven. But financial debts are only half of the equation. In order to bring about God's kingdom, we must be forgiven of a whole different class of debt—the debts we owe to God.

Just to be clear, we do not owe God money. These are debts we have incurred through making mistakes or sins. Why does making mistakes mean that we owe God a debt? Here we have stumbled upon what is one of the most perplexing concepts in the entire Christian religion. Christians claim that when we make mistakes (or sin against God), we become indebted to God. This idea is derived from the Old Testament where Jews were required to pay off a sin debt through the sacrifice of animals. If we take an animal and kill it on an altar as an offering to God, the Bible tells us that God will grant us forgiveness. *(Lv. 4:27-31)* In other words, the Old Testament laws specify that God requires the shedding of blood in order for God to grant forgiveness.

The reason ancient cultures believed there was a correlation between the shedding of blood and God granting forgiveness is complicated. However, their thinking had to do with their perception of the properties of blood. The ancients understood that blood contained the life force of an individual. They had no concept of cells or hemoglobin. All they knew was that, without blood, humans die. In this way, the ancients viewed blood as being sacred to preserving life. However, they also believed that our actions, particularly our mistakes, could taint our life force.[6,7] Thus, the ancients believed that the act of sacrifice had the effect of transferring the sins from our blood to the blood of the animal. Since the animal's blood is pure, it can take our sin and purify our blood.

With this background, you can more easily understand why Christians claim that Jesus died for your sins. Since Christians believe that Jesus lived a perfect life, free from sin, Jesus is acting as the animal whose blood is pure. When Jesus died on the cross, his blood was shed, causing Jesus to become the ultimate and final sacrifice for our sins. The sins in your blood can now be transferred to Jesus' blood and you can achieve permanent forgiveness. Christians argue that Jesus rendered the sacrificial system of the Old Testament unnecessary. With Jesus, we are no longer required to continually sacrifice animals to seek God's forgiveness.

All of this raises a really important question: does it really make any sense that God would require a blood sacrifice in order to forgive humans for their sins? I mean, why do we have to inflict terrible suffering on an animal to show how sorry we are for making a mistake? Can't we simply ask God for forgiveness and can't God simply grant that forgiveness without killing anything or anyone? Whenever I ask these questions of conservative Christians, the answer I receive invariably goes something like this, "Well, I didn't make it up. It's what God says in the Bible. I don't know why God requires blood. He just does. So you can argue with God, because it's God's choice how we are forgiven."

The problem with this argument is that animal sacrifice was utilized by almost every ancient culture in the Middle East as a way of worshiping God. Moreover, Jews were not the first to come up with this concept.[6.8] I think it's clear that Jews incorporated animal sacrifice into their worship of God because animal sacrifice was in vogue at the time the Jewish scriptures were developed. Six hundred years later when Christians were trying to make sense of Jesus' death, they superimposed the Old Testament system of animal sacrifice onto Jesus' death, producing the idea that Jesus died for our sins.

In my opinion, Jesus didn't die so that God could forgive humans. God could always forgive humans for their mistakes, with or without Jesus. The importance of Jesus' death is to help humans comprehend the depth of God's forgiveness. Therefore, our next goal will be to examine how Jesus' life and death help us to unravel the mystery of how God determines who should and should not be forgiven for their mistakes.

THE RED LINE

As a pastor, I am entrusted with many secrets. It is not uncommon for people to tell me things about themselves that they've never told another human being. One of the reasons why is because I am seen as the authority on whether or not their misdeed could jeopardize their afterlife. They want to know if what they did is unforgivable. Could their thoughts or actions cause God to banish them to hell rather than admit them into heaven? Whenever I am pressed with these questions, I am quick to remind them that I am not God and, therefore, I cannot tell them how God feels about their mistakes. However, I am also quick to add that it is hard for me to believe that there is any sin so great that God would not be willing to grant forgiveness to those who are truly sorry.

This might seem like a big assumption on my part. The idea that God will ultimately forgive every sin humans commit is a hard concept for Christians to stomach. I think most of us are good with the idea that God is willing to readily forgive minor infractions because we all make those little mistakes on a daily basis. If God didn't forgive those tiny errors, then God would seem petty. Of course, as we escalate the evil of the sin, the problem becomes how we determine when one has committed a sin that no longer qualifies as being forgivable. The phrase *red line* refers to a point of no return. Crossing a red line is an action that cannot be taken back and forever changes the quality of one's relationship with the world.

Perspectives differ concerning which actions constitute a breach of the red line. I find Jesus' approach to the red line particularly unique. There is a verse when Jesus says, "You have heard that it was said, 'You shall not commit adultery.' But I say to you that everyone who looks at a woman with lust has already committed adultery with her in his heart." *(Mt. 5:27-28)* Jesus is challenging the common wisdom about what constitutes a sin. The laws of the Old Testament tend to emphasize the notion that a sin is an action you perform. You cannot be considered guilty of breaking an Old Testament law unless you actually do something. For example, in the Old Testament, adultery for a man is the action of sleeping with another man's wife. You have to do the deed to be guilty of the sin. In this way, you can think about sleeping with another man's wife all you want and it would not be considered sinful.

Jesus challenges this concept by asserting that contemplating an action is just as sinful as the action itself. The reasoning behind this understanding of sin is that our thoughts are what inspire our actions in the world. One does not simply commit adultery without thinking about the action beforehand. The deed is an actualization of the thought in the real world. If one's thoughts were pure and not focused on adultery, the act of adultery would never occur.

In this approach to sin, every human being falls into the same category because even if we have not committed murder, adultery or theft, it is likely we have thought about those things at one time or another. If thoughts are the basis upon which God judges our sinfulness, then it levels the playing field. According to Jesus, Mother Teresa, one of the noblest human beings to live in the last century, is no different from Amon Goeth, one of the most sadistic officers at the Krakow-Plaszow concentration camp who ruthlessly killed tens of thousands of Jews.

This might seem a bit crazy because, as we know, there's a big difference between thinking about committing murder and actually carrying it out in the real world. When someone actually kills another person, there is real grief and pain that ripples through the world as a result of those actions. Conversely, if you think about killing me, then I might not ever know that you felt that way about me. The practical difference between thought and action seems so insurmountably large that it calls into question whether Jesus' approach to sin actually makes any sense. In fact, my gut reaction was to dismiss his definition of sin as being too severe. What changed my mind about Jesus' view of sin is something that happened to me when I was working as a chaplain intern for a psychiatric hospital.

I ran a small group for patients who were within a year of being released from the hospital. They had shown such substantial improvement that, as long as they followed all the rules and didn't slip back into the symptoms of their mental illness, the court would set them free. One person in this small group was a woman named Emma.*

My supervisor told me that she was in the hospital because she had suffocated her teenage son while he was sleeping. She was found not guilty by reason of insanity and was sent to the psychiatric hospital to undergo treatment. When I first met her, she seemed very cold and distant. The entire time I was working at the hospital, she never once spoke of the reason she was there. This lack of honesty caused me to judge her very harshly. I thought to myself, "How could a mother ever kill her own child?"

Our small group met once a week and, at the end of each month, I was required to place a note into Emma's chart summarizing the highlights of our discussions from the past month. Every time I placed a new note in her chart, I avoided reading the written narrative of her personal history because I didn't want to know the gruesome details of her son's death. However, one day my curiosity got the better of me and I started leafing through Emma's chart. Inside her chart was her entire history, not just the murder of her son, but everything that had preceded it.

When Emma was born, she was given up for adoption. Unfortunately, she was adopted at a time when adoption agencies didn't do their homework very thoroughly. From the time she was 10 until she left home at 18, she was raped every single day by her adoptive father—and that is not an exaggeration. She was smart, so she got a full scholarship to college and became an engineer. She

---

* Name has been changed to protect the patient's identity.

eventually married, had two children and lived all over the world working for a major telecommunications company. But then, one day, all of that abuse and trauma caught up with her and she had a psychotic episode. When I finished reading her story, I thought to myself, "You know, if that happened to me, I probably would have had a psychotic episode as well and who knows what I would have done?"

As human beings, we have the ability to make choices. Unfortunately, many times those choices are the wrong choices. Emma's adoptive father did something that many people would see as unforgivable, but then again, that's what a lot of people said about her when she murdered her son. And though it doesn't make it any better, the records made clear that her adoptive father was doing to Emma the same thing that was done to him when he was a boy.

You see, there isn't a whole lot of justice in this world. We all perpetrate suffering in some form or another and the vast majority of it goes unpunished. Some of us do things that are so egregious that we struggle to comprehend how it ever could have happened. There are times when we want to wipe the slate clean, but we simply cannot, because forgiveness just doesn't seem like an option. There is something inside us that cries out for justice saying, "This is not right and I don't know how to fix it, but something needs to be done!"

The truth is it's hard to make things right. It's hard to bring justice to a world that is so interconnected and complicated. It's one thing to isolate a crime and say, "You're responsible for this happening." Take Emma for example. You could easily say she's responsible for her son's death, but it becomes more complicated when you realize how horribly she was abused and how her past influenced her actions. How do you bring justice to that? How do you unwind all of the factors—the evil thoughts, words and actions—that brought her to the point of suffocating her own son? How do you make that right? The fact is, we can't make it right, but God can.

God is the one who is responsible for giving us the ability to choose good and evil. Thus, God also takes on the responsibility for bringing justice to those choices.[†] God could punish us for making all of those horrible decisions and hold us accountable for the things we've done wrong. That's why you hear a lot of people in the church talk about hell, because hell is the only way some Christians can envision true justice for the wrongs that have been committed on this earth. But the New Testament tells us that God made a different decision and chose to walk down a different path. Rather than hold us accountable, God chose to take on the burden of that punishment. God is willing to take responsibility for the wrongs we have committed and bring justice to them. The reason we believe this to be true is because of Jesus.

God doesn't need Jesus to forgive our mistakes because God can forgive anything. But without Jesus, we as humans could never fully appreciate or comprehend the depth of that forgiveness. In my opinion, without the example of Jesus' life and death, we would never know where God draws the red line. Where is the point of no return? When do our actions cross the line from forgivable to unforgivable? Prior to Jesus, the red line was quite arbitrary. We placed that line wherever we felt a sin was too egregious to warrant forgiveness. After Jesus' death, the first Christians became keenly aware that, from God's perspective, there is no such thing as a red line.

Thanks to Jesus, we can now fully comprehend how the unforgivable is forgivable. Thanks to Jesus, we can understand how God is able to bring love and forgiveness to a world where there is no real justice. Thanks to Jesus, we can now grasp how a woman

---

†   Review p.61-62 for previous discussion of God's responsibility for good and evil.

who was raped every day for eight years and who murdered her own son could be loved and forgiven by God. The beauty of Jesus' movement is that we are now aware that there is no limit to God's love. God is capable of unwinding the web of evil we create for ourselves when our choices hurt other people and when other people's choices hurt us. What we need to tackle next is explaining exactly how Jesus and his movement made us aware of this reality.

1 The formula that has garnered Christianity millions of adherents is no longer viable. The foundation of this formula—belief in Jesus is necessary for a person to be forgiven by God and gain access to heaven—has crumbled under the weight of the atrocities of war inflicted by Christians during the 20th century.

2 The statement, "Jesus died for your sins," is misleading. The idea that God requires the sacrifice of a living being in order to render forgiveness for sins is derived from the sacrificial laws of the Old Testament. The Jewish ritual of animal sacrifice was borrowed from other cultures and was improperly applied to Jesus' death as a necessary condition for God to grant forgiveness.

3 Jesus' death was not necessary for God to forgive humans of their sins. God could always forgive humans with or without Jesus. However, without the example of Jesus' life and death, we as humans could never fully appreciate or comprehend the depth of God's forgiveness.

CHAPTER SEVEN

RETHINKING HEAVEN, HELL AND THE AFTERLIFE

WELCOME TO THE PARTY!

Jesus was famous for telling stories. He used stories as a way to draw people in so they would listen to his message. The most common type of story Jesus told is known as a parable, a story that is told with the explicit purpose of illustrating a moral or spiritual lesson. The parables Jesus told were almost always fictional and he rarely provided any further explanation to his audience beyond the parable itself. The beauty of parables is that, if they are told well, they convey deep truths to the listener.

Perhaps one of the most famous stories Jesus ever told is the parable of the prodigal son. *(Lk. 15:11-32)* This story revolves around a father and two sons. The younger son approaches his father and states that he wants his father to pay him his inheritance now. Of course, this is a horribly insulting request because the son is essentially saying that all he cares about is his father's money and he wishes his father were dead. Practically, such a request would be extraordinarily difficult for the father to grant because it would require the liquidation of assets and land, a process that could be quite complex for a family of means. For the hearers of this parable in Jesus' day, they would have understood that such a request would irreparably damage the relationship between father and son, essentially severing the younger son from the family.

The younger son then takes his inheritance and moves to a foreign land where he indulges his every desire. Today we would say he lived the party lifestyle, meaning he probably ate abundant amounts of food, drank day and night, slept with prostitutes and gambled away his inheritance. This goes on until, one day, he runs out of money. Facing starvation, he seeks employment with a pig farmer, where the pigs eat better than he does. If you take into account the fact that Jesus' audience wouldn't get anywhere near a pig because of the Old Testament kosher laws, they would see this young man as getting exactly what he deserves. As he considers his situation, he thinks back to living in his father's home. In this moment of reflection, he realizes that his father's slaves have better lives than he does. Therefore, he resolves to return back to his father, ask his forgiveness and become one of his father's slaves.

As he gets closer to his home, he is anticipating how his father will react upon seeing him again. No longer part of the family, he is expecting an icy cold reception. But before he gets to the house, his father sees him off in the distance. The father does not become angry, but rather runs out to meet his son. The father embraces his son, hugging him close. The son attempts to state his case as to why his father should accept him back, but his father doesn't seem to be listening. Rather the father calls to one of his slaves to bring out his best robe and to kill a fatted calf so that they can have a party. They are going to celebrate because "this son of mine was dead and is alive again; he was lost and is found!" *(Lk. 15:24)*

As the festivities get underway to welcome back the younger son, his older brother is working out in the fields. The older son calls to one of the slaves to find out what's going on and the slave informs him that his younger brother has returned and that his father is throwing a celebration in his honor. Needless to say, the older son is enraged. In fact, he is so angry that he refuses to join the party. When his father learns that his eldest son is upset, he goes out into the field to plead with his son to come celebrate. The older son berates his father saying that, unlike his younger brother, he has been obedient. He has done everything the father asked of him and never once did his father offer to celebrate all of his hard work. And yet, his younger brother has wasted all of his inheritance on prostitutes and now they are throwing a celebration in his honor. The father then says that all he owns ultimately belongs to his older son and he can do what he pleases with it. However, the father is insistent that they had to celebrate "because this brother of yours was dead and has come to life; he was lost and has been found." *(Lk. 15:32)*

Let's break down who the various characters in this parable represent because that will help us with our interpretation. Clearly, the father in this parable represents God, which is the interpretation in almost all corners of the Christian faith. The two brothers, on the other hand, are not quite as clear cut. I have heard many pastors say that the younger son represents anyone who is not saved by Jesus. However, I think that is a bit of a stretch. There are lots of people who have professed faith in Jesus and continue to live their lives like the younger son. I think based on the way Jesus tells this parable, we can only say for sure that the younger son represents someone who has turned his back on God and has embraced a life of selfishness.

Likewise, the older son represents someone who has embraced God and tries to live according to God's rules. Again, many pastors claim that the older son is anyone who has been saved by Jesus, but I don't agree with this interpretation. This parable is being told in a Jewish context and, therefore, the older son is, more than likely, representing a Jew who is very observant of the 613 laws found in the Old Testament. Thus, the two sons represent two common types of people—the religious who possess a strong faith in God and the non-religious who reject God.

In the context of this story, the religious person is portrayed as being selfless and giving while the non-religious person is portrayed as extremely selfish. We all know this is not a universal truth. There are many religious people who are extremely selfish and many non-religious people who are extremely selfless. That said, the point of the parable is to show these two types of people at their extremes and how God reacts to them. Let's examine God's reaction to the younger son. When the non-religious person turns his back on God and walks away, God is always waiting to welcome him back with open arms. In fact, the kicker in this story is that God is happy to welcome him back *no matter what he has done*. Indeed, God doesn't even require an explanation. Rather, God is simply overjoyed to have him back.

This reality makes the religious person furious, as is indicated by the older son. This unconditional acceptance is hard for the religious person to stomach because he has been obedient to a fault. The religious person is so focused on making sure that none of the rules are broken that he has a tough time forgiving anyone who does not take the rules as seriously as he does. Indeed, he believes he should be the only one rewarded because he's the one who lived the way God expected him to live. When God tries to explain to the religious person that he should be overjoyed by the fact that the non-religious person has come back, the religious person is indignant saying, "How can you accept him back? Don't you care about all the horrible things he did? Don't you care about how he hurt you, me and everyone else?"

The answer is clear, "Yes, I do care that he hurt you, me and everyone else, but that will not prevent me from rejoicing that he has come back home." What Jesus is trying to tell us through this parable is that unconditional love is central to God's being. This means that our actions, regardless of how vile or sinister they might be, will never prevent God from loving us. From God's perspective, the door is always open. We simply have to be willing to walk through it.

Let's step back to appreciate just how radical this concept of God's love actually is. If what Jesus is saying about God is true, then that means the conventional concepts of heaven and hell (where the obedient go to heaven and the wicked go to hell) no longer apply. The doors of heaven are never closed because God is always on the lookout, hoping that one day you might be willing to come home. Regardless of what you do, regardless of whom you hurt, whether it be yourself or others, regardless of what you believe, God will take you back at any time and celebrate that reunion.

In my opinion, Jesus' extraordinary take on God's unconditional love should force us to ask a critical question: are the classical characterizations of heaven and hell conveyed by modern conservative Christians an accurate reflection of what was intended by the New Testament authors? To answer this question, we need to explore the origins of the biblical concepts of heaven and hell.

THE GOLDEN TICKET

You may have read (or seen the movie) Roald Dahl's classic children's story *Charlie and the Chocolate Factory*. The story revolves around the owner of the world's most famous chocolate factory, Willy Wonka, who has decided to allow five children to visit his factory. The way Wonka determines who will be allowed inside is by hiding five golden tickets inside the wrappers of Wonka chocolate bars. Upon entering the factory, the five children are exposed to all kinds of temptations. As the story progresses, four of the five children reveal some kind of major character flaw. The only child who does not have any character flaws is a poor boy named Charlie. Wonka awards Charlie his factory because he is a kind, humble and loving child.

Charlie and the Chocolate Factory is best characterized as a modern morality tale based on conventional Christian concepts of heaven and hell, which became popularized by Christian classics like Dante's *Inferno*. What the children don't know about Wonka's chocolate factory is that it is designed to prey on the weaknesses of the children. Wonka intends for the children to succumb to temptation. Indeed, he is testing the children with the hope that only the most worthy child will inherit his chocolate factory.

To make the correlation with Christianity more direct, imagine that Wonka is God. The chocolate factory is an analogy for hell, even though the kids think they have walked into heaven. When the temptation proves too much, each of the children suffers some kind of punishment. One is sucked up a chocolate pipe, another is thrown out with the trash, still another is transformed into a giant blueberry, and another is shrunk to a miniature size. All of these punishments are fitting to their particular character flaw. Moreover, these punishments are permanent or, in keeping with the analogy, eternal. When Charlie wins, he enters a glass elevator with Wonka which rises to the top of the factory and literally breaks through the ceiling. The analogy, of course, is that Charlie is going to heaven. Since Charlie resisted temptation, he is worthy of inheriting all of God's riches.

Perhaps the best way to summarize this tale is that God will reward those who are good and punish those who are evil. This is precisely what most of us learn of God from a very young age. We see God as a celestial Santa Claus who is keeping a list of who has been naughty and nice. God will give the golden ticket to those who are good and revoke the ticket from those who are bad. As we get older, this concept becomes slightly more refined. We learn that, from God's perspective, there is no such thing as a good person because, in God's eyes, everyone is considered sinful. No matter how good a person you have been in your life, you are not deserving of heaven. Therefore, by default, everyone is going to hell.

Thankfully, God creates a new way of determining who goes to heaven and hell. The way you get your golden ticket is by having faith in Jesus. Those who believe in Jesus will be granted access to heaven, while those who turn their back on Jesus will be destined to hell for all eternity. Sounds like a great system, doesn't it? Simple and easy to understand. The only thing God requires of me to inherit eternal life in heaven is belief in Jesus. I can do that, no problem. Except, what happens if I never hear about Jesus? Let's say I grow up in a country that is predominately Muslim or Hindu or Buddhist or irreligious and I never have the opportunity to hear about Jesus. Will I go to hell? Or what if the person who tells me about Jesus isn't very convincing and I walk away without accepting Jesus? Is my afterlife really dependent upon the action or inaction of other people? Or let's say I accept Jesus when I'm a kid and truly mean it, but then live a horrible life as an adult. Will God allow me to go to heaven, while the person who lived a much better life, but never accepted Jesus, ends up in hell?

These are just some of the many problems with seeing Jesus as a golden ticket that will get you into heaven. When you begin taking this basic idea and applying it to real-world situations, it quickly breaks down. Nor does it have anything to do with the original ideas of heaven and hell as they are portrayed in the Bible. Let's discuss the concept of hell. The word *hell* in the gospels is actually the way we translate the Greek word γέεννα (Gehenna). Gehenna was a valley located directly outside of Jerusalem.[7.1] The sewers of Jerusalem drained into this valley. These sewers were not like sewers of our modern cities, where pipes contain all of the waste. Rather, they were large tunnels that were continually flowing with water. People would throw all kinds of waste into these sewers—human waste, trash and particularly food waste. It was not uncommon for the citizens of Jerusalem to toss dead animals into these sewers.

Eventually, all this waste found its way to the Gehenna Valley, so it was like a trash dump, except much worse. Not only did it smell horribly, but it was quite a sight to behold. In order to make room for the continual outpouring of trash being dumped into the valley, the people who lived there would burn the trash. Any time you walked past the Gehenna Valley, you would see people walking amidst the fires. The fact that there were carcasses in the valley meant that scavengers had a ready food supply. It was not uncommon for dogs to fight over the carcasses. They would gnash their teeth at each other and attack when a carcass with meat found its way into the valley. This is why the phrase "weeping and gnashing of teeth" *(Mt. 13:50)* is associated with the use of the word *hell* in the New Testament.

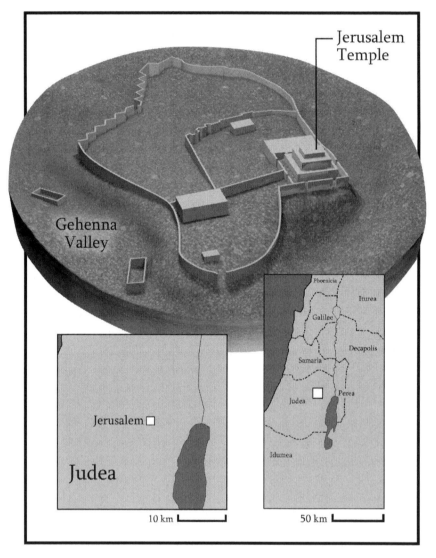

Not surprisingly, the Gehenna Valley was known among the Jewish people as being a pretty horrible place and it was a common illustration of what the Jews believed God's punishment would look like. Jesus was not unique in using Gehenna as an illustration of punishment. In the Jewish rabbinical traditions, Gehenna is considered a place of temporary anguish where the wicked go to be purged of their sins. In their view, the maximum amount of time that God would expect a person to suffer in Gehenna was one year.[7.2]

So let's take a moment to point out the major differences between the common Christian portrayal of hell and the version we just learned about from the Bible. When you hear about hell in Christian churches, it is generally portrayed as a spiritual place of torment where your soul resides for all eternity after you die if you have not accepted Jesus as your savior. However, the biblical version of hell (or Gehenna) is an actual, physical valley here on earth. Gehenna is not underneath the earth or in some other spiritual realm. Gehenna is not a place where your soul resides for all eternity. In fact, quite the opposite. Gehenna is a place where real, live people are punished for their sins for up to a year.

If this is confusing to you because you always thought hell was a place for your soul, it's important to realize that ancient Judaism didn't really have a concept of the soul. In fact, they had little interest in the afterlife.[†] If you scour the Old Testament, you will find that humans didn't go to heaven or hell after they died. In some instances, like in the book of Ecclesiastes, when you die, you simply cease to exist. *(Ec. 3:19-22, 9:5)* In other places, it says that your spirit or "shade" is sent to a place called Sheol, which is kind of like the Jewish version of Hades found in Greek mythology.[7.3] *(Gn. 37:35; Ps. 6:5, 30:3, 88:3, 139:8; Is. 14:9)* This inconsistency is an indication that the Jews were more concerned about what happened to you in this life rather than what was going to happen to you after you die.

A good example of how this affected the writing of the Old Testament is with the concept of judgment. Most modern Jews and Christians assume that humans will be judged by God after

---

†   Review p.68 for previous discussion of the Hebrew/Jewish conception of afterlife.

they die. However, the ancient Jews who wrote the Old Testament believed that God's judgment happened in this life. For instance, the financial status of your family was a reflection of how much God loved or hated your family. Those who struggled to feed their families were thought to be suffering the consequences of the sins their parents or grandparents had committed against God. By contrast, those who were wealthy were considered to be loved by God. Their blessing of wealth showed that their family had done well in God's eyes and, thus, they were favored by God.

The ancient Jews thought in concrete ways, so the physical world was more important to them than the metaphysical. The physical world was made for humans, while the metaphysical world, like heaven, was for God. The division of these two spheres is extraordinarily important for understanding Jesus' version of heaven. Heaven was not something that was generally accessible to human beings. Sure, there was the rare person here or there who had been granted the privilege of going to heaven (Enoch, Moses and Elijah), but those were the exceptions. As a rule, humans could not go to heaven in their afterlife. This is why the Jews believed God was going to create the kingdom of God.

The kingdom of God is something that Jesus talks about a lot in the New Testament. Jesus believed that the kingdom of God arrives when God merges heaven with earth. In other words, since humans cannot gain entrance into heaven, God will literally bring heaven to earth so that they are one and the same. Again, I cannot emphasize enough how extraordinarily concrete this idea is. Heaven will physically reside here on earth. Indeed, many Jews believed that Jerusalem would be the center of this kingdom.

So let's take a moment to point out the major differences between the common Christian portrayal of heaven and the version we just learned about from the Bible. When you hear about heaven in Christian churches, it is generally portrayed as a spiritual place of clouds and angels where your soul resides after you die for all eternity if you have accepted Jesus as your savior. However, the biblical version of heaven (or God's kingdom) is an actual, physical place, right here on earth. God's kingdom is not up in the sky or in some spiritual realm. God's kingdom is not a place where your soul resides for all eternity. In fact, quite the opposite. God's kingdom is a place where real, live people go to be rewarded for their allegiance to God. Furthermore, if the center of God's kingdom is in the city of Jerusalem, then hell (or the Gehenna Valley) is right next to heaven. People only have to stay in the Gehenna Valley for a year to be purged of their sins and then they will be welcomed into God's kingdom.

If this notion of heaven and hell sounds similar to the parable of the prodigal son, that's because they are talking about the same ideas. More than likely, Jesus never believed that a human's soul would go to heaven after death. Like most Jews in the first century, Jesus believed that physical human beings would reside in God's kingdom. This is why the concept of resurrection (the bringing back to life of the physical body) is so important in early Christianity. If the kingdom of God is a real, physical place on earth, then you need real physical people to inhabit that kingdom. Only those who are alive can enjoy God's kingdom, which means that the dead must be physically brought back to life.

If the notion that humans need to be physically brought back to life sounds crazy to you, then you're not alone. When I first encountered the idea that Christians believe that all human bodies would be reassembled by God at some undetermined point in the future, I literally laughed out loud. I thought, "If this is what Christians actually believe, then Christianity is not for me." What I have found in my time as a pastor is that few Christians actually subscribe to this belief. The vast majority of Christians, including myself, believe that when you die your soul goes to heaven or hell and that is the end of it.

Clearly, the important factor for many Christians, whether they believe in physical resurrection or the soul separating from the body, is that God rewards those who are good and punishes those who are bad. We care a lot about God doling out justice after we die because the world is so unjust. However, the question I would like to explore next is whether or not God's version of justice is really the same as our version of justice because, like most things in the Bible, what we want from God often differs from what God wants from us.

IT'S ELECTION TIME!

I'm associated with Presbyterianism. The man most credited for founding Presbyterian theology is John Calvin (1509-1564 C.E.). Perhaps one of Calvin's most famous and most controversial ideas about Christianity is called the Doctrine of Predestination. If I had to summarize predestination, I would say predestination is the idea that God is the one who determines your salvation, not you.

Calvin believed very strongly that God is in control of everything, in particular, our salvation. Calvin called the people whom God chooses "the elect." These special people are the ones God chooses to go to heaven. But then Calvin takes this concept of election one step further. Calvin says that if God has chooses some, God also rejects others. Calvin comes to this conclusion because, near the end of the Old Testament, the prophet Malachi, a man who was supposedly speaking on behalf of God, says, "I have loved Jacob, but I have hated Esau." *(Ml. 1:2-3)*

Jacob and Esau were twin brothers whose story is told in the book of Genesis. *(Gn. 25-27)* This scripture from Malachi is interesting because it claims that God loves some people and hates others. Calvin was intrigued by this idea and wanted to know the criteria God uses for determining whether to love or hate someone. Since Malachi develops this idea based on the story of Jacob and Esau, Calvin uses the brothers to shed light on the subject.

Later in their lives, Jacob and Esau have an encounter where Esau comes in from hunting in the fields and is hungry. Jacob, who mostly spends his days cooking inside his mother's tent, takes advantage of Esau's hunger and coerces Esau into selling his birthright in exchange for bread and a bowl of lentil stew. In this story, Jacob is crafty and unethical (because he shouldn't have taken advantage of his brother) and Esau doesn't respect his birthright (which was a big deal at this juncture in history because the first-born male inherited the father's legacy and a double portion of everything the father owned).[7.4]

This type of interaction happens over and over again with Jacob and Esau. Neither Jacob nor Esau is particularly ethical. They both look out solely for their own self-interest. The more you read about these two brothers, the harder it is to discern why God chose one over the other. Calvin comes to the conclusion that it is impossible for us to know why God chooses some over others. All we know is, if the scriptures are to be believed, that's just how God operates. Of course, if we take this doctrine to its logical conclusion, then those whom God loves will go to heaven and those whom God hates will go to hell.[7.5]

I'm sure you can understand why this doctrine causes a lot of anxiety for people. If God chooses some but not others and we have no idea whom God chooses and why God chooses them, then we have no idea whether or not we will go to heaven or hell. People during Calvin's day got very upset about this and they started asking him, "Is there any way we can know whether or not we are one of God's chosen?" Calvin, seeing how perturbed people were, provided one answer to this question: if you truly believe in Jesus, if you truly have faith in your heart and live the life that Jesus expects you to live, then more than likely you are one of God's elect. But the reality is that you can never really know for sure.

I know for most Christians the idea that God determines whether you go to heaven or hell seems crazy. Based on this doctrine, I could believe everything God wants me to believe and do everything God wants me to do and, in the end, God could still send me to hell because I am not one of God's elect. Although I disagree with many of the conclusions Calvin derives from the Doctrine of Predestination, I fell in love with the idea that God is the one who determines my salvation. All my anxiety went away because I realized I couldn't do anything to change what happens after I die and I didn't need to waste my time thinking about it anymore.

The beauty of God being in control of your salvation is that it changes your focus. Many Christians think that the work of Christianity is saving people's souls from going to hell. They spend their time trying to make people believe in Jesus and they neglect the important work that we are supposed to be doing as Christians. But if our salvation is predestined by God, then we can throw that problem out the window. We don't need to worry about it. God's got that covered, so rather than spend our time converting everyone to Christianity, we are freed to spend our time doing what Jesus asked us to do when he said to feed the hungry, clothe the naked, care for those who are sick, welcome the stranger and love the outcast. *(Mt. 25:34-40)* In other words, we are free to focus on building God's kingdom here on earth.

If you're wondering whether or not I actually care about my soul ending up in hell, let me be very clear, I don't. First of all, you have to understand that I don't think getting into heaven is the *point* of Christianity. The idea that I should believe in Jesus so that I can get a ticket into heaven is a selfish motivation, which to me is inherently contradictory to the point of following Jesus in the first place. In Chapter 10 we will discuss Jesus' teachings in further depth, but one of the most important principles Jesus teaches is that becoming his disciple requires you to deny yourself. *(Mk. 8:34-38)* One of the central tenets of following Jesus is understanding that it's not about you. Therefore, the idea that one should believe in Jesus in order to get into heaven contradicts the very essence of Jesus' movement because the golden ticket mentality is a lot more about self-preservation than self-denial.

Second, I believe that God wants all God's creatures to be saved. If the story of the prodigal son is any indication of the kind of love God has for us, then I believe that God wants all humans to find redemption.[†] Personally, I disagree with the prophet Malachi and Calvin. I do not think God loves some and hates others. What I think is that we as humans make choices that end up separating us from God. Not unlike the prodigal son who leaves and goes off on his own, we often turn our backs on God through the choices we make. We believe those choices will lead us somewhere better than where we were when we started. However, those choices will often lead us into a state of hell—a place of separation from God.

I don't know about you, but when I look at the world, I don't need to imagine some place of eternal torment where my soul will burn forever. I am continually astonished by the human ability to inflict pain and suffering on others. We are masters of creating hell right here on earth and I think it is a mistake to assume that God desires to treat us the same way we treat our fellow human beings. In fact, the scriptures convey a message that the exact opposite is true. God is willing to love us when no one else will. Not only is God always waiting with outstretched arms to welcome us whenever we are ready to return, but if there is any penalty to be incurred for our bad behavior, God would rather take the consequences on God's self than have us suffer those consequences. In other words, there is nothing we can do, think or say as human beings that could prevent God from loving us. Nothing.

---

†   Review p.68-69 for previous discussion of redemption.

Does that mean everyone is destined to go to heaven? Yes. Is my opinion on this matter some kind of fringe theology that nobody really believes to be true? No. The first person to articulate this point of view was the apostle Paul in his letter to the Romans in the New Testament. As Paul spread Christianity throughout the Mediterranean world, some of his new converts became concerned about how the Jews were not accepting Jesus as the messiah. If belief in Jesus is the only way for humans to be part of God's kingdom, then will Jesus' own people, who have rejected him, not be allowed into God's kingdom?

Paul dealt with this question by saying that God's promises to the Jews in the Old Testament can never be erased. In essence, the covenant God made with Abraham in Genesis *(Gn. 15:18-21, 17:1-8)* takes precedence over the covenant God made through Jesus. Thanks to Jesus, Gentiles (non-Jews) can now gain access to the promises God made to Abraham, making them honorary Jews. Paul believed that, no matter what, "all Israel will be saved." *(Rm. 11:26)* Ultimately, Paul felt that once enough Gentiles (or non-Jews) believed in Jesus, the Jews would undergo a mass conversion and accept Jesus as the messiah. Indeed, Paul was confident that *everyone*, given enough time, would eventually come to accept God's love and mercy: "For God has imprisoned all in disobedience so that he may be merciful to all." *(Rm. 11:32)*

Around 150 years after Paul's death, a theologian named Origen expanded on Paul's ideas. Origen believed that God's goal was to seek the redemption of the entire universe.[7.6] Origen also believed we have a choice as to whether or not we want to return to God. Therefore, God will not achieve the goal of total and complete redemption until every being in universe has made the choice to turn back to God. Origen believed, given enough time, God's love could melt the most hardened hearts.

Therefore, whether a person is dead or alive, God is always seeking to have them be a part of his kingdom. There is no such thing as permanent separation from God. But God can't prevent us from separating ourselves from the party. Like the older son in the parable of the prodigal son, we may choose, for whatever reason, to have nothing to do with God. This self-imposed separation from God is what hell is all about. The reality of hell is that it is never imposed on us by God. We impose hell on ourselves through our choices. Thankfully, even if we choose to separate ourselves from God, Jesus provides us with a way back.

1 Unconditional love is central to God's being. This means that, regardless of how vile or sinister our actions might be, they will never prevent God from loving us.

2 The standard depictions of heaven and hell promoted by conservative Christians are distortions of heaven and hell as found in the New Testament.

3 Heaven is not a spiritual realm up in the sky where souls reside for eternity. The biblical version of heaven (or God's kingdom) is an actual, physical place, on earth. Jerusalem is at the center of God's kingdom and the residents are not souls, but real, live people.

4 Hell is not a spiritual realm where the soul endures eternal torment. Rather, hell (or the Gehenna Valley) is located right next to Jerusalem and the people who inhabit Gehenna will be there for up to one year before being released back into God's kingdom.

5 When we subscribe to the idea that God determines our salvation, we are freed to stop worrying about whether or not we are going to heaven or hell. This allows us to spend our time doing what Jesus asked us to do on earth by serving those in need.

CHAPTER EIGHT

BUILDING UP THE JESUS OF HISTORY

THE BLACK SWAN

During my time at Oxford University, I developed a close friendship with a young man from Mississippi named JR who was a true renaissance man. He was brilliant at everything he did. Not only was he incredibly gifted academically but, when he was a teenager, he was widely considered to be one of the best young classical guitarists in the country. He could achieve anything he set his mind towards.

One day during the spring semester, JR approached me about going punting. I had no idea what that was, but I soon discovered that a punt is a boat used on inland waters that are relatively shallow, like a river or canal. The driver stands at the end of the punt, like on a gondola, and propels the boat using a large pole. It just so happens that Oxford has a large series of canals that allow you to travel through the town and out into the countryside. JR had been reading up on how to operate a punt and had reserved one for our group of friends.

As JR skillfully propelled us along, we came to a beautiful open spot where the canal broke off into several different streams. While we were debating which way to go, three white swans made their way out of the brush. They were regal and beautiful, so mesmerizing that we all stopped talking and just stared at them. Then from the other direction came a single black swan. The black swan mingled with the white swans and then they swam off together. To this day it is still one of the most beautiful things I have ever seen.

For the better part of human civilization, black swans were presumed not to exist. The Roman poet Juvenal once said, "A rare bird in the lands and very much like a black swan."[8.1] The English used the term "black swan" in their vernacular the same way we use the expression "when pigs fly." In other words, a black swan represents something that is very unlikely to occur. Today the phrase *black swan* usually refers to unforeseen events that occur in the financial markets. The economist and mathematician Nassim Nicholas Taleb wrote a book *The Black Swan* expanding this concept to include major events that have shifted the tide of human history. Taleb's idea has become known as Black Swan Theory and it attempts to explain three recurrent phenomena: 1) why black swan events have such a huge impact on the world in which we live; 2) why it's impossible for us to predict what events will become black swans; and 3) why we tend to be blind to how these events have shaped our lives.

One example that Taleb uses in his book is September 11, 2001. The events of 9/11 shifted the geopolitical landscape in ways that no person could have ever predicted. But many people believe that 9/11 could have been prevented. After the event, U.S. intelligence services scoured all of the intelligence data and found that the U.S. had evidence that could have led to uncovering the plot, preventing it from happening. Taleb walks us through a thought experiment built around this particular assertion.[8.2]

Let's say somebody had connected the dots. Let's say somebody knew that there was a plan being developed to crash planes into the

World Trade Center, the Pentagon and the White House. What if that person told Congress, "I think it would be in our best interest to make sure all the pilot cabins on airplanes are equipped with bullet proof doors that are continuously locked so that a terrorist cannot hijack the plane and crash it into a building." Today that kind of thinking makes total sense. I doubt that you would find anybody who would think that having secure cockpit doors on airplanes is not a good idea. However, prior to 9/11 that person would have been laughed out of Congress.

The notion that airlines should spend billions of dollars on a preventive measure like that would have been intensely fought by the airlines. It is only in the aftermath of a statistically improbable event like 9/11 that such thinking makes total sense. This is what makes a black swan a black swan. Until it happens, nobody can imagine how that event could change the world.

Jesus is a black swan. His influence on the course of Western civilization over the last 2,000 years cannot be overstated. How Jesus became a black swan that transformed the world into its present state is an important question that we will endeavor to answer during the next three chapters. And yet, I know there are many people reading this book who think they already possess the answer to that question: Jesus was God, so of course he was going to change the course of human history. Although this may be the conventional Christian approach to Jesus' influence, when you start examining Jesus' life from a historical perspective, you come to realize that his movement wasn't really set up to succeed in the way that it did.

Even though everyone today knows the name of Jesus, he may never have been called Jesus during his lifetime. Jesus is a Greek rendering of the Aramaic word *Yeshua*, which we translate into English as Joshua. So Jesus' real name is Joshua, but because of how it translates into Greek, the language of the New Testament, we call him Jesus. Moreover, Jesus was a very common name in the ancient world.

Since so many people were named Jesus, the ancients would tack identifiers to the end of the name. For instance, Jesus son of Sira, Jesus Justus, Jesus son of Ananias. However, the Jesus whom Christians worship is called Jesus of Nazareth. Apparently, that's the factor that differentiated the Christian Jesus from every other Jesus—his town of origin. Therefore, if we're going to talk about Jesus, it's important for us to know something about Nazareth. If you take some time to research the ancient village of Nazareth, you will quickly find that we don't know much about it.

Today Nazareth is a sprawling metropolis that is home to more than 75,000 people. In Jesus' day, Nazareth was located in a remote corner of an area known as Galilee. If you look at descriptions of Galilee from that era—descriptions that identified to the Roman government where people lived for purposes of taxation—Nazareth isn't anywhere to be found.[8.3] This tells us that Nazareth was so remote and inconsequential that tax collectors didn't even bother to log it in their official records.

Essentially, Nazareth was a backwater town in the middle of nowhere. A good analogy might be to think of the remote communities clustered in the hills of the Appalachia Mountains. There are small groupings of homes in the Appalachia region that are so far off the beaten path with so few people living in them that Google Maps doesn't even register their existence. Appalachia is also a good analogy because of the distinct nature of their accent. If you've always imagined Jesus speaking in a very refined and dignified manner, it's time to revise your assumption. In the eyes of educated Jews, Jesus would have sounded like a country boy.

You get hints of how people regarded Nazareth from the gospel stories of Jesus' ministry. For instance, in the gospel of John, a Jewish man named Nathanael hears about Jesus from his friend Philip. When Philip reveals that Jesus is from Nazareth, Nathaniel responds, "Can anything good come out of Nazareth?" *(Jn. 1:46)* Nathanael says this because he hails from Jerusalem. If Nazareth was like a remote town in Appalachia, then Jerusalem was like New York City. The Jews from Jerusalem were cultured and well educated, and they often looked down on Jews who were from other parts of the world.

Nathaniel is skeptical of Philip's claim that the messiah would come from Nazareth. Why would the messiah come from there? In the same way that most Christians have a picture in their minds of Jesus being cultured, educated and respected, that's exactly what many of the Jews during Jesus' day believed the messiah would be. But in Nazareth there was no formal education. There was no synagogue. The hundred or so families that resided in Nazareth were farmers who lived in poverty.[8.4] The likelihood that Jesus could even read is extremely low. And yet, this poor, uneducated peasant, Jesus of Nazareth, changed the world. Jesus' movement shouldn't have succeeded; in all honesty, we shouldn't even know his name, and yet, Christians around the world worship him every Sunday. To begin the journey of understanding how Jesus became this black swan that nobody could have anticipated, we need to understand the culture and environment into which Jesus was born.

IT'S THE ECONOMY, STUPID!

New Testament scholars estimate that Jesus of Nazareth was born sometime between 7 B.C.E. and 4 B.C.E.[8.5] At the time of Jesus' birth, Rome had become the dominant force in the Mediterranean. Rome's empire was enormous, which was both a curse and a blessing. It was curse in the sense that it was hard to control such a vast territory. Rome's primary tactic for keeping the populace in line was to crush any resistance with brutal force. One of the ways Rome ensured compliance was by stationing Roman soldiers in as many places as possible. No matter where you went, it felt as if Rome was watching. Due to the fact that any minor infraction of the law was met with violence, the subjects of the Roman Empire were often too scared to engage in uprisings and revolts.

However, violence was not the only tactic of control. The new Emperor, Caesar Augustus, understood that if his subjects were financially prosperous, then there would be no need for violence.[†] Therefore, Augustus set out to stabilize the economy with the release of standardized coinage throughout the empire.[8.6] This coinage made it far easier for nation states to engage in commerce with one another. Thus, the blessing of such a large empire is that everybody was allowed to do business with everyone else, which created a booming economy in many places. Wealthy Jews loved being able to do business under the new Roman regime and, for the first 40 years of the empire's existence (26 B.C.E – 14 C.E), Rome helped to create an incredibly robust and diversified economy in Judea and Galilee. During this period, everyone from aristocrats to artisans to peasants enjoyed an improved standard of living.[8.7]

For example, not long after Jesus was born, the new Roman ruler of Galilee, a man by the name of Herod Antipas, built two large cities intended to house the wealthiest citizens in Galilee. One of these cities was Sepphoris, which was located only five miles away from Jesus' hometown of Nazareth. The second was Tiberias, which was located right on the Lake of Galilee (often referred to as the Sea of Galilee in the gospels).[8.8] The construction of these cities meant that the peasant population, who were often relegated to subsistence farming, could earn extra money by assisting with the various building projects within these two cities (in the next section we will discuss how scholars have speculated that Jesus may have been a day laborer on the construction of Sepphoris). Therefore, even if their own personal crops did not perform well, the peasants who worked on these building projects could afford to buy extra

---

†   Review p.113-114 for previous discussion of Roman emperors.

food at market. For a group of people who were often malnourished, such economic benefit brought real stability to their lives.

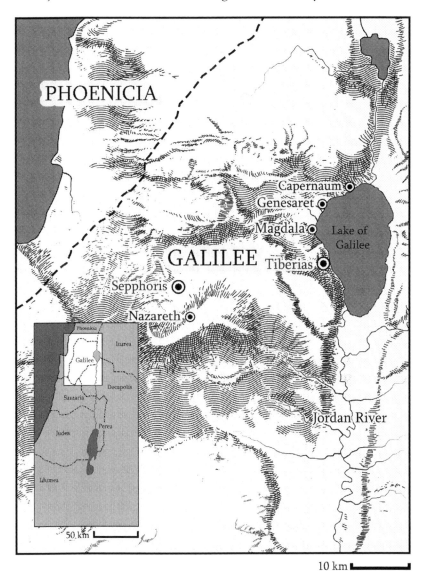

Unfortunately, the prosperity of the first 40 years of the Roman Empire would slowly be undone when Emperor Tiberius, Augustus' successor, came to power in 14 C.E. Tiberius made a foolish decision when he began hoarding coinage in the Roman Treasury.[8,9] As you can imagine, this hoarding had extremely negative effects that could be felt throughout the empire.[8.10] As coinage was removed from circulation, interest rates began to soar. Within six years, the repercussions of the credit crisis were noticeable in the region of Galilee.†

By 20 C.E., most of the major building projects at Sepphoris and Tiberias had been completed, drying up the extra income that had subsidized the peasant population. What's more, since coinage was in short supply, there was pressure on the provincial government to locate enough funds to operate.[8.11] The burden to cover this deficit fell on the tax collectors, who heavily inflated their tax rates. The peasants, who mostly traded in grain, were being squeezed for every resource in their possession. By the mid-20s, a growing number of peasants were so far behind on their payments they had to forfeit their land in order to remediate the debt.[8.12] The sad irony of these circumstances is that their land was now owned by the same wealthy Jews for whom they had built homes in Sepphoris and Tiberias.

Jesus' movement arose at the height of the credit crisis.[8.13] He watched as families who formerly made a living wage became unable to support themselves. A good example of this was the fishing industry around the Lake of Galilee. If you look at ancient maps of the Lake of Galilee, you will see the shoreline dotted with little coastal villages. For centuries prior to Roman rule, these little villages were home to families that fished the lake and made a decent income.[8.14] Many of Jesus' disciples were fisherman: what made them leave behind a comfortable lifestyle to follow Jesus?

Many Christians want to believe that the reason the disciples left behind their families, children and jobs to follow Jesus is because he was irresistibly charismatic. Although this is a wonderful notion, the reality is a little clearer once you understand the disciples' situation. People don't typically abandon their responsibilities if things are going well. The only way a movement like Jesus' would

---

† Review p.129 for previous discussion of the financial debts of peasants.

be appealing is if Jesus' disciples believed that following Jesus was going to lead them to a better life than the one they currently had.

As Jewish fisherman living in Capernaum, Simon, Andrew, James and John were subject to the same market forces as the farmers in Galilee. As the credit crises loomed large, Herod Antipas tightened his control over the Lake of Galilee, forcing the smaller fishing enterprises to hand over more and more of their daily catch to tax collectors.[8.15] By the late 20s, the little mom and pop fishing businesses that had been around for centuries all of a sudden struggled to stay afloat because they were bringing so few fish to market. It is not surprising that these young men, who were working so hard for so little benefit, believed that it was worth it to leave their jobs and families to follow Jesus.

If we look at all the various elements surrounding this small window of time (20-30 C.E.) in which Jesus started his movement, it becomes clear how it was a perfect storm for apocalyptic, end-of-the-world thinking. Thanks to Rome, the lives of the Jewish peasants in Galilee were becoming increasingly unbearable. They were under constant threat of violence from the Roman soldiers in their midst. Many peasants couldn't afford to feed their families and what little money they did have was being taken by tax collectors, which helped to fund the very oppression they loathed.

Therefore, it makes sense that the Jews were waiting for someone to save them from their oppression. Surely God would see their persecution and fulfill the promises of the scriptures to send them a savior who would relieve them of their suffering. Surely God would not abandon them in their moment of greatest need. Surely God was preparing a leader to free them from the rule of the Roman government. The time was ripe. The question on everyone's mind was, "Who? Who will rise up and become the messiah, the king that will lead the Jewish people out of their oppression?"

ONLY THE FACTS, MA'AM

If you've ever done any digging into Jesus' life, you probably discovered that we know remarkably little about him. In fact, beyond the documents found in the New Testament, there is very little historical evidence to corroborate Jesus' existence. All we know about Jesus comes from his followers, people who were dedicated to his cause following his execution by the Roman government. Although there is a lot of information in the New Testament about Jesus' life, we cannot approach this information as wholly factual. I'm not saying everything written about Jesus in the New Testament is false. Rather, we have no way of confirming the events depicted. Therefore, I want to extract five basic plot points about the trajectory of Jesus' life that seem the most reliable to scholars:

1. Jesus was born in the town of Nazareth. (7-4 B.C.E.)
2. Jesus was baptized by John the Baptist. (28-30 C.E.)
3. Jesus travelled all over Galilee, preaching about the coming of God's kingdom and healing the sick. (28-30 C.E.)
4. Jesus disrupted the business transactions taking place in the Jerusalem Temple, an act which led to his arrest. (30-33 C.E.)
5. Jesus was convicted of treason by the Roman government and executed by means of crucifixion. (30-33 C.E.)

Though this might not seem like much, each of these plot points provides us with a wealth of information and will allow us to paint a fairly complete picture of Jesus' life. First, Jesus was born in the town of Nazareth, a small village of approximately 100 families located in the lower corner of Galilee. Though we don't know much about Nazareth itself, we know quite a bit about the area right outside of Nazareth. Five miles away from Nazareth was a city called Sepphoris that was fully excavated by archaeologists in the 1980s. Sepphoris was home to some of the wealthiest citizens of Galilee and, in 4 B.C.E., was attacked by a group of peasants led by a man named Judas who raided the royal armory. Using these weapons, Judas ransacked the homes of the wealthy, slaughtering members of the Jewish aristocracy in the process.[8.16]

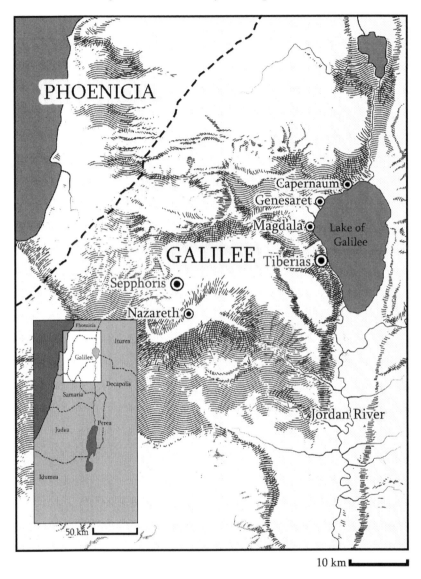

In response, Rome sent soldiers who captured Judas. Not only did they execute him, but they crucified some 2,000 of Judas' followers and sympathizers. The Roman army then turned their sights on the citizens of Sepphoris and punished them for not better guarding their arsenal of weapons. The soldiers captured the inhabitants and auctioned them off as slaves before burning the city to the ground.[8.17] The villagers in Nazareth would have been able to see Sepphoris burning at night. During the day, if one travelled out of Nazareth, the roads would have been lined with persons hanging from crosses; hundreds of them, with no end in sight. Some were dead, rotting and being picked apart by birds and insects; some were alive waiting to die. All of them had endured horrible suffering.

Can you imagine what it would do to your psyche to see something like that? Can you imagine how it would get inside you and change who you are? You'd never look at the world the same way. You would always know that what happened to them could easily happen to you if you weren't careful. Jesus' mother would have warned Jesus about the perils of challenging Rome's authority, and yet, more than 20 years later, Jesus would face the exact same fate. Why Jesus wasn't more afraid of the consequences of challenging the Roman government can be attributed to what he experienced during the intervening years prior to beginning his ministry.

After the destruction of Sepphoris, Herod Antipas decided to rebuild the city. The wealthiest citizens of Galilee were willing to fund the rebuilding project, but it would require a lot of cheap labor. Jesus is described in the gospels as a τέκτων (tekton), which is often translated as *carpenter* into English. A better translation would be *handyman*.[8.18] Jesus was a guy whom you would hire to do odd jobs. However, Nazareth is such a small village that Jesus would not have been able to find enough work to support himself, so more than likely, he was part of the rebuilding effort in Sepphoris during his teenage years. In the gospels, Jesus is portrayed as speaking passionately about the negative influence of money on a person's relationship with God. *(Mk. 10:23, Mt. 6:24, Lk. 12:13-21, 14:25-33, 16:19-31)* One can imagine how Jesus' thinking about the disparity between the wealthy and the poor would have been shaped as he built lavish homes for the wealthy.

Although we have no record of how Jesus spent most of his early adult life, we can make an educated guess as to some of the events that might have inspired him to begin his ministry. By the time Jesus was entering his early 20s, he would have become more aware of how the economic suffering of Galilee was directly linked to the Roman occupation of Jewish lands. Like many people in Jesus' situation, he would have been looking for ways to express his frustration. In our modern world, a common pattern among young men and women who live in oppressive situations is to join groups of like-minded people. We see this in places like modern Egypt, Syria and Libya where impoverished youth band together to create movements for change. During Jesus' day, one such movement that attracted disaffected youth was led by a man named John the Baptist, which is the second plot point on Jesus' timeline. Certain scholars have speculated that Jesus may have been one of John's disciples before venturing out on his own.[8.19] John was called the baptizer because he would ritually cleanse his disciples by immersing them in water.

The word *baptize* comes from the Greek word βαπτιζω (baptiz-do), which literally means *to dip*.[8.20] The concept of dipping people into water to cleanse them is an ancient tradition in Judaism and rooted in rituals where priests would purify themselves with water before offering a sacrifice to God. *(Nu. 19:1-9)* Over the years, this concept of priestly purification trickled down into the general Jewish population. Archaeologists have found baths all over Israel where people would go to ritually cleanse themselves.[8.21] John's movement borrowed from this tradition. The purpose of John's ritual cleansing was to prepare for the coming of God's kingdom.

Many of John's followers believed that John was the messiah. *(Lk. 3:15)* Although John plays a supporting role in the Christian scriptures, to this day, there is a small sect of individuals called the Mandaeans in the Middle East who proclaim John the Baptist as their true teacher.[8.22]

Today, Jesus is clearly the more historically important of the two men, but had you been alive in early first century Galilee, you would not have guessed that to be the case. Although the Christian scriptures portray Jesus as being this wildly popular figure who could never get a moment alone, John the Baptist was more famous than Jesus ever was during his lifetime. John was the preeminent prophet of his day. We know this because there was a historian called Flavius Josephus who lived a few decades after Jesus and wrote about the history of the Jewish people. In one of his works, he mentions John the Baptist and how his prominence among the Jewish peasantry led to his execution by Herod Antipas sometime between 28 and 30 C.E., about two to three years before Jesus was crucified.[8.23]

Interestingly, Josephus only makes one passing mention of Jesus in his histories. This seemed like a glaring omission to Christians in later centuries who were trying to preserve Josephus' work, so to correct this problem, some of these Christians took it upon themselves to insert a few short sentences about Jesus into Josephus' histories.[8.24] The fact that Christians had to forge these passages on Jesus' behalf is telling. It seems that during his lifetime, Jesus was barely a blip on the radar screen of the Jewish people. Even in the early decades following his death, the early church was an unknown entity to anybody of importance among the Jewish people. How Jesus eventually came to have prominence over John the Baptist leads us to the third plot point along Jesus' timeline—Jesus' ministry.

TOPSY-TURVY

From what we can tell, Jesus' ministry was short. Depending on which gospel you read, it was between one and three years.[8.25] That's not a lot of time to get your name out in the world, and yet, this short period of time would prove potent enough to redirect the course of human civilization. It is within this timeframe that Jesus began preaching and healing. There are two events that propelled Jesus to venture out on his own. The first is his baptism. Although this scene is highly dramatized in the gospels, clearly something important happened to Jesus when he was baptized by John. The way this event is portrayed in the Gospel of Mark seems to indicate that Jesus' baptism is where he acquires his ability to preach and heal. *(Mk. 1:9-11, 6:1-3)* Indeed, I would suggest that it is during his baptism that Jesus acquires his fully formed God consciousness.[†] Therefore, even though Christians tend to think of Jesus as possessing these abilities since his birth, the earliest and most reliable portrayal of Jesus' life seems to dispute this notion. Prior to his baptism, Jesus was a nobody. Following his baptism, Jesus became someone of note.

The second event that influenced Jesus' movement is the arrest of John the Baptist by Herod Antipas. There is speculation among scholars as to whether Jesus simply took over John's movement after John's arrest or launched his own ministry. Regardless, Jesus picked up where John left off by preaching about the coming of God's kingdom.

The concept of God's kingdom is an amalgamation of a lot of different ideas from various religious traditions. The basis for the concept begins in Zoroastrianism, which states the messiah will usher in a cosmic renovation where heaven and earth are merged as one.[8.26] God will destroy those who perpetrate evil, chaos and violence, creating an era of unprecedented peace and prosperity. Beyond this, the Jewish prophets describe God's kingdom as a place where nobody suffers. Everyone has enough to

---

†   Review p.116-117 for previous discussion of God consciousness.

eat; everyone has clothes to wear and a roof over their heads; everyone is treated for their illnesses; nobody is forgotten. *(Is. 11:1-8, 58:6-11, 65:17-25, Mc. 4:1-3)*

Jesus retains all of these elements, but adds his own nuances concerning those who will be granted entrance into God's kingdom. In God's kingdom, the normal social order is reversed. The ones you would expect to be first will be last and those you would expect to be last will be first. In particular, Jesus tells us that the wealthy will have a difficult time gaining entrance into God's kingdom. Jesus lets us know in no uncertain terms that the poor are favored in God's kingdom: "How hard it will be for those who have wealth to enter the kingdom of God." *(Mk. 10:24)*

I cannot emphasize enough how radical this slight twist on the concept of God's kingdom was at the time. Jews talked about the imminent arrival of God's kingdom all the time, but most Jews assumed that the parameters of entrance would hinge on whether or not you were Jewish—one of God's chosen people. Jesus up-ends this dynamic by undercutting many of the basic traditions of Jewish piety.

First century Jews believed that your life was a reflection of how much God loved or hated your family.[†] For instance, if you had a child with a physical or mental handicap, the Jews believed that such maladies were the result of God punishing your family for their sins.[8.27] An example of this mentality can be found in the book of 2 Samuel. When David commits adultery with Bathsheba and she becomes pregnant, she ends up losing the child shortly after it is born. This is interpreted in the Bible as David being punished by God for committing adultery and orchestrating the death of Bathsheba's husband. *(2 Sa. 12:13-14)*

Another example of this type of thinking was a family's financial status. Those who lived in generational poverty and struggled to feed their families were thought to be suffering the consequences of the sins their parents or grandparents had committed against

---

†   Review p.147-148 for previous discussion of the Jewish view of generational sin.

God. By contrast, those who were wealthy were considered to be loved by God. The blessing of wealth showed that their family had done well in God's eyes and, thus, they were favored by God. *(Gn. 24:35, 26:12-13, 32:13-15; Jb. 1:1-8)* The idea that the wealthy might not be able to gain entrance into God's kingdom was unthinkable. Even Jesus' disciples are portrayed as being bewildered by this concept *(Mk. 10:23-27)* because, in their way of thinking, God's kingdom is essentially a mirror of the world as it stands right now, with the major change being that Jews would be in control.

One can imagine how Jesus' message would have been welcome news for the peasant population whose economic circumstances were becoming increasingly dire. However, what really enticed them to listen to Jesus was the fact that he was a healer. Many Christians assume that Jesus was such an amazing speaker that people were compelled to listen to him, but skill in oratory had little to do with whether or not you could draw an audience in Jewish culture. Not dissimilar to our mentality today, we listen to people because of the expertise they bring to a topic. Therefore, because Jesus lacked formal education, he also lacked authority among the larger Jewish community to speak about religious matters. But Jesus, being a man of no education, was able to buck this trend by using his healings as leverage to entice people to listen to his teachings.

Another misconception held by Christians is that people flocked to Jesus because he was the only person they had ever met who could perform healings. There were many people during Jesus' day who called themselves healers. If you were able to gain a positive reputation, it could be a very lucrative profession. However, what differentiated Jesus from his competition was that Jesus didn't charge money to perform his healings.[8.28] It seems the only compensation Jesus required was that you listen to his teachings. Jesus' willingness to heal for free probably stemmed from experiencing how the poor were increasingly unable to help their loved ones who suffered from illness and disease.

Therefore, it was the combination of these two factors—his healings and his teachings—that gave Jesus standing in the community. Had Jesus only been a healer and not a teacher or only a teacher and not a healer, we would not know the name of Jesus of Nazareth today. But he was both and this was rather unusual in the ancient world. In fact, this is what set Jesus apart from every other person who claimed to be the messiah. Jesus was not the only itinerant preacher in the countryside claiming messiahship, but he was the only one who used his talents to alleviate the plight of the poor. In this way, Jesus not only proclaimed the coming of God's kingdom but also was able to model what the kingdom was supposed to look like by creating instances of the kingdom among the people he encountered.

JESUS' MASTER PLAN

Somewhere along the way Jesus made a decision that he wanted to make a statement against the wealth and corruption that had brought so much suffering upon the Jewish people. Perhaps the greatest symbol of corruption in the Jewish tradition was the Jerusalem Temple. The Temple was where members of the Jewish faith would come to offer animal sacrifices to God. As we discussed in Chapter 6, the Jewish people felt compelled to sacrifice animals to God because it was mandated by the laws of the Old Testament. In order for your sins to be forgiven, you needed to offer a sacrifice to God. Once the priest offered the sacrifice on the altar in the Temple on your behalf, then you would be cleansed of your sins for a period of time.

Observant Jews would try to make a pilgrimage to Jerusalem once a year, often during the Passover. Many of the Jews who visited the Temple had traveled great distances and, therefore, did not have a sacrifice to offer. As a result, they needed to purchase the sacrifice there at the Temple. This continual need for sacrifices had given rise to an entire industry built around the buying and selling of sacrifices.[8.29]

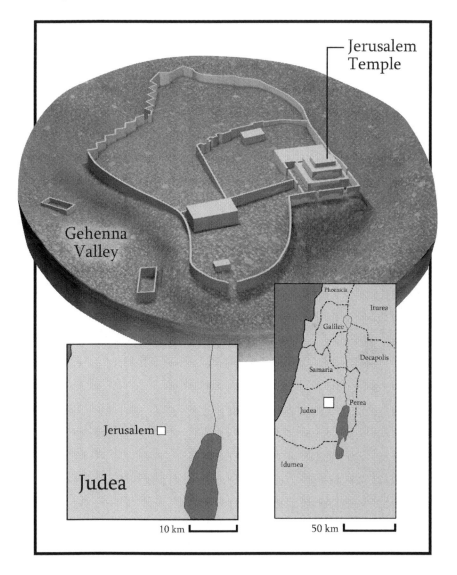

Those coming in from out of town might not have the correct type of money to purchase the sacrifice, so they would have to exchange their money into the right currency. Of course, the money changers charged a hefty fee for their services. The next step in the process was to purchase the sacrifice, which meant buying from the sellers of the sacrifices. The sacrifice options could range from a small dove to a full-sized bull. Again, every seller was trying to get top dollar, which meant that the poor would often bear the brunt of these high prices. The less money you had at your disposal, the harder it was to worship God and the deeper you had to go into debt to do something that should be a fundamental right of being Jewish.

Furthermore, the priests performing the sacrifices, many of whom were members of the aristocracy, took a cut of the profits reaped from this massive industry. When Jesus makes the statement, "You cannot serve God and wealth," *(Mt. 6:24)* I cannot help but assume that his reference point was the corruption taking place at the Jerusalem Temple. In an act of defiance, Jesus walked into the Temple and overturned the tables of the money changers and the sellers of the sacrifices (the fourth plot point on Jesus' timeline). All of the gospels portray Jesus as being able to walk away from this incident without consequence. Indeed, the gospels tell us that Jesus was able to move about freely in Jerusalem and teach for almost a week before he was arrested and crucified. The timeline of Jesus' last week tends to look something like this:

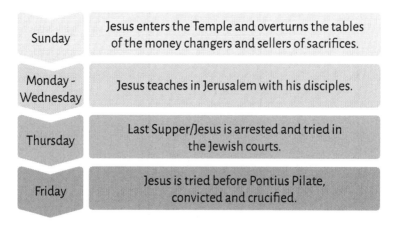

Sunday	Jesus enters the Temple and overturns the tables of the money changers and sellers of sacrifices.
Monday - Wednesday	Jesus teaches in Jerusalem with his disciples.
Thursday	Last Supper/Jesus is arrested and tried in the Jewish courts.
Friday	Jesus is tried before Pontius Pilate, convicted and crucified.

This timeline is highly unlikely for several reasons. Let's start at the beginning of the week. First of all, there were soldiers stationed all around the Temple courts. During the Jewish festivals, when Jerusalem swelled with worshipers, Rome wanted to remind the Jewish people who was in charge.[8.30] The aristocracy didn't mind the extra security since there was so much money changing hands. Anybody walking into the Temple with the intention of stealing or disrupting these transactions would quickly be arrested. Therefore, there are only a couple of different scenarios that make sense: 1) Jesus never disrupted the business transactions in the Temple, as portrayed in the gospels; 2) Jesus only overturned the tables of one or two money changers (which the guards might have overlooked as a business transaction gone wrong); or 3) Jesus did exactly what the gospel authors claimed, except he didn't walk away freely. My belief is that Jesus entered into the Jerusalem Temple with the understanding that he would be arrested for disrupting the business transactions. Indeed, I believe he wanted to be arrested. In order to explain why, I need lay out an alternate timeline for Jesus' last days, which is a little different than the portrayal we find in the gospels.

If you read the gospels closely, it appears that Jesus believed his role as the messiah was to usher in God's kingdom.[†] He planned on doing this by suffering on the cross. It seems that Jesus believed that his execution on the cross was the pivotal component that would usher in the new kingdom of God. That said, Jesus didn't simply want to suffer on a cross anywhere. He wanted to be crucified in Jerusalem, the epicenter of Judaism. The gospels lead us to believe that Jesus was a known entity to the Jewish authorities and they were looking for ways to have him arrested, *(Mk. 3:6, 14:1, Mt. 12:13-14, Lk. 22:2, Jn. 11:53)* but I think it is within reason to believe that Jesus' movement was unknown to anyone outside of the Jewish peasantry. Therefore, Jesus needed to do something that would get the attention of the Jewish aristocracy. His plan was to enter the Temple and disrupt the business transactions, knowing this would entice the Jewish aristocracy to hand him over to Rome for execution.

---

†   Review p.100-101 for previous discussion of the Jewish messiah.

Therefore, the last supper probably occurred the night before the entry into the Jerusalem Temple. In other words, I don't think the disciples were as ignorant about Jesus' intentions as the gospels make them out to be. *(Mk. 9:32, Lk. 9:45, 18:34)* I think they knew full well that Jesus was going to be arrested and executed for his actions in the Temple. In my mind, this sheds a different light on the tradition of Jesus using the bread and wine as a symbol of his suffering. Jesus was not simply establishing a ritual of remembrance, as is portrayed in the gospels. Jesus and the disciples believed this was truly their last supper in this present world before God would establish God's kingdom on earth. They assumed that the next day, after Jesus was arrested by the Roman soldiers, Jesus would be ushering in the new world order. This perspective sheds new light on Jesus' statement, "Truly I tell you, I will never again drink of the fruit of the vine until that day when I drink it new in the kingdom of God." *(Mk. 14:25, Mt. 26:29, Lk. 22:18)*

All of the gospels portray Jesus as going through two trials—one with the Sanhedrin (a group of priests with legal authority for conducting trials against the Jewish people) and one with the Roman government, where he was sentenced to crucifixion, but that's probably not what happened. After Jesus' arrest in the Temple, the aristocracy would have wanted to make a quick example of Jesus. Since the aristocracy had a comfortable relationship with the Roman authorities, Jesus was probably immediately handed over to the Romans to be tried for treason against the Roman government (the fifth plot point on Jesus' timeline).

The person responsible for executions in this region of the world was a man named Pontius Pilate.[†] Even though Pontius Pilate is portrayed as being sympathetic to Jesus' plight, we know from historical documents that Pontius Pilate was extremely cruel and heartless. Pilate was outspoken in his hatred of the Jews and he had no qualms expressing how much he disliked his assignment to this area of the world.[8.31] Pontius Pilate was known for putting Jews to death without trial. Given this reality, the likelihood that Jesus even had a trial is quite low. If Jesus did have a trial, you can be sure that Pontius Pilate was more than happy to sign Jesus' death warrant. Given this information, let's look at the revised timeline:

Day 1	Last Supper with Jesus' disciples.
Day 2	Jesus enters the Temple and overturns the tables of the money changers and sellers of the sacrifices leading to Jesus' arrest.
Day 3	Jesus is tried before Pontius Pilate, convicted and crucified.

Leading up to Jesus' crucifixion, you will notice that I am essentially dismissing all of the drama that we find in the gospels of Jesus being betrayed by Judas. To be clear, I don't think that ever happened. The reason is quite simple—the same story occurs in the book of Genesis when Joseph is betrayed by his brother Judah for 20 pieces of silver. *(Gn. 37:25-28)* The name Judah in Hebrew translates into Judas in Greek. Therefore, I think Mark took this story and superimposed it onto Jesus' story to create a nice literary parallel. Mark wants the reader to associate Jesus' story with Joseph.[‡] In the same way that Joseph being sold out by Judah results in the salvation of the family of Israel by saving them from starvation,

---

†   Review p.93 for previous discussion of Pontius Pilate.
‡   Review p.65-67 for previous discussion of Joseph's story.

when Jesus is sold out by Judas, his suffering results in the salvation of the Jewish people.

Once Jesus is on the cross, I am of the opinion that Jesus believed this event would be enough to initiate a chain reaction that would establish God's kingdom on earth. As God's chosen one, I think Jesus believed God would save him. Jesus felt that by being crucified at the hands of the Jewish aristocracy, the very people who were colluding with the Roman government and causing so much suffering for God's people, God would see his suffering, intercede, save him, save the Jewish people and bring God's kingdom to earth. If you think my interpretation might be a stretch, all you need to do is look at Jesus' last words: "My God, my God, why have you forsaken me?" *(Mk. 15:34)* Christians have puzzled over these words for centuries. If Jesus knew he was going to die, why, in his last moments of life, would he proclaim that he felt abandoned by God? Well, you could come up with elaborate theological answers to this question or you could acknowledge the simple answer staring us in the face—Jesus didn't think he was going to die.

This is where the topic we discussed at the end of Chapter 5—how Jesus' God consciousness does not imbue Jesus with special insight into the future—becomes really important. Remember, I stated that the same rules apply to Jesus as to everyone else. God can only work with the decisions that Jesus makes and sometimes those decisions turn out to be mistakes.[†] I think Jesus and his disciples were convinced that God would intervene and pull him down from the cross. I think Jesus incorrectly believed what was written in Psalm 91 applied to him: "For he will command his angels concerning you to guard you in all your ways. On their hands they will bear you up, so that you will not dash your foot against a stone." *(Ps. 91:11-12)* There are allusions to this line of thinking in three places in the gospels.

[†]   Review p.58-60, 74-75, 117 for previous discussion of God's interaction with free will.

The first is when Jesus is being arrested: "Then Jesus said to him, 'Put your sword back into its place; for all who take the sword will perish by the sword. Do you think that I cannot appeal to my Father, and <u>he will at once send me more than twelve legions of angels</u>?'" (*Mt. 26:52-53 – emphasis added*) The second occurs during Jesus' crucifixion. In the gospel of Luke, Jesus exchanges words with the two criminals being executed next to him. One of the criminals says to Jesus, "...remember me when you come into your kingdom." Jesus replies, "Truly I tell you, <u>today you will be with me in Paradise</u>." (*Lk. 23:42-43 – emphasis added*) Read in the context just described, Jesus' response to the criminal would indicate that Jesus felt God would establish the kingdom that very day.

The third reference is also from Jesus' crucifixion and is found in Mark and Matthew: "When some of the bystanders heard it, they said, 'This man is calling for Elijah.' At once one of them ran and got a sponge, filled it with sour wine, put it on a stick, and gave it to him to drink. But the others said, 'Wait, <u>let us see whether Elijah will come to save him</u>.' Then Jesus cried again with a loud voice and breathed his last." (*Mk. 15:35-36, Mt. 27:47-50 – emphasis added*) I believe these oral traditions found their way into the scriptures because they were part of the original thinking of the movement. However, when Jesus unexpectedly died on the cross, these oral traditions had to undergo major revision.

The fact that Jesus' disciples had the opportunity to revise their thinking about Jesus is astounding. Frankly, Jesus' movement should have dissolved the moment he died on the cross. The disciples should have seen Jesus as a crackpot who made a promise he couldn't deliver. He was not the messiah after all. He was not the one who would usher in God's kingdom. Indeed, when you look at Jesus' life in totality, you realize that he should have been lost in the annals of history. At best, Jesus should have been a footnote, one among the throngs of people claiming to be the messiah. But he wasn't forgotten. His movement and his cause became the focal point around which Western civilization was formed. The reason for this relates to an event that falls outside the scope of normal historical study. This event differentiated Jesus from everyone else claiming to be the messiah and would cement him as the black swan that would change the course of human history—Jesus came back from the dead.

CHAPTER 8 RECAP: WHAT YOU NEED TO KNOW

1 The factor that differentiated the Christian Jesus from every other Jesus in the ancient world was his town of origin—Nazareth.

2 Jesus' movement arose at the height of the credit crisis in the Roman Empire. Those who followed Jesus were disenfranchised by the lack of economic opportunity in Galilee.

3 Jesus was likely a disciple of John the Baptist and, following John's arrest, Jesus either took over John's movement or branched out on his own.

4 The stated goal of Jesus' movement was to usher in God's kingdom. Jesus' version of God's kingdom was shocking because he reverses the normal social order. For example, the poor are favored over the wealthy.

5 As God's chosen messiah, Jesus likely believed that being placed on the cross would usher in God's kingdom. When God did not intervene to save Jesus and create the kingdom, Jesus felt abandoned by God as indicated by his last words, "My God, my God, why have you forsaken me?"

CHAPTER NINE

THE RESURRECTION

A SHADOW OF A DOUBT

When I was growing up, even though I went to church every Easter, I never understood the celebration of Easter. I knew it involved bunnies and chocolate and hunting for painted eggs, but I never grasped why my mom insisted that we go to church. I mean, why ruin all the fun? Church would inhibit my ability to eat all of the candy in my Easter basket. It didn't make sense to me as a kid and it still didn't make sense to me as a teenager.

I remember the first time I understood what Christians were actually celebrating on Easter. In college, my roommate Grant told me that Easter was the day Christians celebrate Jesus' resurrection. I said, "Well, what does that mean? What is a resurrection?" He said, "It means something that was dead has come back to life. So three days after Jesus was executed by the Roman government, he came back to life." I couldn't believe what I was hearing. I said, "All these years I've been celebrating Jesus becoming a zombie?" Grant didn't appreciate my humor and said, "He's not a zombie, Alex. He's not a dead body that can walk around. Jesus was dead and then he came back to life." I thought about this for minute and said, "I'm surprised that people actually think this is true."

Although Grant looked at me as if I was crazy for questioning whether Jesus came back to life, I eventually discovered that I was in good company. A Rasmussen Reports research poll from 2013 estimates that 36 percent of the American population does not believe in Jesus' resurrection (19 percent reject the resurrection as untrue and 17 percent are unsure).[9.1] So it seems I'm not the only one questioning the validity of this claim. And frankly, can you blame people for questioning the resurrection? It's an outlandish concept that a man who was executed could come back from the dead.

There are three ways to reconcile what the disciples claimed to have happened: 1) Jesus wasn't dead when they thought he was; or 2) he was dead and they imagined he came back; or 3) they completely made it up. Why do we think this way? Because we've grown up in a world where things are testable. If I throw something up in the air, unless there's a rocket attached to it, it's going to come back down. Gravity is testable. If my heart stops beating and no one resuscitates me, then I will die. It's medically verifiable. No heartbeat leads to death. Yes, there are instances when people "die" for short periods of time and come back, but with Jesus we are talking about coming back to life after being dead for 36 hours or more. More importantly, without a time machine, this claim is not testable or verifiable.

Even though we cannot prove or disprove the resurrection, something happened after Jesus' execution. Exactly what happened is hard to say, but what we know for certain is that Jesus' disciples, friends, family, and followers experienced something profound. The way they describe this event is that Jesus was with them. What exactly the resurrection entailed is unclear because the New Testament describes Jesus' resurrection in three different ways. In Matthew and Luke, Jesus physically comes back to life. In portions of John's gospel, Jesus is portrayed as a ghost or spirit who can walk through walls. Finally, in Paul's letters, Jesus' appearance is a vision experienced by hundreds at a time. Although these are three distinct encounters with Jesus following his death, Christians tend to group all of them under the category of the same resurrection appearances.

When I began studying Christianity, I assumed that this discrepancy was a matter of interpretation. Like everything we experience in the world, different people present at the same event come away with different understandings of what took place. But the more I examined each of the resurrection accounts individually, the more I realized that these three versions are not perceptual differences. Indeed, these authors are talking about very different kinds of resurrection. Similar to the idea we discussed in Chapter 5 of Jesus slowly becoming God over the course of the New Testament, we also see an evolution in the way the resurrection is portrayed as the documents in the New Testament trend further away from Jesus' life. So let's examine these differing accounts of the resurrection because, if we don't thoroughly understand the resurrection, then we cannot understand Jesus, the purpose behind his message or the meaning of his movement in the 21st century.

NOT ALL RESURRECTION ACCOUNTS ARE CREATED EQUAL

In order to understand how each of the resurrection accounts converge and diverge from one another, we need to walk through them in the order that they were written. As we discussed earlier, Paul's letters are the earliest documents in the New Testament. Paul describes Jesus' resurrection in terms of a vision that many people witnessed individually and as whole groups at different times following Jesus' death.[9.2] Indeed, Paul claims that he is the last person to have interacted with the resurrected Jesus. *(1 Co. 15:8)* Although he never provides details as to what this vision looked like, we can glean some important information from how Paul describes Jesus' second coming at the end times.

In his letter to the church in Thessalonica, Paul says these words: "For the Lord himself, with a cry of command, with the archangel's call and with the sound of God's trumpet, will descend from heaven, and the dead in Christ will rise first. Then we who are alive, who are left, will be caught up in the clouds together with them to meet the Lord in the air; and so we will be with the Lord forever." *(1 Th. 4:16-17)* Clearly, Paul believes that when Jesus returns to earth, his entry point will be from the sky. Part of the reason why he describes Jesus' return this way is because the Jews believed that the entry point into heaven was in the sky. However, the other reason for describing Jesus coming from an aerial location is possibly because, when Jesus appeared to him and the crowds, they saw Jesus in the air.

There are not many tangibles to grasp when it comes to Paul's account of the resurrection. Indeed, the speculative nature of the earliest accounts of the resurrection may be the reason that the first gospel about Jesus' life does not contain a resurrection narrative. In Mark's gospel the women come to the tomb in order to anoint Jesus' body with spices. When they arrive, they find the stone has been rolled away and upon entering find a young man sitting in a white robe. Mark ends when the women, after being told of Jesus' resurrection, flee from the tomb "for terror and amazement had seized them; and they said nothing to anyone, for they were afraid." *(Mk. 16:8)* There is no resurrection appearance in Mark's gospel.[9.3]

In the original version of Mark's gospel, we only *hear* about Jesus' resurrection, we never see it. A big reason Mark does this is because he doesn't want to define what the resurrection looks like due to the fact that it is unclear exactly what they saw. However, if we fast-forward 10 years, the gospels written after Mark are not so shy about portraying Jesus' resurrection. Both Matthew and Luke portray Jesus as physically coming back from the dead. Although the disciples do not immediately recognize Jesus, there is no doubt that he is a real, live, breathing person. They portray Jesus this way because they were reacting to something specific that was happening in the Jewish religion around the time they were writing their gospels.

In 66 C.E., the Jewish people were protesting against the heavy taxation of the Roman government. The Romans responded by robbing the Jewish Temple and executing some 6,000 Jews in Jerusalem. This violence provoked a full-scale rebellion and, for the next 4 years, the Jews engaged in a guerilla battle with the Roman army. These guerilla battles were led by different leaders, many of whom claimed to be the messiah. In fact, these messiahs would get into fights with one another because each one believed that he was the rightful leader of Jews.[9.4]

By 70 C.E., Titus, the general in charge of the Roman troops, devised a different strategy to defeat the Jews—he decided to starve them to death. Titus' soldiers built a stone wall to encompass the city of Jerusalem.[9.5] Initially, the Jews were able to work their way around these walls by sneaking in weapons and food through underground tunnels. Once the Romans discovered these tunnels and blocked them off, all Titus had to do was sit back and wait. You can imagine how the situation in Jerusalem would have become unmanageable as the food in the city quickly ran out.

When most of the Jews had died of starvation, Titus ordered his troops to storm the city. The soldiers worked their way through the streets, systematically burning the entire city to the ground and killing anyone who had not already died from hunger. When the Roman soldiers finally made their way to the Temple, they found that the last remaining Jews had locked themselves inside. The soldiers then set the Temple foundation on fire, burning the building to the ground. The only part of the Temple that survived is called the Western Wall (or more pejoratively the Wailing Wall), which you can still visit in Jerusalem to this day.

At the time when Jerusalem was decimated by the Romans, there were a number of different Jewish sects. A sect is similar to a denomination in Christianity (think Presbyterians, Methodists, Baptists, Lutherans, Catholics—they're all Christian, but interpret the Bible and tradition in different ways). There were the Pharisees, the Sadducees, the Essenes, and the Zealots.

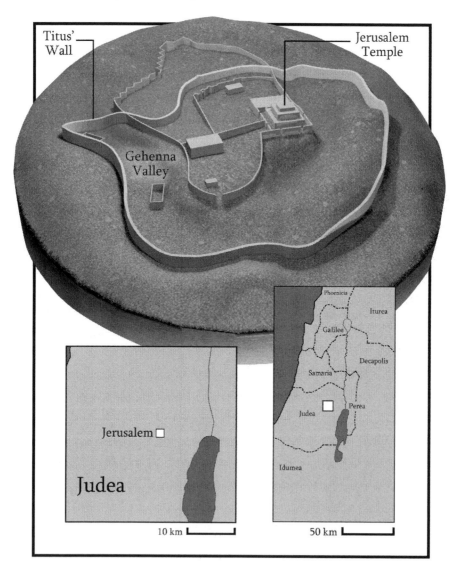

After the destruction of the Temple, most of these sects were wiped out. With the Temple no longer the central point for Jewish worship, the focus of Judaism shifted to the local synagogue. The primary sect in the local synagogues prior to the destruction of the Temple was the Pharisees. The Pharisees were focused on educating people in the synagogues and wanted everyone who was Jewish to have the opportunity to learn about their religious tradition. As a result, within 10 years of the destruction of the Temple, the Pharisees had established themselves as the dominant force in Judaism, which is why the Pharisees are portrayed as being the primary opponents of Jesus in Matthew and Luke's gospels. Even though Jesus probably had some interaction with the Pharisees when he was alive, Matthew and Luke portray Jesus as continuously debating the Pharisees.

One of the key beliefs that distinguished the Pharisees from other Jewish sects is the belief in the resurrection of the physical body.[†] During the first century, the Pharisees had a practice of allowing a dead body to decompose and then taking all the bones and placing them within a box called an ossuary. They would place the ossuary inside the tomb so that God could reassemble the person during the resurrection.[9.6]

Since Matthew was writing his gospel to appeal to a primarily Jewish audience who believed in physical resurrection, he portrayed Jesus' resurrection in terms they would understand—Jesus' body came back to life and walked around just like any other person. Luke, on the other hand, writes his gospel for a primarily Gentile (non-Jewish) audience. Although Luke is not concerned with converting Jews to believe in Jesus, Luke is concerned with portraying Judaism accurately, which means adhering to a bodily resurrection account.

The last variation on Jesus' resurrection is found in John's gospel written 5-10 years after Matthew and Luke.[‡] John's gospel is partially written from a Gnostic Christian perspective.[9.7] The term Gnostic comes from the Greek word γνῶσις (gnosis), which means *knowledge*.[9.8] In Greek culture, one of the most valued assets was knowledge, particularly hidden knowledge. The teachers who garnered the most respect in Greek culture were those who revealed

---

† Review p.148-149 for previous discussion of physical resurrection.
‡ Review p.15-17 for previous discussion of John's community.

the secrets of hidden knowledge. Gnostic Christians believed Jesus brought with him the hidden knowledge of the afterlife following his resurrection. They were not particularly concerned with what Jesus said or did prior to his crucifixion. John's gospel reflects this perspective because none of the characters in John's gospel understand what Jesus is saying until after he is resurrected. This is why the character of the beloved disciple (John) is so important because he is the only one in the gospel who understands Jesus prior to his crucifixion.

Another place where we find the Gnostic leanings in John's gospel is how Jesus' body is described during the resurrection accounts. Following Jesus' crucifixion the disciples are gathered together inside a house. The text continues, "Although the doors were shut, Jesus came and stood among them and said, 'Peace be with you.'" *(Jn. 20:26)* Jesus walks through walls like a ghost and appears in the disciples' presence. Although this might seem like an insignificant detail, the fact that Jesus is not bound by physical limitations like walls would have been important to Gnostic readers. The Gnostics believed that all physical matter in the universe was inherently evil. By contrast, they believed spirit to be the most pure form of being. If Jesus is no longer bound by his physical body following his crucifixion, then that validates the superior hidden knowledge that Jesus gained following his resurrection.[9.9]

Understandably, the Gnostic belief that Jesus was merely a spirit following his resurrection did not sit well with the Christians who believed that Jesus' resurrection was physical and bodily. Therefore, a group of Christians who favored bodily resurrection added Chapter 21 to John's gospel at a later time.[9.10] In this chapter, we find the resurrected Jesus sitting on the lakeshore eating breakfast with his disciples. Jesus fries fish and bakes bread, engaging in what is perhaps the most necessary of all bodily activities—the consumption of calories. The author of Chapter 21 wants us to know that when our bodies are resurrected, food is still a requirement.

With this historical context, we are in a position to answer the most pressing question which has eluded us thus far: which of these three resurrection accounts is most likely?

THE FLY IN THE OINTMENT

Most Christians choose to accept all three variations on the resurrection as part of the same experience. However, each variation represents a distinct notion of what the resurrection entails. Therefore, I would contend that, if Jesus did in fact appear to his disciples following his crucifixion, only one version can be correct. Since John's account is the furthest from Jesus' actual life and is clearly influenced by Gnostic thinking, I think we can say with a pretty high degree of certainty that John's version of the resurrection never happened. It seems logically inconsistent to me that Jesus would be walking through walls like a ghost one day and then cooking breakfast on the shore with his disciples the next.

This leaves us with two possible options—the physical resurrection described by Matthew and Luke or the vision of Jesus described by Paul. Which of these two options is most likely? The answer lies in how the gospels describe Jesus' last hours on earth. The fact that Jesus was crucified tells us something important about the crime of which Jesus was accused. Crucifixion was only used as punishment for extreme political crimes—treason, sedition, rebellion or banditry. Jesus was accused of treason.

Treason is the crime of betraying one's country, typically by attempting to overthrow the government. This might seem like an odd accusation to level against Jesus, but it makes sense when you understand two facts about Jesus' life: 1) Jesus called himself the messiah, which, as we discussed earlier, means that he has kingly ambitions and 2) Jesus overturned the tables of the money changers and the sellers of the sacrifices in the Temple, an act that was a direct threat to the Jewish aristocracy who were in league with the Roman authorities. Thus, it was the act of declaring himself the messiah combined with the act of disrupting the business transactions in the Temple that determined Jesus' fate.

The punishment of crucifixion was not unique to the Roman government. Crucifixion was used by many different empires, including the Persians, Assyrians and Greeks. The reason it was utilized as a form of capital punishment is because it was efficient and public. All you needed to crucify someone was a plank of wood and some rope or nails. Often, the executioner was given discretion as to how the accused was to be attached to the cross. Some were hung right side up, others upside-down. Sometimes they would be hooded, but it was common to have the accused stripped naked for maximum shame. Interestingly, it often happened that the accused would be executed prior to being hung on the cross. In this way, the cross was more of a display case than an instrument of torture.[9.11]

Matthew, Mark and Luke (the synoptic gospels) tell us that after being convicted of treason and sentenced to death, Jesus is flogged and then forced to carry his cross, a task handed to all criminals sentenced to crucifixion. Jesus is unable to carry the cross on his own. The soldiers have to compel a passerby, a man by the name of Simon of Cyrene, to help Jesus carry his cross. When Jesus arrives at the hill on which he is to be crucified, Jesus is stripped naked, nailed to the cross and after six hours cries out his last words, "My God, my God, why have you forsaken me?" *(Mk. 15:34)*

It is here, after Jesus' death, where the synoptic gospels do not match up with the historical reality of what we know to be true about crucifixion. The gospels say that, after his death, Jesus was taken down off of the cross and placed in a tomb. If you study the history of crucifixion, you realize that the purpose of this type of execution was quite simple—the government wanted to demonstrate to the public that, under no circumstances, will rebellion, in any form, be tolerated. Crucifixion was always performed in a public space where lots of people could see the results. The purposes of hoisting someone up in the air were visibility and deterrence.

Crucifixion was a public display of torture and this is why Jesus was led to a hillside outside of Jerusalem. This hillside was public enough that it would be hard for anyone to miss as they went about their daily activities. This hillside was nicknamed Golgotha, otherwise known as the place of the skull, because the hillside was littered with skulls from others who had been crucified.[9.12] The skulls were there because the bodies of the crucified were left on the cross to decompose after they had died. The whole point of crucifixion was to leave the body on the cross to serve as a recurring reminder that you don't want to be like this person. What many Christians don't realize is that the removal of an executed individual from the cross for burial was extraordinarily rare. Pulling the body down for burial would defeat the entire purpose of being crucified. Why go through all that trouble to hoist them up in the air if you were going to take them down as soon as they were dead? In my opinion, it doesn't make a lot of sense that Jesus, a poor Jewish peasant from Nazareth, would be shown such treatment. It's not impossible, but it is highly unlikely.

Jesus was probably left on the cross like everyone else and, when his bones had fallen to the ground, his remains were likely thrown into a mass grave along with others who had been crucified alongside him.[9.13] One piece of evidence in the Bible that supports this point of view is the fact that Paul's letters, which predate the gospels, never refer to Jesus as being buried in a tomb. Paul talks a lot about Jesus being crucified and resurrected, but he never discusses how Jesus was buried. Therefore, since the physical resurrection of Jesus' body found in the gospels seems to revolve around Jesus' body being buried in a tomb, a reality that, from a historical perspective, seems unlikely, then we are forced to conclude that Jesus' physical resurrection is also unlikely. Thus, our best option as to what occurred after Jesus' death is Paul's version of events.

Since Paul's is the earliest of the accounts of Jesus' resurrection, I am inclined to believe that Jesus' resurrection was like a vision. In the same way that people in our modern world experience mass visions of important religious figures (e.g. the Virgin Mary, saints, even Satan), I think what they experienced was a series of visions of Jesus. It is impossible to know whether these visions were authentic appearances of Jesus or mass hallucinations. Regardless of what actually happened, I have no doubt that every person who saw it was greatly transformed by that moment and, for Jesus' disciples, this vision inspired them to continue what Jesus had begun. I am also inclined to believe that there was some auditory component that accompanied these visions. In other words, some of the people who experienced Jesus' appearance believed they heard Jesus speaking to them. What Jesus said to them is unclear, but Paul's experience of the resurrection reveals that whatever he heard was powerful enough to cause him to change the course of his life and commit himself to Jesus' cause. Therefore, if we are to truly understand why Jesus' movement persisted as it did and why it should be meaningful to us today, then we must decipher what this moment meant to those who experienced this vision.

ANY DAY NOW

When we take the time to look at the documents in the New Testament in the order in which they were written, it becomes apparent that the earliest Christians believed that Jesus was going to return to establish God's kingdom at any moment. In Paul's earliest letter, 1 Thessalonians, he describes how Jesus will come like "a thief in the night" and that "there will be no escape!" *(1 Th. 5:1-3)* If you compare 1 Thessalonians, which was written in 51 C.E., with Paul's last letter, Philippians, which was written in 60 C.E., Paul has changed his tune quite a bit. Paul is writing Philippians from prison and knows that, depending on his sentence, his life could be near its end. As a result, Jesus is no longer coming back tomorrow, but rather Paul says, "For to me, living is Christ and dying is gain. If I am to live in the flesh, that means fruitful labor for me; and I do not know which I prefer. I am hard pressed between the two: my desire is to depart and be with Christ, for that is far better; but to remain in the flesh is more necessary for you." *(Pp. 1:21-24)*

Paul is struggling with the idea that Jesus may not return to earth within his lifetime. This is a problem for Paul since a big part of his message to the converts in his churches is that Jesus is coming back any day. Therefore, Paul wants to adjust his audience's expectations, because they may be faced with the same fate as Paul and die before Jesus' return. Thus, Paul poses a question: which is better, to die and be with Jesus now or to live and spread the gospel? If Jesus is coming back tomorrow, then dying is not the better option of the two. Interestingly, Paul chooses death, which means that he has begun to doubt his original message that Jesus will return at any moment.

Although we can't say for sure, this shift in thinking could be one of the major reasons why many of Paul's churches failed. By continually pushing back the date of Jesus' return, Paul's disciples may have begun questioning the validity of his beliefs. Indeed, it seems that the whole Christian movement had to reassess its message in light of the reality that Jesus wasn't coming back anytime soon. The longer Jesus postponed his arrival, the longer God postponed merging heaven with earth and creating the kingdom of God. Why would God put off what seemed inevitable with Jesus' resurrection appearance? The answer came with the destruction of the Jewish Temple and decimation of Jerusalem.

During the battle with Rome between 66-73 C.E., there were several different men who rose up and claimed to be the messiah. When the Roman army finally starved the Jewish people into submission and all of those messiahs met their end, there was a lingering question among the survivors who had not been a part of this battle: Why didn't God intervene? Why didn't God come from heaven and stop the massacre of the Jewish people like in the book of Exodus when God intervened to help the Hebrew slaves? Although many answers were provided, the Christian answer to this question resolved the issue of why Jesus had not returned to earth—God allowed the destruction of Jerusalem so that everyone might know that Jesus was the one true messiah.

You might be thinking, "How does the destruction of Jerusalem and the deaths of tens of thousands of innocent Jews prove that Jesus was the real messiah?" When the Temple was destroyed in Jerusalem, the Jews could no longer offer sacrifices.[†] According to the laws of the Old Testament, without these sacrifices the Jews could not receive forgiveness. Christians used this event as a way to explain why Jesus' sacrifice was so important. They said that Jesus' sacrifice on the cross was the final sacrifice for all the sins of the world. They claimed that Jesus' sacrifice rendered the sacrifices in the Temple unnecessary. Prior to the destruction of the Temple, it was hard for the Jews to accept this reality. However, with the Temple gone and all those other messiahs dead, it was easier for the Jews to understand why God had sent Jesus as the true messiah to die 40 years prior to the destruction of the Temple. What's more, the only requirement for forgiveness is belief that Jesus is the messiah.

It all made perfect sense and it achieved the shift Christians were looking for—no longer were they so concerned with the future of Jesus' return. With the destruction of the Temple, Christians could focus on the present because Jesus can forgive you right now. What's more, that forgiveness means a place at the table when God establishes the kingdom on earth…whenever that might be. In other words, the destruction of the Temple changed the argument for why Jesus should be a pressing need in our lives. Prior to the destruction

---

†   Review p.130-131, 174-177 for previous discussion of the sacrificial system in the Jerusalem Temple.

of the Temple, the argument was that Jesus could come back at any time. When that proved inaccurate, the destruction of the Temple provided a new pressing need for Jesus in our lives—without Jesus we cannot be granted forgiveness from God.[9.14]

What this tells us is that not everyone in the early years after Jesus' execution was on board with the notion that Jesus died for your sins. Indeed, the earliest Christians were not certain what Jesus' death on the cross meant for them.[9.15] Different groups had different takes on Jesus' execution. For instance, some groups, like Gnostic Christians, didn't think Jesus dying on the cross held any particular significance. These Christians saw Jesus' execution as a necessity that allowed Jesus to get to the resurrection, which was the pivotal event of Jesus' life.

Other groups, like Paul's churches, interpreted Jesus' death on the cross as removing sins. Paul interpreted the cross as having so much value because his audience was comprised mostly of Jewish-Gentiles. Jewish-Gentiles are people of Jewish descent who lived outside of Israel in areas around the Mediterranean. They tended to be people who had a limited background in the Jewish faith. They might have lived according to certain Jewish customs, but lacked a working knowledge of the Torah. That said, they did have a sense of who the Jewish messiah was supposed to be and they understood that the messiah was not supposed to die.

Therefore, Paul had to prove to them that their understanding of the messiah was not entirely accurate. This is why, when Paul references Jesus dying for your sins, he says, "For I handed on to you as of first importance what I in turn had received: that Christ died for our sins in accordance with the scriptures…" (1 Co. 15:3 – emphasis added) Because Jesus did not fit the traditional pattern for what the Jews expected from the messiah, Paul is trying to make an argument that Jesus fits the scriptural definition of messiah; it's just different from the one they're used to hearing about. By finding the right scriptures, Paul convinced these Jewish-Gentiles that the messiah was supposed to die for the purpose of forgiving sins.

With the destruction of the Temple, Paul's notion that Jesus died for the sins of humanity took on a whole new importance.[9.16] When the primary reason for believing in Jesus began to shift from Jesus returning to earth to Jesus forgiving our sins, other parts of Christianity had to adjust to complement this new focus. This adjustment is particularly evident in the ways that Christians began thinking about God's kingdom.

Most Jews believed that God was going to bring about the kingdom through a massive cosmic renovation where God merged heaven with earth. There would be a complete overhaul of the present national power structures. All of them would be toppled to the ground and subsumed into God's kingdom, allowing God's messiah to become the ruler over everyone and everything. This led to verses like this one where Jesus says, "Truly I tell you, some who are standing here will not taste death before they see the Son of Man coming in his kingdom." *(Mk. 9:1, Mt. 16:28)*

Jesus' delay in returning to earth to rule the kingdom provoked Luke to write this verse: "The coming of the kingdom of God is not something that can be observed, nor will people say, 'Here it is,' or 'There it is,' because the kingdom of God is within you." *(Lk. 17:20-21)* Through this verse Luke changed God's kingdom from a physical place here on earth to something that takes place within your heart. In doing so, Luke reframes the kingdom of God as something intensely spiritual and personal to every human being. He does this because he wants to draw attention away from the expectation that Jesus needs to be physically present to rule God's kingdom. Luke is promoting the idea that Jesus can create God's kingdom by ruling our hearts through the Holy Spirit.

Did you catch what just happened? We made a huge leap. We moved from a concept of God's kingdom where the physical world is overturned by God's presence to a concept of God's kingdom where our hearts are overturned by God's presence. So even though

Jesus' original intention was to bring about God's physical kingdom, this new way of thinking about God's kingdom will come to dominate the Christian mindset. Because this is so important, I want to take special care to explain how and why this happened.

When the earliest Christians started coming to the realization that Jesus wasn't coming back soon, they felt abandoned. In order to make them feel better about Jesus' absence, certain Christian leaders said that God's spirit would be present with us until Jesus' return. These early Christians referred to God's spirit as the Holy Spirit. This idea had been floating around in Judaism for some time. Since God is not a physical, tangible being, God's spirit is what remains in the world as our way of feeling God's presence in our lives.

In Paul's letters, Paul uses the presence of the Holy Spirit as evidence that God is with the members of Paul's churches. The Holy Spirit is what gives people the ability to prophesy, to speak in tongues, to teach and serve others. The work of the Holy Spirit in their lives is evidence that they have accepted Jesus as the messiah. In Paul's letters, the presence of the Holy Spirit is a symbol that when God's kingdom is established on earth, you will be in Jesus' good graces.

However, the farther away you get from Jesus' death and resurrection, the more the Holy Spirit takes on the role of filling in for Jesus until he returns. For instance, in Mark's gospel, which is written 40 years after Jesus' death and resurrection at a time when Jesus' return was still widely anticipated by most Christians, the Holy Spirit is mentioned only twice in the entire gospel. By the time we get to Luke's gospel, which is written 55 years after Jesus' death and resurrection, the entire focus of the gospel is on the presence of the Holy Spirit where it is mentioned some 20 times. By the time John's gospel is written, this idea of the Holy Spirit filling in during Jesus' absence is so prominent that Jesus says these words: "But the Advocate, the Holy Spirit, whom the Father will send in my name, will teach you all things and will remind you of everything I have said to you." *(Jn. 14:26)*

This new model of having the Holy Spirit fill in for Jesus during his absence forced Christians to reinterpret how Jesus would bring about God's kingdom on earth. As Christians realized that they were not going to live to see God merge heaven with earth, they decided that, in the meantime, it was their responsibility to build God's kingdom on earth. The way this would happen is by everyone individually doing their part to positively impact the world by living out Jesus' teachings. But in order for you as an individual to create the kingdom of God in the world, God had to first create the kingdom of God within your heart. The way God accomplishes this is through the Holy Spirit, which is how you experience God's forgiveness when you believe in Jesus. This complements the notion that forgiveness is now the motivation for believing that Jesus is the messiah.

Let's recap that last part because this progression is essential to understanding the core message of the Christian faith. When you believe in Jesus, you experience God's forgiveness in your heart through the Holy Spirit. This forgiveness allows the Holy Spirit to create God's kingdom inside your heart, which, in turn, allows you to do your part to create God's kingdom in the world. In essence, we are Jesus' hands and feet in the world that allow for the kingdom to be built in his absence. So what exactly does Jesus expect us to do in order to build the kingdom? In Matthew's gospel, Jesus tells us that those who build the kingdom do as follows: "For I was hungry and you gave me something to eat, I was thirsty and you gave me something to drink, I was a stranger and you invited me in, I needed clothes and you clothed me, I was sick and you looked after me, I was in prison and you came to visit me....Truly I tell you, whatever you did for

> one of the least of these brothers and sisters of mine, you did for me." *(Mt. 25:35-36, 40)*

In other words, when you serve the least and the lost of this world, then you are doing Jesus' bidding to build God's kingdom on earth. By emphasizing that Christians are the ones responsible for creating God's kingdom on earth, Matthew and Luke change the focus of Christianity from a faith primarily concerned with the future of Jesus' return to a faith concerned with the present. But this shift begs an important question: does one necessarily need to be Christian to perform all of the actions listed above? The answer to that question is a resounding "No!"

Clearly, there are millions of people in the world who have no connection with the Christian faith, and yet, they spend their time feeding the hungry, giving drink to the thirsty, housing the stranger, clothing the naked, caring for the sick and visiting those in prison. Likewise, there are millions of people who identify as Christian and perform none of these actions. So how does this reality square with Luke's assertion that in order to create the kingdom of God in the world, we must first build the kingdom of God in our hearts through the presence of the Holy Spirit? My first instinct when I see an inconsistency like this is to say, "You're wrong!" Christianity cannot claim to have a corner on the market of good deeds. However, upon closer examination, I have come to realize that Jesus is not making the claim that Christians are the only ones who can make a positive contribution to the world, far from it.

The verse from Matthew quoted above depicts the judgment of the world. Jesus sits on his throne as the messiah and separates the sheep from the goats. The sheep are those who have lived according to his commands and the goats are those who have not. Nowhere in this section does Jesus mention one's beliefs or faith as the defining factor that determines where one is placed. The determination is based completely on one's actions. According to Matthew 25, whole swaths of people could be judged righteous because they did all the things that Jesus expected of them in spite of never having been a Christian a day in their life. Whereas people who claim to be a follower of Jesus and believe all the "right" things about the Christian faith could be rejected by Jesus because they never served the least and the lost. What are we to make of this?

For me, it highlights the reason why I choose to follow Jesus. I believe that we can create the kingdom of God here and now, in this place and time. Indeed, I believe it is our responsibility, not as Christians, but as humans to create God's kingdom on earth. I believe this because the Bible teaches that within every human heart there is infinite capacity for good. It doesn't matter where we are from; it doesn't matter what our religious or cultural background might be, inside every human heart resides the potential to perform the deeds Jesus asks of us. In my opinion, the difference between those who release that potential and those who don't has to do with one factor—love. Is your heart open or closed to love?

If your heart is open to love, then God will be actively building the kingdom of God inside your heart, providing you with the opportunity to build God's kingdom in the world. Likewise, if your heart is closed to love, then God cannot build the kingdom in your heart, which prevents you from building the kingdom in the world. Therefore, what I will focus on next is what I feel is one of the best ways to open our hearts to love—Jesus' teachings.

1   The New Testament describes Jesus' resurrection in three different ways:
- Jesus' appearance is portrayed as a vision that was experienced by hundreds at a time (Paul).
- Jesus is portrayed as physically coming back to life (Matthew/Luke).
- Jesus is portrayed as a ghost or spirit who can walk through walls (John).

2   The most probable of these three options is Paul's version of the resurrection because his is the only firsthand account provided by the authors of the New Testament.

3   Following Jesus' resurrection appearances, many of the disciples believed that Jesus would be returning from heaven at any moment to establish God's kingdom on earth. As the decades passed and Jesus still had not returned, many of the original churches began to fail due to attrition.

4   Once Christians stopped anticipating Jesus' return, they began focusing on the Holy Spirit as a surrogate for Jesus during his absence. Furthermore, Christians began to think of God's kingdom as something that Jesus establishes in your heart through the Holy Spirit.

— CHAPTER TEN —

THE TEACHINGS OF JESUS

ALL YOU NEED IS LOVE

We established earlier that Jesus' ministry lasted between one and three years. If we assume the reality is somewhere in the middle, Jesus would have only been known among the public for two years before he was captured and killed. Just take a moment and let that sink in to your mind. The man who has shaped Western civilization for the last 2,000 years did so on the basis of two years of solid work. It's not as if Jesus had a publicist to market his ideas. Everything Jesus said had to be spread by word of mouth. Jesus' words are still well known because of the power and simplicity of his teachings. Jesus was an itinerant preacher. More than likely, he could not read and had no formal training in Jewish law. But what you'll notice if you read the gospels is that Jesus was very good at distilling a teaching down to its essence. Jesus got to the point quickly and didn't provide a lot of background information to support his points, perhaps because he didn't have formal training in the laws of the Torah. Therefore, Jesus simply said what he thought and moved on.

I think this is why Jesus' movement caught on the way it did. Most people like things simple. Make it easy to digest and it's going to appeal to a broad range of people. There is wisdom in simplicity. He gives you the essential information and allows you to form your own conclusions. Of course, the downside to Jesus' method is that there is no single definitive interpretation of what his teachings mean. Had Jesus been more precise in his statements, there wouldn't be 9,000 different Christian denominations, all of whom believe they have the correct interpretation.

In the end, there tends to be only one teaching of Jesus that every Christian agrees is important. It is called the Greatest Commandment:

> "The first is, 'Hear, O Israel: the Lord our God, the Lord is one; you shall love the Lord your God with all your heart, and with all your soul, and with all your mind, and with all your strength.' The second is this, 'You shall love your neighbor as yourself.' There is no other commandment greater than these." *(Mk. 12:29-31)*

Just to be clear, Jesus is not the originator of these teachings. The first part about loving God is known in Hebrew as the Shema (which means *hear* or *listen* in Hebrew) and it is found in Deuteronomy, "Hear, O Israel: The Lord is our God, the Lord alone. You shall love the Lord your God with all your heart, and with all your soul, and with all your might." *(Dt. 6:4-5)* The second is from Leviticus, which states "You shall not take vengeance or bear a grudge against any of your people, but you shall love your neighbor as yourself: I am the Lord." *(Lv. 19:8)*

Both of these laws are found in the Old Testament. Jesus placed them together into a single unit. Furthermore, he was not the first to do so. It was common in ancient Israel for teachers to ask each other for their summation of the law. Often times they would draw their formulations from other Jewish thinkers. For instance, the

Testament of Dan, a book that didn't make it into the Bible but was written shortly before Jesus' birth, states: "Love the Lord with all your life, and another with a sincere heart." (5:3) Another example is the Testament of Issachar, which states, "I loved the Lord with all my strength; likewise, I loved every man with all my heart." (5:2) So clearly these combinations had been formulated prior to Jesus' lifetime and this combination represents the foundational principle of our growth toward achieving Jesus' God consciousness.[†]

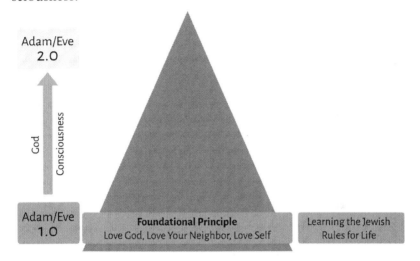

This pyramid represents the population relative to the achievement of the step in the process of approaching Jesus' God consciousness. The higher up the pyramid, the fewer people who are able to achieve the next step in the process.

Like these prior combinations, Jesus starts with loving God. For those outside of religion, the idea of loving God might seem strange. How does one love something that you cannot see and cannot prove exists? Furthermore, why does God require us to love him/her/it? Is God so needy that without our love God will feel inadequate? Finally, what exactly does loving God achieve? Is it a 1-to-1 relationship where the more we love God, the better God will treat us? Likewise, if I don't love God, does that mean God

---

†   Review p.116-117 for previous discussion of God consciousness.

will not love me? Will that choice cause God to negatively affect my life? These are all valid questions that should not be treated lightly, and to answer them, I want to return to something we discussed in Chapter 3—being made in God's image.

As I explained earlier, being made in God's image reflects how there is a bit of God present in all human beings. You could call this the soul or a divine spark, but we all carry God's spirit in our hearts. I believe humans have a physical nature and a spiritual nature. Our spiritual nature is the image of God that is spoken of in Genesis Chapter 1. As humans, we tend to focus on our physical well-being to the detriment of our spiritual well-being, but without the spiritual, we can never be whole. Thus, a major part of the equation of becoming a whole person is investing in our spiritual development, and perhaps one of the best ways to develop spiritually is to figure out how we can love God.

The God I believe in does not require our love out of need on God's part. Nor does God intend to impose consequences on us for not loving God enough. In the parable of the prodigal son, God loves us no matter what we choose to do with our lives.[†] It is important for us to love God because the action of loving God fills a void in our souls. If you don't believe there is a void in your soul, then you may disagree with me that this is necessary. However, if you are willing to grant me that there might be a connection between loving God and enhancing our spiritual well-being, then I can explain how the process of loving God will lead to becoming a whole person.

The first issue we need to address is how one loves God. More than one person has posed this question to me. Loving God is not like loving a person, a pet, or a possession. There is nothing physical upon which you can focus your love and, without that visual representation, love becomes much more challenging. This is why ancient peoples worshiped objects like the sun, the moon, trees, and carved statues. Indeed, one of most commonly employed

---

† Review p.139-143 for previous discussion of the parable of the prodigal son.

arguments by conservative Christians for why God became human is that Jesus provides Christians with an appropriate visualization for God that would otherwise be lacking.

I agree that humans need a visual representation when loving God, but I don't limit those representations to Jesus. We established in Chapter 3 that God is transcendent, which means that God is in everything. You, me, and all existence is God because God is what makes existence possible. Therefore, when the question of how one loves God is posed to me, I always say that by showing love to everyone and everything you encounter, you are showing love to God. By pouring love into the world, you are loving God. The only problem with this way of thinking about loving God is that your definition of what love means and my definition of what love means can be drastically different. Thus, to gain a clearer definition of how God expects us to love, we need to move to another way that people attempt to nurture their spiritual nature: coming together with a group of people to worship God.

The act of worship is more than just expressing belief in, or reverence for, God. It is also learning how to live the way God expects you to live. If you attend a Christian church, in worship you affirm that you want to follow Jesus' version of God and you are given the tools to live out Jesus' teachings in the world. By trying to shape your life to the teachings of Jesus, you will be on the journey to finding spiritual well-being in your soul. This happens because, by living out Jesus' teachings, you are placed in a position of having to embody and reflect the unconditional love God has for you in your relationships with others, which leads us to the second commandment: loving your neighbor as yourself.

Like the other formulations, Jesus is borrowing from the Old Testament. However, Jesus does something unexpected in his formulation. When he talks about loving your neighbor, he quotes Leviticus 19:18. However, Jesus doesn't include the whole verse. He truncates the verse, leaving some words out. These words might not seem all that important, but in this case, the words he leaves out mean everything. Notice that in the Leviticus verse, the words preceding the phrase "love your neighbor as yourself" are, "You shall not take vengeance or bear a grudge against any of your people." The original context of this verse defines your neighbor as *your people*. And who are your people? In Leviticus it means anyone who is Jewish. So God requires you to love your neighbor if they are Jewish. However, if they are not Jewish, then that requirement does not apply. By leaving out the first part of Leviticus 19:18, Jesus avoids defining who is and is not your neighbor, meaning that your neighbor could be anyone.

This is huge! This omission is critically important for Jesus' teaching on love. You do not get to discriminate about whom you love and don't love. You must love everyone equally, no matter who they are. So whether it's your spouse, your best friend, your next door neighbor, the stranger you meet on the street, the criminal in jail or the terrorists who attacked on 9/11, you are supposed to love them, which is incredibly difficult. Some might say that it's impossible because, let's be honest, do you really love everyone equally? No, of course not! There's a hierarchy of the people you love in your life. We love our families first and foremost. We might love some close friends. Finally, there might be some mentors or leaders we admire and love, but our love for others does not generally extend beyond this small inner circle.

This is a problem because if we're going to live up to Jesus' expectations of how we're supposed to love others, then we need to explore the question of why we are so bad at loving those who are outside our inner circle of family and friends. The answer to this question is found in the last part of the phrase—love your neighbor as yourself. It's not just "love your neighbor," it's "love your neighbor *as yourself*." So if you don't know how to love yourself, then you won't be able to love your neighbor. And the truth is that we are not very good at loving ourselves.

In order to love yourself, you have to be able to look in the mirror and accept what's staring back at you. You have to be able to say, "I am who I am and I can't be anybody else." But most of us are incapable of doing this. Most of us are constantly striving to be someone other than ourselves. We live in a society where we are bombarded by images of who we should and should not be. Every day the average person is exposed to thousands of advertisements and these advertisements not only sell us products, but they sell us ideals of beauty, success and happiness.[10.1] They convey to us what a successful life looks like: if you look like these people who own these products and are doing these activities, then you will be happy.

Unfortunately, the standards of beauty and success created by advertising are impossible for us to achieve and we are left feeling inadequate. Society is constantly telling us that we are not good enough as we are, that we need more than what we have right now to be complete. You need to have the perfect body so you can marry the perfect person so you can have the perfect family who wear the perfect clothes and live in the perfect house that is all paid for by the perfect job. And you need to make all of this look effortless.

I'm not saying there aren't areas we could improve about ourselves, but the improvements advertised by society are precisely what prevent us from truly loving ourselves. Loving yourself is hard because you must accept your own limitations. You have to be willing to admit that you don't know all the answers, that you have weaknesses, and that you are sometimes frail, weak and lost. In other words, in order to love yourself, you have to be vulnerable. And we don't like being vulnerable.

We like to pretend we have it all together, that we are strong and invincible, that we are only a step away from those ads we see on television. Ironically, the only people who are allowed to see our weaknesses are the people we love. The people we love know all of our weaknesses. We allow them to see those things because we love them. This is why truly loving our neighbor is so hard. To truly love our neighbor means being vulnerable with them like we are with our family and friends. It means being open about our weaknesses with people we don't know well and that can feel threatening.

So rather than love our neighbors, we tolerate them. We get to know them from a distance and, if they prove themselves worthy, we might allow them a glimpse of our true self. But that's not what Jesus tells us to do. He doesn't tell us to test our neighbors to determine if they are worthy of our love. He tells us to love our neighbors—full stop—and because none of us are naturally inclined towards this type of love, it means we have to work at it. We have to practice being vulnerable with ourselves so that we can be vulnerable with others, which leads us back to loving God.

One of the most important aspects of loving God is the recognition that, as human beings, we need something more than ourselves to make it through this world. I believe that when we open ourselves to loving God, we also open ourselves to the understanding that we need more than ourselves if we are going to make it through life. Yes, we need each other but, even more than that, there are things we have to do by ourselves that no one else can do for us. And when we face those obstacles in our lives, we can either try to do it alone or we can dig deep down inside ourselves, admit that we need help, and find God's presence in our souls so we can make it to the other side.

In opening ourselves to God's presence, we open ourselves to vulnerability, which is the key to truly loving others. The beauty of Jesus' version of the Greatest Commandment is that it's circular. You start by loving God. The more you love God, the more you will live out God's love in the world by loving your neighbors. The more you love your neighbors, the more you become vulnerable with yourself, which leads you back to loving God.

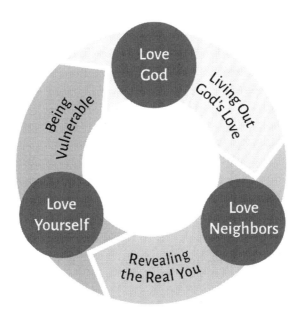

What Jesus is saying through this teaching is quite simple: all you
need to be a complete person is love. You don't need to look a
certain way. You don't need to buy anything. You don't need to be
different than you are. The person staring back at you in the mirror
right now is enough. All you need to do is choose love. Choose
to love God. Choose to love others. Choose to love yourself. If
you strive to embrace these three things, then you will find a life
worth living.

WINNING BY LOSING

My father is a stockbroker. From a very young age, I remember
him getting up early in the morning, leaving the house in a nicely
pressed suit, and driving an hour to Richmond, Virginia to begin
working before the markets opened in New York. I have always
admired my father's work ethic. It's part of the reason he has been
so successful in life. He never cuts corners and people trust him.
Once my father believes in you, he will go to the ends of the earth
to help you. However, the other reason he has been successful is
because of how he pitches his potential clients. My father always

begins by saying, "If you invest with me, I guarantee that you will lose money." After a short pause to allow that sentence to sink in, he continues by saying, "But if you stick with me over the long term—10, 15, 20 years—I guarantee that you will make money."

In the short term, you are going to lose. You're going to experience lots of little failures that may feel discouraging. But given enough time and use of the right strategy, you will win. My father's words have always stuck with me because they apply to many aspects of life. My successes in life came after many smaller failures where I didn't deliver as I hoped. By continually coming up short, I gradually learned how to do better so that when a bigger opportunity arrived I could take advantage of it. This life strategy is more universally known as winning by losing and it is the reason why Christianity has survived as long as it has throughout the bumpy road of history.

Christianity should not have survived beyond Jesus' lifetime. After Jesus' death, his disciples should have felt deceived. God wasn't bringing the kingdom to earth as he had promised and Jesus wasn't the messiah they expected him to be. In this sense, the pinnacle of Jesus' movement revolves around what most would label a monumental failure: the public execution of its leader. But that failure became an asset when Jesus' disciples adapted to the circumstances. After Jesus appeared to them in a vision, they used the failure of the crucifixion to redefine their movement. Indeed, Jesus' crucifixion would come to define the core message of Jesus' movement.

Jesus says, "If any want to become my followers, let them deny themselves and take up their cross and follow me. For those who want to save their life will lose it, and those who lose their life for my sake, and for the sake of the gospel, will save it. For what will it profit them to gain the whole world and forfeit their life? Indeed, what can they give in return for their life?" *(Mk. 8:34-37)* This is one of Jesus' most important teachings because it is the foundation on which all of his other teachings are built.

Although we can argue about Jesus' motivations for getting up on the cross, it is clear that Jesus embraced sacrifice and made sacrifice the core principle of his teachings. This core principle became known as The Way among early Christians. The term *Way* is not unique to Christians. It was used by the Jews, and the Greeks before them, to describe how a person should go about living the correct kind of life. Usually, the term *Way* refers to a particular philosophy where the best kind of life is the result of taking the difficult path as opposed to the easy path.

One really good example of The Way in our modern world is the premise of healthy living through exercise. The easy path that many people take is to not exercise at all. Most people wake up in the morning, go to work and are so tired by the end of the day that all they want to do when they get home is eat a meal, relax and go to bed. Unless you work at a job where you burn calories doing physical labor, this type of lifestyle is sedentary and could eventually result in health problems. The reason so many people have trouble breaking out of these sedentary patterns is because exercise is difficult. When you work hard at the gym, through doing cardio or lifting weights, it hurts. So if you don't go to the gym with the mentality that physical discomfort is a good thing that will benefit you in the long run, then you're not going to see any results.

This is true of so many aspects of life. The things that will benefit you the most are often the most difficult. If you want to succeed in school, then you're going to have to work hard to learn the information required to pass your classes. If you want to succeed in your relationships, then you have to work through the conflicts that will inevitably arise. If you want to be respected in your profession, then you need to make moral and ethical decisions, even when those choices are not popular. The best kind of life always comes as a result of taking the difficult path and this is why the Christian Way is defined by sacrifice.

Jesus begins with the premise that sacrifice is something you should embrace. As we read above, Jesus states that "if any want to become my followers, let them deny themselves and take up their cross and follow me." *(Mk. 8:34)* This is one of the most challenging statements in the entire Bible. Jesus is essentially saying that if you're going to be part of his movement, you need to be okay with the fact that you're going to embrace sacrifice. Indeed, it seems that self-preservation is not an option. If you sign up with Jesus, you need to be willing to lay everything on the line. You need to know that your life will be harder as a result of following Jesus, not easier. You need to know that there is no exit strategy and that the path you are walking is going to lead to sacrifice, suffering and possibly death. This concept leads us to the second step in our movement towards achieving Jesus' God consciousness.

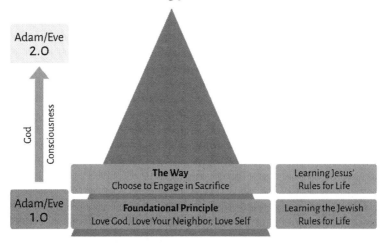

This raises a really important question: if Jesus' whole message revolves around sacrifice, does that mean that God wants humans to suffer? In the last section, I stated that God is primarily defined by love. If God's being is truly one of love, then God would not desire for human beings to suffer. By contrast, I have also explained that I believe Jesus speaks on behalf of God because Jesus possessed a fully formed God consciousness. In this way, when Jesus tells us that his followers should embrace sacrifice, which often leads to suffering, that statement is grounded in God's being. On the surface, this might seem contradictory. On the one hand, I subscribe to Jesus' version of God where suffering is necessary, but, on the other hand, I believe that a God of love would not want us to suffer. To address this paradox, it's important to appreciate that there are two different types of suffering in the world.

One type of suffering is the kind that the world imposes on us. Sometimes it happens through natural disasters; sometimes through diseases or cancer; and sometimes when another person intentionally tries to hurt us or when we intentionally engage in behaviors that hurt ourselves. In my opinion, all of these represent the types of suffering that God does *not* want us to endure because it hurts God's spirit to see us suffer in that way.[10.2] The other kind of suffering comes as a result of us choosing to sacrifice for the benefit of ourselves and others. These are the situations in which we are willing to suffer because we believe that suffering will benefit others in the long run. Earlier, I spoke of Kayla Mueller, a young woman who was an aid worker for *Support to Life* who intentionally sacrificed her comfortable life in the United States for the purpose of helping Syrian refugees fleeing into Turkey because of the Syrian civil war. Her sacrifice of travelling to a war-torn area of the world so she could help those in need caused her to suffer. Her sacrifice represents the kind of suffering God *does* want us to endure because it furthers God's love in the world.

The act of intentionally engaging in sacrifice to help those around us is what Jesus means by *carry your cross*. Whenever a person was sentenced to death by crucifixion, it was common for the guilty party to be forced to carry the cross to the location of crucifixion. It was a form of public shaming that drew further attention to the person and discouraged potential offenders. In one sense, the notion that one should carry a cross is literal because that's what Jesus did. Some of Jesus' followers would suffer a similar fate by being sentenced to death by crucifixion. However, if every person who followed Jesus had to be crucified, then there would quickly be no Christians left.

Therefore, Christians took the sequence of events that occurred after Jesus' conviction (where Jesus carried his cross, died from crucifixion and then—some days, weeks or months later—appeared to his disciples in a resurrection vision) and transformed this sequence into a roadmap that all of Jesus' disciples are supposed to follow. To summarize this roadmap: we need to sacrifice and die in order to find new life. However, rather than performing this sequence by literally dying, Jesus explains that we must experience a metaphorical death and resurrection within our hearts by dying to self. If Christians are to find true life, they must engage in self-denial by letting go of the world and dying to self, which is the third step in our movement towards achieving Jesus' God consciousness.

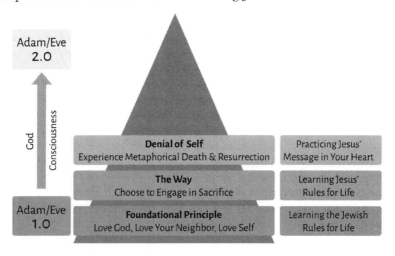

I'm the first to admit that this is a tough concept to understand, so let's break it down. There are certain basic needs every human has—food, shelter, clothing. We are programmed to seek out these things because, without them, we will have a tough time surviving. But these needs are also the reason why humans can be very selfish. You might not consider yourself to be a selfish person, but if I take away your food, shelter and clothing, you will become selfish very quickly.

Indeed, what many people fail to recognize is that our drive for success in the world is really a reflection of those three basic needs. The more successful we are, the more those needs recede into the background of our lives so we don't have to think about them. In fact, these three needs are the underlying reason why people are so reluctant to share their wealth. There is more than enough money in the world to end poverty, but we have this primal worry in the back of our minds that one day we may not have enough to care for ourselves, so we hold on tight to our resources just in case something happens.

Denial of self is about not letting those three needs rule your life. When you die to yourself and let go of the concerns of the world, there's a new person who rises in place of the old. This new person is not concerned with serving oneself or with the ambition to have everything the world has to offer. This new person is only concerned with being selfless, with loving others. This new person finds their worth and value not in gaining for themselves, but in gaining for others. They know that they are not nearly as important as the people whom they serve. I refer to this way of being in the world as the Resurrected Life.

THE RESURRECTED LIFE

At the beginning of this book, we talked extensively about the fact that many Christians believe that if you have not accepted Jesus Christ as your Lord and savior, then God will send your soul to hell. Everything you've read up to this point should indicate how much I disagree with this belief. I do not think that accepting Jesus is a necessary requirement for one to be with God in the afterlife. I think God welcomes the souls of all people with open and loving arms regardless of their religious background. This, of course, begs the question: if Jesus is not a ticket into heaven, then what is my motivation for caring about what Jesus has to say? The average Christian doesn't seem any better off than their non-Christian counterpart. Will my life be lacking something substantial if I don't dedicate myself to Jesus' Way?

The answer is both yes and no. You are correct that the average Christian is no better off than someone who is not Christian. However, this is true because the average Christian is not following Jesus' Way but believes in Jesus for the selfish reason of gaining access to heaven. On the other hand, those I have met who have invested heavily in Jesus' Way through the denial of self for the benefit of others are some of the most remarkable people I have encountered. In fact, the first person I met who really embodied this type of lifestyle enticed me to dig deeper into what Christianity had to offer.

When I was studying theology at Oxford University, I was paired with a professor named Henry Wansbrough. Father Wansbrough is a Benedictine monk, which means that he lives a simple life devoid of worldly possessions. I remember he once showed me a closet in his office with a small bed. He said, "This is where I live. You could fit all of my worldly possessions in a small box." My first thought was that Father Wansbrough was missing out on all the things that the world has to offer. How could he get by with nothing but a few books and keepsakes from his life? But the more time I spent with him, the more I came to realize that there's something to this idea of living simply.

Father Wansbrough was a joyous individual who cared deeply about everyone he met. Rather than judge you for your shortcomings, he could look inside you and see the best of what you could become. At the time I came to him, I was a horribly insecure, super-sensitive kid who was highly skeptical of religion and Christianity. Each week I would have to write a paper for him on a subject of his choosing. Rather than simply submitting the paper and being given a grade, I would have to go into his office and read the paper aloud. This is perhaps the most difficult aspect of being at Oxford because you are one-on-one, reading a paper to a world-renowned scholar in whatever field you are studying. Unlike American schools where we are often coddled by our teachers, their goal is to tear your argument to shreds.

Though my other professors at Oxford often would make me feel worthless, Father Wansbrough would always let me know how much he appreciated my efforts, even when my research was not as thorough as it could have been. He would say, "You write very well and carry out your argument to a logical conclusion even when you're wrong." That was awfully generous, given that Father Wansbrough is a brilliant scholar who published his own translation of the Bible. However, what truly amazed me is that he had a deep belief in Jesus' Way and lived out those teachings in everything he did. As a result, Father Wansbrough was the first person I ever met who was truly content with his life. He needed nothing more than what he had. Furthermore, he was willing to give and sacrifice for the benefit of others. He made the lives of everyone he encountered better as a result of his presence, and I wanted to have a life like his.

When I asked him how he became the man sitting before me, he responded that he learned it from trying to embody Jesus' teachings. He imparted to me that my life could mirror his if I took those teachings seriously. Father Wansbrough wanted me to understand that he was not unique. Anyone could do what he did if they spent time learning Jesus' teachings concerning The Way. He also emphasized that his journey was not something achieved in isolation from the world. Although he dedicated himself to being a monk, Father Wansbrough was part of a larger community of monks who nurtured and gave him guidance as to how he needed to grow as a person to better reflect the ideals that Jesus taught in the gospels. Indeed, the Resurrected Life is something that cannot be achieved apart from community.

Father Wansbrough was not transformed in a single moment. Rather, he went through an extensive process.[10.3] When I studied under Father Wansbrough, he was in his late 60s. He became a monk at the age of 18. Therefore, I met a man who had the benefit of decades of instruction and failure among the members of his monastic community. His peace was the result of a lengthy period of time where he reformed his habits and behaviors. He wanted me to appreciate that the man sitting before me was not the result of an instantaneous transformation.

Father Wansbrough stressed how embracing the Resurrected Life generally takes years or even decades because the thinking and behaviors that Jesus asks us to adopt are not natural to our way of being. It's not natural for us to give our money away so we can depend more on God. It's not natural for us to stand up for the oppressed and the downtrodden. It's not natural for us to love our enemies and pray for their well-being. Therefore, as each of these teachings become part of our lives, a different part of us has to die and be reborn into something new. Sometimes it takes several iterations of death and rebirth to really live into the most difficult of Jesus' teachings.

The relationship between involvement in a church community and our ability to live out Jesus' Way in the world cannot be overemphasized. One of my goals for those reading this book is that you might take the time to study Jesus' teachings closely (particularly those found in the Sermon on the Mount from Matthew Chapters 5-7) and attempt to emulate them in your own life. However, studying these teachings in isolation from a church community will greatly hinder your ability to experience the fullness of the Resurrected Life. I know that might be hard to hear since churches often contain some unpleasant people, but I want to explain to you why those people are so important in finding the fullness of life that Jesus is promoting in the Bible.

I view the church as a sort of training room, akin to a dojo (which literally means *place of the way*) for learning martial arts. The church allows us to practice the skills that are necessary for creating God's kingdom in the world.[†] The church is a place where (theoretically) everyone is welcome, regardless of their background. This means that the church is one of the last places in the world where you can find people with many different viewpoints gathered together. Therefore, within the church, we are able to practice loving our enemy and forgiving those who have wronged us when we find ourselves in the presence of people with whom we disagree. Within the church, we are able to practice hospitality by welcoming strangers into our midst and not judging them for their past. Within the church, we are able to practice serving the poor by giving our resources to feed the hungry, clothe the naked and care for the sick, while also accepting those same things when we need them for ourselves. Practicing Jesus' message in Christian community is the fourth step of our movement towards achieving Jesus' God consciousness.

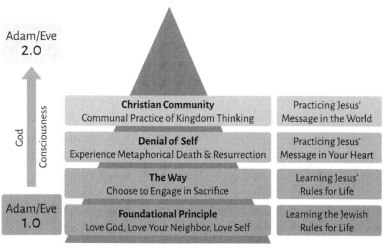

Adam/Eve
2.0

God Consciousness

Christian Community Communal Practice of Kingdom Thinking	Practicing Jesus' Message in the World
Denial of Self Experience Metaphorical Death & Resurrection	Practicing Jesus' Message in Your Heart
The Way Choose to Engage in Sacrifice	Learning Jesus' Rules for Life
Foundational Principle Love God, Love Your Neighbor, Love Self	Learning the Jewish Rules for Life

Adam/Eve
1.0

---

† Review p.171-173 for previous discussion of God's kingdom.

In this way, the church is a microcosm of God's kingdom. The skills that you learn within the church are designed to help you create God's kingdom in the world beyond the walls of the church. Indeed, this is where the right kind of pastor can make all the difference to your growth as a follower of Jesus' Way. A good pastor is like the Sensei of the dojo. The Sensei is a master of his particular discipline and can assist those who seek to become masters in the same discipline. Similarly, a good pastor can guide you in the training that will enable you to feel strong enough and motivated enough to progress in Jesus' Way and do your part to build God's kingdom beyond the church.

This is why not just any church will do because not every pastor teaches the same discipline of Christianity. Too many pastors focus on the life to come and not enough on this life. The emphasis on soul-saving means that they tend not to care about Jesus' call to serve those who are suffering now. A church with the wrong focus is not going to be able to provide you with the right training to follow Jesus' Way. However, a growing number of churches, including my own, emphasize this world over the next. If you are willing to take the time to find such a church, then that community will help you find the strength to die to self and embrace the Resurrected Life.

Father Wansbrough was my Sensei and he made it clear that the goal of the Resurrected Life is not to memorize verses from the Bible and mimic them in the world. Those verses lay the foundation for what comes next. The ultimate goal of the Resurrected Life is to move beyond those rules. As we see from our pyramid of progression towards a fully formed God consciousness, learning Jesus' teachings is one step in the process. Once Jesus' teachings are fully integrated into your life and once you have gone through the process of death and resurrection enough times, you are capable of seeing the world totally and completely through the prism of God's love, which is the fifth step of our movement towards achieving Jesus' God consciousness.

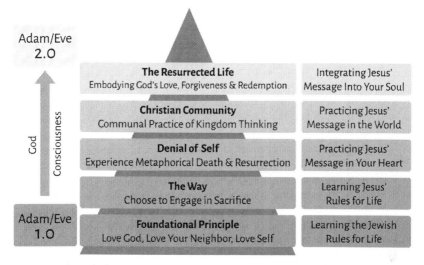

Adam/Eve 2.0	**The Resurrected Life** Embodying God's Love, Forgiveness & Redemption	Integrating Jesus' Message Into Your Soul
	Christian Community Communal Practice of Kingdom Thinking	Practicing Jesus' Message in the World
God Consciousness	**Denial of Self** Experience Metaphorical Death & Resurrection	Practicing Jesus' Message in Your Heart
	The Way Choose to Engage in Sacrifice	Learning Jesus' Rules for Life
Adam/Eve 1.0	**Foundational Principle** Love God, Love Your Neighbor, Love Self	Learning the Jewish Rules for Life

Even though these steps are laid out in a sequential order, it's important to understand that these steps are not one and done, like a check-list. In my experience, as you move up the pyramid, you must return to prior steps several times and rework your way upward. This is necessary because, as you grow into the Resurrected Life, your understanding of previous steps is altered by the integration of Jesus' Way into your being.

That's how Father Wansbrough saw the world. Everything was about God's love. He didn't have to think about loving his enemies because, when you see the world through the prism of God's love, you're going to love them no matter what. He didn't have to think about giving money to the poor. When you see somebody who's cold and hungry, you buy them a meal and find them a place to stay. He didn't have to stop himself from judging me for being insecure because he accepted me and loved me just as I am. When you see the world through God's love, the rules don't matter anymore because you will accomplish everything that Jesus expects of you. That's the beauty of the Resurrected Life—there are no more rules because you have transcended them with love.

THE KINGDOM OF GOD IS AT HAND

If you take time to observe humans in the way you observe wildlife, you will notice a fascinating paradox: humans want and desire to be around other humans, but we have limited tolerance for how long we can handle being with other people before we get into conflict. Schools are a great example of this. You pack hundreds of kids into a building for eight hours a day and expect them to get along. For the first month or two, they are able to tolerate the close quarters because they've had the summer away from school. They can get outside and burn off their excess energy because the weather is still warm. But beginning in November, when the weather gets cold and everyone is sequestered inside, conflicts become much more commonplace. In middle school and high school, November is the beginning of fight season for administrators. As the school year wears on, the number of fights escalates well into the spring. I remember in my high school, during springtime, there could be two or three fights a day. The kids are weary of being around the same people all the time.

In the adult world, these skirmishes play out on a much larger stage. When adults disagree over the distribution of resources, the role and purpose of government, even fundamental ideas of how we should live, tensions can escalate and we find ourselves in conflict within our own society and with other nations. This conflict can be resolved through diplomacy (talking it out), sanctions (the withholding of resources) and war (the removal of opposition through violence). What I find fascinating about these global problems is that we use the same strategies for resolution when we are in conflict with one another on an individual level.

Take my sons, for instance. When they are in conflict over a toy and want to use it at the same time, they are dealing with disagreement over the distribution of resources. Their go-to tactic is violence. One will try to overpower the other to gain possession of the toy. However, my older son does not always go down this path. Sometimes he'll say to his younger brother, "Well, if you get the toy, then you won't be able to have any of the juice that you like." That's a sanction that he's imposed. He's withholding resources from his younger brother to entice him to get what he wants.

And then there's the rare occasion when they'll use diplomacy. They'll talk it out. Now if it were up to them, they would never use diplomacy. They would fight it out because conflict is innate to our DNA. Diplomacy, on the other hand, is a learned skill. It takes work and effort to learn how to resolve your problems through conversation, but when it's done well, conversation is the most effective means for resolving conflict. Why? Because true conversation is an act of empathy, which means that you are able to understand and share the feelings of another.

The essence of true conversation is that both sides are not only listening to what the other person is saying, but they are also trying to see the world from the other person's perspective. The art of conversation takes work. It's not easy to commit to true conversation because it requires each side to momentarily let go of what's important to them and assume the vantage point of what's important to someone else. It's an incredibly transformative experience because it opens you up to entirely new ways of thinking. Indeed, those new ways of thinking can transform the world. Let me give you an example.

In the 1980s, America was in the midst of the cold war with Russia. President Reagan, like many people in the United States, saw Russia as the most serious threat to freedom and democracy. Early on in his presidency, Reagan took a hardline stance in his dealings with Russia and leaned heavily on his military advisors as to the tactics he should employ against them. At that point, Reagan was not interested in having conversations with Russia. He was interested in winning the cold war.

That all changed in 1984 when Reagan met Suzanne Massie, an American who was the daughter of a Swiss diplomat. Massie spoke Russian and had an intimate knowledge of the Russian people and culture. Reagan became interested in Massie when he read her book *Land of the Firebird: The Beauty of Old Russia.* After their initial encounter at the White House, Massie was invited back some 20 times to have conversations with Reagan.[10.4] Sometimes these meetings would take place in the presence of national security advisors, other times they would have these conversations in private. What became clear to the people who worked with Reagan in the White House is that Massie was changing the way Reagan understood the Russian people.

Perhaps the most important piece of wisdom that Massie imparted to Reagan is that the Russian people are not evil. They are human beings just like everyone else. They want what everyone else wants—a good life in which their families can prosper. Because Reagan was willing to listen and learn from Massie, he broke with his party and began to engage diplomatically with Mikhail Gorbachev, which put an end to the cold war. In this way, a series of conversations literally transformed the world. That's the power of the right kind of conversation.

What the Reagan example proves to me is that when people are having the right kind of conversations and find common ground, then we as a species can progress in the dynamics of our thinking. The fact that we were able to move beyond the cold war without it escalating points to an evolution in our thinking as humans. I think modern humans are far more aware of the costs of war than our ancestors. As an example of how humans used to think about war, examine this passage from 1 Chronicles: "In the spring of the year, the time when kings go out to battle, Joab led out the army, ravaged the country of the Ammonites, and came and besieged Rabbah." *(1 Ch. 20:1)* Notice how it says that the springtime is when kings go out to battle. They did this to maintain and expand their borders, but what this verse clearly indicates is that war was a regular part of the Hebrew culture. This type of thinking, where war is built into your yearly schedule, is about as far away as you can get from Jesus' teachings on God's kingdom.

Some might argue that our thinking as a species has not progressed much further than what we read in 1 Chronicles. Humans remain violent creatures that are prone to conflict. However, what gives me hope is that, for the first time in human history, our species is beginning to engage in global conversations. Perhaps the most significant of these conversations concerns the subject of war. Over the last 70 years, since the end of World War II, the global population has become increasingly anti-war in their thinking. Part of the reason for this is because World War II was the most destructive war in the history of the world. When the war ended and the civilian population began to learn about the aftermath—death tolls incurred from soldiers on the battlefield, concentration camps and the atomic bomb—many people became conscious of the fact that this devastation should never be repeated. I think many people realized that the consequences of warfare are simply too great to warrant the costs.

This is kingdom thinking. Kingdom thinking is the idea that countries and nations should not take what they want by force. Kingdom thinking is the idea that war and violence are unacceptable. Jesus told us that in God's kingdom, there's no more pain and suffering, and a big reason why this pain and suffering wouldn't exist in God's kingdom is because we would not inflict it on each other any longer. We are moving towards that kind of thinking as a species and it's because we are having these larger conversations with each other.

Indeed, I would argue that we are closer than we ever have been to creating God's kingdom on earth. Our changing perspective on war is only one example. Others would be our attitudes towards food and medicine. In ancient societies, when there wasn't enough food, large portions of the population would starve to death. Only the wealthy were immune from drought or famine. However, in the last 100 years we have made extraordinary leaps in our technological capabilities to produce food. We have the capacity with our present technology to ensure that every person in the world has enough calories to sustain their existence. Because of these advances, humans have shifted in their thinking about food. Since there is enough food to feed everyone in the world, humans have begun to think, "Food is a fundamental right. No one should have to starve to death." This type of thought is kingdom thinking because, in God's kingdom, everyone has enough food to eat.

The same evolution in thinking is true of medicine. In the ancient world, if you got sick, your only hope was that your immune system was strong enough to recover. However, modern medicine is moving in the direction where we are able to heal and cure all manner of sickness. With each advance in the medical field, there is a larger conversation around how every human should have access to vaccines and medical care for their illnesses. Again, this is kingdom thinking. Indeed, similar types of conversations are happening all the time around the ideas of housing and education. Everyone deserves the right to a roof over their head and a proper education. The more we have these conversations, the closer we will come to creating God's kingdom on earth.

What I find to be so fascinating about these advances in human thinking is that the vast majority of people having these conversations are not Christian. In fact, quite the opposite. Christians are often on the periphery of these conversations inhibiting forward progress. Why? Because many Christians have bought into the notion that humans are incapable of creating God's kingdom. They think Jesus must return in order to create God's kingdom. I couldn't disagree more!

First of all, I don't think Jesus is coming back. I know such a statement is heresy to some Christians, but we've discussed how sure the disciples were that Jesus was going to return during their lifetimes. Here we are, nearly 2,000 years later, and Jesus still hasn't come back. I'm open to Jesus proving me wrong, but I'm not holding my breath. Therefore, I think it's irresponsible for Christians to sit back and wait for Jesus to clean up our mess.

Second, God has provided us with everything we need to create the kingdom here and now. All we need is the will to choose love of neighbor over selfish ambition. Clearly, this is easier said than done. The people who are willing to give up what they have for the benefit of others tend to be the exception and not the rule. The key question is what will compel us as a species to make the necessary changes in our society to create the kingdom?

Given that it will be some time before we will evolve as a species to be less selfish, our only other option at present is to embrace a life philosophy that will achieve the same end. Left to our own devices, I do not think this will happen. Humans can hardly agree on the color of the sky, let alone a life philosophy. However, history teaches us that when humans are backed into a corner, circumstances force us to make decisions about what is most important for the benefit of the whole. During World War II, millions of men and women sacrificed their lives so that Nazism would not become a dominant life philosophy in the world. People all over the world examined the situation and eventually came to the conclusion that the sacrifice of resources and lives was worth the cost. I think we are quickly approaching a time in our modern world where such decisions will have to be made again.

We exist at a time where the necessary technological factors have come together to create the possibility for God's kingdom on earth. What is also clear to me is that we are at a perilous moment in the history of our species. The paradox we face is that the same technology that will help us create the kingdom is the very thing that may destroy us. The difference will be in how we use that technology. If we view our technological innovation as something to be used for the benefit of the many, then we will open the door for the kingdom to become a reality. However, if our technology continues to be reserved for those who can afford to pay for it, then the door will remain shut and we may not survive. The difference comes down to consistently being willing to share what you have for the benefit of others. The more people are willing to make this sacrifice, the greater the possibility of creating the kingdom. This is why Jesus' teachings are so important, particularly in developed nations, where much of this conversation around kingdom thinking is already taking place.

As I stated previously, kingdom thinking is already prevalent in our culture. Both secular and religious people believe in these ideals. Unfortunately, we often lack the will to implement these ideals in our world because they have been divorced from Jesus' teachings on sacrifice and love. Kingdom thinking cannot be successful independent of Jesus' teachings. Without Jesus' teachings, we lack the instructions to build the kingdom. This is why Christianity remains relevant in our world today. Therefore, when we commit ourselves to following Jesus' teachings and seeking out the Resurrected Life, then we enable the creation of God's kingdom in our world. By doing so, we tear down the greatest barrier preventing the kingdom from coming to fruition: the conflict within ourselves.

Of all the conflicts we face as a society, the most profound are the conflicts we face within our own minds and spirits. These problems of self are the genesis of all other conflicts we face. If you resolve the conflict inside yourself, then you will eliminate the conflict you have with others. Indeed, if all the people who called themselves Christian actually subscribed to Jesus' Way of life, then the positive ripples would be so enormous that the kingdom would be here within a few generations. Unfortunately, few Christians adhere to Jesus' Way of life and, as a result, the kingdom feels far away from the modern church.

Despite all of this, I see the future of the church as very bright. Two generations from now, the church as we know it today will be dead. When this church dies, something new will rise in its place. My hope is that this new church will be filled with a vibrant group of people who clearly see the possibility of what the Christian faith holds for their lives and the world. These will be people who follow Jesus because they want the Resurrected Life for themselves. No longer will these people be motivated by the antiquated doctrines of the old church—original sin, fear of hell, a God who looks down on them with disapproval. No, these people will follow Jesus because his teachings represent the kind of God that is worth believing in—a God of unconditional love who is always waiting with outstretched arms. Most importantly, they will use that love as a force for positive change in the world so that God's kingdom can become a reality. I believe this is what the new church will look like because I see it happening right now. Slowly but surely, the new church is emerging out of the old. My hope is that, before long, the words Jesus pronounced 2,000 years ago will come to fruition: "The kingdom of God is at hand."

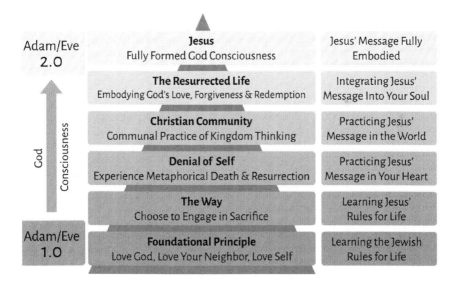

1 Jesus' greatest commandment is a circular pattern of love that provides the foundation for becoming like Jesus. The core principle of this love is vulnerability. The willingness to be open and expose our limitations and weaknesses is the key to loving God, neighbor and self.

2 Jesus' *Way* of life is defined by intentionally engaging in sacrificial suffering to help those around us. The act of sacrificial suffering allows us to die to self, resulting in a new person who finds their worth and value in gaining for others rather than themselves.

3 The Resurrected Life comes as a result of engaging with Jesus' teachings within a supportive Christian community. Each teaching requires a different part of us to die and be reborn into something new, creating the possibility of seeing the world exclusively through the prism of God's love.

4 Humans are the closest they ever have been to creating God's kingdom on earth, thanks to technological advances. As a result, humans are now engaged in kingdom thinking via global conversations about food, education, housing and medicine as fundamental human rights.

5 Christianity remains relevant in our world today because this type of kingdom thinking cannot be successfully implemented independent of Jesus' teachings on love and sacrifice. Humans are simply too selfish. Jesus provides the necessary guidelines that make God's kingdom possible.

THE NEW GOSPEL

A few years ago, one of my colleagues asked me, "Alex, what do you think the church is going to look like in 50 years?" This is an important question because statistics indicate that nearly every Christian church in America is in decline.[B.1] Some are dying faster than others, but we are all slowly being phased out and replaced with something different. A new version of Christianity is rising out of the ashes of the old church. This book is my attempt to identify what I think that new Christianity should look like. I refer to this new version of Christianity as the New Gospel.

Over the last ten chapters, we have covered a lot of ground. If you're having trouble seeing how the various sections of this book come together into a cohesive whole, I want to provide you with a short summation of the message I am attempting to convey. In the Christianity of the 21st century, we are dispensing with the old ways of thinking about the Bible, God and Jesus. When it comes to the Bible, we need to openly admit that the Bible was not written directly by God, but by human beings who had agendas and biases just like you and I do. Furthermore, we need to acknowledge that many of the stories written in the Bible are not historically factual.

These stories were created as way for a group of people (the Jews) to express their beliefs about God. Our job in reading the Bible is to extract the core spiritual message from a scriptural text, while simultaneously disposing of the unbelievable elements that alienate modern readers. With this new interpretive lens, not only does the Bible become more palatable, but we are able to correct the problems that plague the classical conceptions of God found in the Bible.

The ancient Jews believed God to be the source of all existence in the universe, which means that God takes ultimate responsibility for all things that transpire. In this new version of Christianity, we openly admit that good and evil are the result of God allowing us to make choices. We stop believing that God intervenes in the universe with miracles, but rather, chooses to work through human free will. This means that God does not have a plan for our lives. Instead God imbues us with a spirit of redemption, embedding within us the ability to restore the world.

This capacity for restoration is best expressed through the person of Jesus. In following Jesus' Way of life, we can fully exploit the potential that exists inside us. The problem with embracing Jesus' Way is that we have to disentangle Jesus from the mythology that enshrouds his life. The New Gospel discards the four non-starters that prevent modern people from embracing Jesus:

1. Jesus was not born of a virgin (Jesus was born of normal sexual relations, like everyone else)
2. Jesus did not die for your sins (God can forgive you without Jesus)
3. Jesus did not physically rise from the dead (Jesus' disciples saw a vision of Jesus)
4. Jesus was not God in the flesh (Jesus was a normal human being with a fully formed God consciousness)

This last point is critical to the New Gospel because Jesus' God consciousness means that his example and teachings reflect God's being. Moreover, because Jesus is human, not divine, his achievements can become our achievements if we follow his path. We too can possess a fully formed God consciousness.

This notion is very different from the way modern conservative Christians portray Jesus. They believe that Jesus was sacrificed by God so that our sins could be forgiven, allowing our souls access to heaven when we die. With the New Gospel, salvation is no longer the aim of Christianity. What matters is how we live here and now. What matters is whether we are able to bring restoration to the world. This is why we follow Jesus. His teachings guide us towards the Resurrected Life, the fruits of which create God's kingdom. In this way, the New Gospel is best defined as restoration. We can't control what happens to us after we die, but we can contribute to the restoration of ourselves and the world.

In truth, this book can be summed up with two Hebrew words—*tikkun olam*. These two words are best translated into English as *repair the world* or, more broadly, *repair the cosmos*.[B.2] In the Jewish mystical tradition, this phrase indicates the special purpose for which God created human beings. In order to fully understand this special purpose, one must understand the mystical story of creation attached to this purpose:

In the beginning, when God resolved to create the world, God determined that it was necessary to reduce part of God's self into vessels of light. Unfortunately, these vessels shattered causing the wholeness of the world to be broken into an infinite number of fragments. Rather than allowing these fragments to disappear into the cracks and crevasses of the universe, God created human beings. God endowed humans with the unique ability to see the hidden light that is scattered throughout the world. This light is hidden everywhere, but our gift allows us to observe this hidden light in two specific places—people and events.

Every time we catch a glimpse of that light in the people and events of our lives, our job is to point it out for others to see. The more people who see it, the more wholeness is restored to the universe. Thus, the purpose of humanity is *tikkun olam* or the restoration of the world through the lifting up of hidden light. This task cannot be sustained by the work of a few, but requires the collective effort of every human on the planet. As each generation exposes more hidden light, the world edges closer to wholeness. In this way, we each possess the ability to bring healing to the universe and that is the point of this book—you are a healer of this world. You simply have to choose to embrace the role that God bestowed upon you from your birth.

BIBLIOGRAPHY

Alpine, Max. *Was Jesus Ever a Disciple of John? A Historical Study.* Edinburgh: University of Edinburgh Publishing, 2011.

Amsel, Nachum. *The Jewish Encyclopedia of Moral and Ethical Issues.* Northvale: Jason Aronson Inc., 1994.

Andrew, George. *The Epic of Gilgamesh: The Babylonian Epic Poem and Other Texts in Akkadian and Sumerian.* London: Penguin Books, 2003.

Aslan, Reza. *Zealot: The Life and Times of Jesus of Nazareth.* New York: Random House, 2013.

Augustine. *Confessions.* Translated by R. S. Pine-Coffin. New York: Penguin Books, 1961.

Bar, Shaul. *A Letter That Has Not Been Read: Dreams in the Hebrew Bible.* Pittsburgh: Hebrew Union College Press, 2001.

Barrett, David B., George Thomas Kurian, and Todd M. Johnson. *World Christian Encyclopedia: A Comparative Survey of Churches and Religions in the Modern World.* Oxford: Oxford University Press, 2001.

Bietak, Manfred. "On the Historicity of the Exodus: What Egyptology Today Can Contribute to Assessing the Biblical Account of the Sojourn in Egypt." In *Israel's Exodus in Transdisciplinary Perspective Text, Archaeology, Culture, and Geoscience.* Ed. Thomas E. Levy, Thomas Schneider, and William H.C. Propp. Cham: Springer, 2015.

Brecht, Martin. *Martin Luther.* Translated by James L. Schaaf. Philadelphia: Fortress Press, 1985–93.

Brown, F., S. Driver, and C. Briggs. *The Brown-Driver-Briggs Hebrew and English Lexicon.* Peabody: Hendrickson Publishers, Inc., 2001.

Brown, Raymond E. *An Introduction to the New Testament.* New York: Doubleday, 1997.

Calvin, John. *Institutes of the Christian Religion.* Translated by Henry Beveridge. Michigan: W. B. Eerdmans Publishing Company, 1998.

Cobb, Matthew. *The Egg and Sperm Race: The Seventeenth-Century Scientists Who Unlocked the Secrets of Sex and Growth.* London: Simon & Schuster, 2006.

Crossan, John Dominic. *The Historical Jesus: The Life of a Mediterranean Jewish Peasant.* San Francisco: Harper Collins, 1992.

Danker, Frederick William. *The Concise Greek-English Lexicon of the New Testament. Chicago: University of Chicago Press, 2009.*

Douglas-Klotz, Neil. *The Hidden Gospel: Decoding the Spiritual Message of the Aramaic Jesus.* Wheaton: Quest Books, 1999.

Erlikman, Vadim. *Loss of Population in the 20th Century.* Moscow: Russian Panorama, 2004.

Ehrman, Bart D. *How Jesus Became God: The Exaltation of a Jewish Preacher from Galilee.* New York: HarperOne, 2014.

Fiensy, David A. and Ralph K. Hawkins. *The Galilean Economy in the Time of Jesus.* Atlanta: Society of Biblical Literature, 2013.

Fitzmyer, Joseph. "The Languages of Palestine in the First Century A.D" in *The Language of the New Testament,* Ed. Stanley E. Porter. Sheffield: Sheffield Academic Press, 1991.

Glass, Ira and Brian Reed. "547: Cops See It Differently." *This American Life.* Podcast audio, February 6th, 2015. https://www.thisamericanlife.org/radio-archives/episode/547/cops-see-it-differently-part-one

Greenblatt, Stephen. *The Rise and Fall of Adam and Eve.* New York: W. W. Norton & Company, 2017.

Grull, Tibor. "The Legendary Fate of Pontius Pilate." *Classica et Mediaevalia, Danish Journal of Philology and History* 61 (2010): 151-54.

Hanson, K.C. "The Galilean Fishing Economy and the Jesus Tradition." *Biblical Theology*   Bulletin 27 (1997): 99-111.

Hoffmeier, James K. *Israel in Egypt: Evidence for the Authenticity of the Exodus Tradition.* New York: Oxford University Press, 1996.

Homer, Sidney. *A History of Interest Rates.* New Brunswick: Rutgers University Press, 1963.

Hopkins, Ian W. J. "The City Region in Roman Palestine," *Palestine Exploration Quarterly* 112, no. 1 (July 1980) :19-32.

Isbouts, Jean-Pierre. *The Biblical World: An Illustrated Atlas.* Washington, D.C.: National Geographic, 2007.

Isometsa, E. T. "Psychological Autopsy Studies—A Review." *European Psychiatry* 16 no. 7 (November 2001), 379-385.

Jenni, Ernst and Claus Westermann. *Theological Lexicon of the Old Testament.* Volume 2 and 3. Translated by Mark E. Biddle. Peabody: Hendrickson Publishers. 1997.

Josephus, Flavius. *The Antiquities of the Jews.* Brookfield: First Rate Publishers, 2013.

Josephus, Flavius. *The Wars of the Jews.* Charlotte: Information Age Publishing, 2009.

Juvenal. *Satires of Juvenal: Book 1.* Translated by Thomas B. Lindsay. New York: American Book Company, 1890.

Kee, Howard Clark, Emily Albu, Carter Lindberg, J. William Frost, and Dana L. Robert. *Christianity: A Social and Cultural History.*, 2nd ed. New Jersey: Prentice-Hall, Inc., 1998.

Kelber, Werner H. "Jesus and Tradition: Words in Time, Words in Space" in *Semeia 65: Orality and Textuality in Early Christian Literature*, ed. J. Dewey. Atlanta: Scholars Press, 2004.

Kelber, Werner H. *The Oral and the Written Gospel: The Hermeneutics of Speaking and Writing in the Synoptic Tradition, Mark, Paul, and Q.* Minneapolis: Fortress Press, 1983.

Lambert, Wilfred G., and A. R. Millard. *Atrahasis: The Babylonian Story of the Flood.* Oxford: Oxford University Press, 1969.

Light, Jonathan Fraser. "Longest Throws" in *The Cultural Encyclopedia of Baseball.* Jefferson: McFarland & Company Inc., 2005.

MacCulloch, Diarmaid. *The Reformation: A History.* New York: Penguin Books, 2003.

Martyn, J. Louis. *History and Theology in the Fourth Gospel, 3rd Edition.* Louisville: Westminster John Knox Press, 2003.

Morford, Mark P. O. and Robert J. Lenardon, *Classical Mythology Sixth.*, 6th ed. New York: Longman, 1999.

Nagy, Gregory, Stephen A. Mitchell, and Albert Bates Lord. *The Singer of Tales, 2nd Edition.* Cambridge: Harvard University Press, 2000.

Niswonger, Richard L. *New Testament History.* Grand Rapids: Zondervan Publishing, 1992.

Origen. *An Exhortation to Martyrdom, Prayer, First Principles: Book IV, Prologue to the Commentary on the Song of Songs, Homily XXVII on Numbers.* Translation and Introduction by Rowan A. Greer, preface by Hans Urs Von Balthasar. New York: Paulist Press, 1979.

Origen. *On First Principles.* Translated by George William Butterworth. London: SPCK Publishing, 1936.

Orme-Johnson, David W. et al., "International Peace Project in the Middle East: The Effects of the Maharishi Technology of the Unified Field." *The Journal of Conflict Resolution* 32 no. 4 (1988): 778.

Pagels, Elaine. *Adam, Eve and the Serpent.* New York: First Vintage Editions, 1989.

Parker, Theodore. *Ten Sermons of Religion.* London: Trubner & Co., 1879.

Petropoulou, Maria-Zoe. *Animal Sacrifice in Ancient Greek Religion, Judaism, and Christianity, 100 BC-AD 200.* New York: Oxford University Press, 2008.

Pew Research Center: Religious and Public Life. *America's Changing Religious Landscape.* Last Modified May 12, 2015. http://www.pewforum.org/2015/05/12/americas-changing-religious-landscape/

Rasmussen Reports. "64% Believe Jesus Christ Rose From the Dead." Last modified March 29, 2013. http://www.rasmussenreports.com/public_content/lifestyle/holidays/march_2013/64_believe_jesus_christ_rose_from_the_dead

Roberts, Alexander. *Saint Irenaeus of Lyons: Against Heresies.* Ex Fontibus Company, 2015.

Ryan, William and Walter Pitman. *Noah's Flood: The New Scientific Discoveries About the Event That Changed History*. New York: Touchstone, 1998.

Schleiermacher, Friedrich. *The Christian Faith*. Ed. H.R. MacKintosh and J.S. Steward. Philadelphia: Fortress Press, 1976.

Singer, Isidore and Cyrus Adler. *The Jewish Encyclopedia: A Descriptive Record of the History, Religion, Literature, and Customs of the Jewish People from the Earliest Times to the Present Day*. London: Funk and Wagnalls Company, 1901.

Souter, Alexander. *A Glossary of Later Latin to 600 A.D.* Oxford: Clarendon Press, 1949.

State of Connecticut, Office of the Child Advocate. "Shooting at Sandy Hook Elementary School." Last modified November 21st, 2014. http://www.ct.gov/oca/lib/oca/sandyhook11212014.pdf

Story, Louise. "Anywhere the Eye Can See, It's Likely to See an Ad." In *The New York Times*. Last modified January 15, 2007. https://www.nytimes.com/2007/01/15/business/media/15everywhere.html?pagewanted=all&_r=0

Stroumsa, Guy G. The End of Sacrifice: Religious Transformations in Late Antiquity. Translated by Susan Emanuel. Chicago: Chicago University Press. 2009.

Sull, Donald N. "The Dynamics of Standing Still: Firestone Tire & Rubber and the Radical Revolution," *Business History Review* 73, no. 3 (Autumn 1999): 430.

Weems, Mason Locke. *The Life of Washington the Great*. Augusta: George P. Randolph, 1806.

Weems, Mason Locke to Mathew Carey, January 12, 1800, in Paul Leicester Ford, *Mason Locke Weems: His Works, His Ways: A Bibliography Left Unfinished*, 3 vols. New York: Plimpton Press, 1929.

NOTES

CHAPTER 1: HOW DID WE GET HERE?

TURNING BACK THE CLOCK

1.1 Martin Brecht, *Martin Luther* (Philadelphia: Fortress Press, 1985–93), 1:48.

1.2 Howard Clark Kee, Emily Albu, Carter Lindberg, J. William Frost, Dana L. Robert, *Christianity: A Social and Cultural History.*, 2nd ed. (New Jersey: Prentice-Hall, Inc., 1998), 265.

1.3 Alexander Souter, *A Glossary of Later Latin to 600 A. D.* (Oxford: Clarendon Press, 1949), 345.
Redemption comes from the Latin root *redemptio*, which literally means *price or payment*. This word was commonly used during debt collection. Imagine you owe someone money and you give them your property as collateral until you've saved enough money to pay the debt. During that time your property is in someone else's possession. However, when the time comes for redemption, you are buying back your property and paying the debt. This is how the Catholic Church justified indulgences. In the New Testament, this concept is used to illustrate our relationship with God. You are God's property, but you have been separated from God because you have sinned. The sins are the debt and it was believed that sinners were in Satan's possession. God, desiring to have us back, must redeem the debt and buy us back. Luther used Romans to justify his belief that Jesus' sacrifice is the only way those debts can be paid.

1.4 Howard Clark Kee, Emily Albu, Carter Lindberg, J. William Frost, Dana L. Robert, *Christianity: A Social and Cultural History.*, 2nd ed. (New Jersey: Prentice-Hall, Inc., 1998), 265-66.

1.5 Diarmaid MacCulloch, *The Reformation: A History* (New York: Penguin Books, 2003), 166-67.

1.6 Howard Clark Kee, Emily Albu, Carter Lindberg, J. William Frost, Dana L. Robert, *Christianity: A Social and Cultural History.*, 2nd ed. (New Jersey: Prentice-Hall, Inc., 1998), 268.

1.7 David B. Barrett, George Thomas Kurian, and Todd M. Johnson, *World Christian Encyclopedia: A Comparative Survey of Churches and Religions in the Modern World* (Oxford: Oxford University Press, 2001), 16.

CONTEXT IS EVERYTHING

1.8 Raymond E. Brown, *An Introduction to the New Testament* (New York: Doubleday, 1997), 334.

THE PROBLEM

1.9 J. Louis Martyn, *History and Theology in the Fourth Gospel.*, 3rd ed. (Louisville: Westminster John Knox Press, 2003), 164. The expulsion of John's community from the synagogue is a theory that was first promoted by J. Louis Martyn, professor of Biblical Theology at Union Theological Seminary. In this book, Martyn outlines his thesis that John's gospel was written shortly after the final rift between Jewish Christians and Pharisaic Jews around 90 C.E.

1.10 Raymond E. Brown, *An Introduction to the New Testament* (New York: Doubleday, 1997), 373-75.

CHAPTER 2: GRAINS OF TRUTH

THE JESUS PROBLEM

2.1 Frederick William Danker, *The Concise Greek-English Lexicon of the New Testament* (Chicago: University of Chicago Press, 2009), 52.

2.2 Raymond E. Brown, *An Introduction to the New Testament* (New York: Doubleday, 1997), 7-8.

2.3 Ibid. 164.

2.4 Ibid. 362-371. The gospel of John was written independent of Mark, Matthew or Luke and is derived from vastly different source material, most of which has nothing to do with the actual historical Jesus.

CAN I GET A QUOTE?

2.5 Werner Kelber, "Jesus and Tradition: Words in Time, Words in Space" in *Semeia 65: Orality and Textuality in Early Christian Literature*, ed. J. Dewey (Atlanta: Scholars Press, 2004), 139-68.

2.6 John Dominic Crossan, *The Historical Jesus: The Life of a Mediterranean Jewish Peasant* (San Francisco: Harper Collins Publishers, 1992), 24-26.

2.7 For more information on this study see Gregory Nagy, Stephen A. Mitchell, and Albert Bates Lord. *The Singer of Tales.*, 2nd ed. (Cambridge: Harvard University Press, 2000).
   Due to an untimely death, Parry's work was brought to fruition by his assistant, Albert Lord.

2.8 Werner H. Kelber, *The Oral and the Written Gospel: The Hermeneutics of Speaking and Writing in the Synoptic Tradition, Mark, Paul, and Q* (Bloomington: Indiana University Press, 1983) xxiii.
   "[The author of Mark] was plugging into a copious reservoir of memories, retrieving and reshuffling what was accessible to him memorially. In the end, I venture the suggestion that the gospel composition is unthinkable without the notion of cultural memory, which serves ultimately not the preservation of remembrances per se but the preservation of the group, its social identity and self-image...Mark avails himself of a rich cultural memory for the purpose of securing the Christian identity for a postwar generation."

THE REAL STORY OF NOAH AND THE ARK

2.9 For a good translation of the Epic of Atrahasis see Wilfred G. Lambert and A. R. Millard's *Atrahasis: The Babylonian Story of the Flood* (Oxford: Oxford University Press, 1969).

2.10 If you are interested in exploring Gilgamesh and other Sumerian mythical texts that are in the same milieu as Genesis 1-11, I would recommend George Andrew's *The Epic of Gilgamesh: The Babylonian Epic Poem and Other Texts in Akkadian and Sumerian* (London: Penguin Books, 2003).

2.11 Ian W. J. Hopkins "The City Region in Roman Palestine," *Palestine Exploration Quarterly* 112, no. 1 (July 1980): 19-32. Hopkins studied settlements that emanated from the city of Joppa and using Central Place Theory determined that settlements in antiquity were spaced "at ten to twelve mile intervals." Hopkins claims that, "The key factors which determine this pattern of settlement location are commerce, especially local marketing functions, and administrative functions, through which the cities serve the towns and the town the villages and even the villages may – in Europe at any rate – serve a small area of farms and hamlets." Thus, most peasants in antiquity would have lived within a 15 mile radius of a larger village or major urban center that would have served their basic needs and would often never venture beyond that radius.

2.12 For more on William and Pitman's research, read their book *Noah's Flood: The New Scientific Discoveries About the Event that Changed History* (New York: Touchstone Press, 1998). Their journey towards the development of this theory is fascinating, but it didn't come without consequence. As evidence that the Noah story has acquired a wholly negative connotation within secular culture, the promotion of this theory caused William and Pitman to be shunned in certain corners of academia.

DOES THE END JUSTIFY THE MEANS?

2.13 F. Brown, S. Driver, and C. Briggs, *The Brown-Driver-Briggs Hebrew and English Lexicon* (Peabody: Hendrickson Publishers, Inc., 2001), 427-28.

2.14 Ibid. 628-629.

CHAPTER 3: THE GOD YOU KNOW

THE GLASS IS HALF FULL

3.1 "Shooting at Sandy Hook Elementary School," Office of the Child Advocate, State of Connecticut, last modified November 21st, 2014, http://www.ct.gov/oca/lib/oca/sandy-hook11212014.pdf

3.2 Based on statistics provided by the Anxiety and Depression Association of America: https://adaa.org/about-adaa/press-room/facts-statistics#

3.3 E. T. Isometsa, "Psychological Autopsy Studies—A Review," *European Psychiatry* 16 no. 7 (November 2001), 379-385. This number is derived from an instrument known as psychological autopsies (PA) and as Isometsa says, PAs "established that more than 90% of completed suicides have suffered from usually co-morbid mental disorders."

WORD PLAY

3.4 Listening to Presbyterians: The Presbyterian Panel Report. "Religious and Demographic Profile of Presbyterians, 2011: Findings from the Initial Survey of the 2012-2014 Presbyterian Panel." *Church Attendance and Other Religious Participation.* http://www.pcusa.org/media/uploads/research/pdfs/presbyterian_panel_survey_fall_2011_religious_and_demographic_profile_of_presbyterians.pdf, iv.
The median age of the congregants in the Presbyterian Church being 63. Since the median age rose from 60 to 63 between 2008 and 2011, we can correctly assume that the median age has increased in the interceding years.

3.5 For a less academic version of Diogenes Allen's theology, read *Theology for a Troubled Believer: An Introduction to the Christian Faith* (Louisville: Westminster John Knox Press, 2010). In this book, Dr. Allen provides a brief overview of the main problems with the application of Greek philosophy to the Hebrew religion.

3.6 Alexander Souter, *A Glossary of Later Latin to 600 A. D.* (Oxford: Clarendon Press, 1949), 425.

Of all the scriptures expressing God's transcendent nature, Exodus 3:13-14 is the most profound. When God tells Moses the divine name of "I am", the utilization of the verb *to be* implies that God is existence itself.

3.7 Joseph A. Fitzmyer, "The Languages of Palestine in the First Century A.D." in *The Language of the New Testament*, ed. Stanley E. Porter (Sheffield: Sheffield Academic Press, 1991), 126-162.

The reason the New Testament is written in Greek as opposed to Aramaic, the language spoken by Jesus, is because Greek culture had a wide-reaching influence on countries all over the Roman Empire. Commonly referred to as Hellenization, almost all people who were literate wrote using some form of Greek. If the New Testament had been written in Aramaic, few people would have been able to read it and Christianity would not have had broad reach.

3.8 Neil Douglas-Klotz, *The Hidden Gospel: Decoding the Spiritual Message of the Aramaic Jesus* (Wheaton: Quest Books, 1999), 27-28.

BATTLE OF THE WILLS

3.9 F. Brown, S. Driver, and C. Briggs, *The Brown-Driver-Briggs Hebrew and English Lexicon* (Peabody: Hendrickson Publishers, Inc., 2001), 871-73.

CHAPTER 4: THE GOD OF REDEMPTION

SUFFERING FOR SALVATION

4.1 Jean Pierre Isbouts, *The Biblical World: An Illustrated Atlas* (Washington D.C: National Geographic, 2007), 85.

What made Joseph's coat special was that "it was long and hemmed, a garment usually worn by persons of wealth and authority."

4.2 Shaul Bar, *A Letter That Has Not Been Read: Dreams in the Hebrew Bible* (Pittsburgh: Hebrew Union College Press, 2001), 44-77.

Bar makes clear that biblical authors do not believe that every dream in the human mind comes from God. Some dreams are "vain and meaningless," while others are "significant symbolic messages from God." This is why men like Joseph and Daniel were so sought after because they could tell the difference between the two and accurately interpret dreams from God "to decipher their meaning."

4.3 Manfred Bietak, "On the Historicity of the Exodus: What Egyptology Today Can Contribute to Assessing the Biblical Account of the Sojourn in Egypt" in Thomas E. Levy, Thomas Schneider, and William H.C. Propp, eds., *Israel's Exodus In Transdisciplinary Perspective: Text, Archaeology, Culture, and Geoscience* (Cham: Springer, 2015), 17-38.

The details reflected in the archaeological record are 1) in the city of Avaris, the capital of the Hyksos administration of the Lower Kingdom, archaeologist Manfred Bietak has found signet rings with the inscription of the Hyksos king Yaqub-hor (Jacob). This Jacob and his sons who served in his administration may have served as inspiration for the biblical Jacob and 2) archaeologists have found grain silos all over northern Egypt for the storage of grain.

THE REDEMPTIVE ARC

4.4 Theodore Parker, *Ten Sermons of Religion* (London: Trubner & Co., 1879), 49.

"I do not pretend to understand the moral universe; the arc is a long one, my eye reaches but little ways; I cannot calculate the curve and complete the figure by the experience of sight; I can divine it by conscience. And from what I see I am sure it bends towards justice."

THE RIPPLE EFFECT

4.5 David W. Orme-Johnson, et al., "International Peace Project in the Middle East: The Effects of the Maharishi Technology of the Unified Field" in *The Journal of Conflict Resolution* 32 no. 4 (1988): 778.

The effects of prayer have been widely documented by psychologists and sociologists. David W. Orme-Johnson, a psychologist at Maharishi International University working in conjunction with John L. Davies at Harvard University, researched the effect of collective consciousness on real world events. In 1983, during the Lebanese civil war, Orme was able to document that the quality of life in Jerusalem, Lebanon and Israel was tangibly improved by the positive thinking of a collective of individuals committed to prayer. For the short period of time these community members joined as one to pray for relief from their oppression, violence and crime decreased. One logical reason for these results is that a normally divided and individualistic community separated by violence is now operating as a cohesive unit. Yet, there were gaps in the results that could not account for the decrease in violence overall, giving rise to the conclusion that the unaccounted factor was the influence of prayer on the community at large. In short, the conclusion of Orme's study is that prayer does indeed affect change in the world in dramatic ways.

THE IMPURITIES IN THE CLAY

4.6 Ira Glass and Brian Reed, "547: Cops See It Differently" on *This American Life*. Podcast audio, February 6th, 2015. https://www.thisamericanlife.org/radio-archives/episode/547/cops-see-it-differently-part-one

4.7 Expansion on the statement: "The raw material of humanity is shaped by so many genetic and environmental variables that God can only work with situations we have created for ourselves." I believe that when God created the universe, God set into motion an evolutionary process that would eventually produce us—sentient, conscious beings who can recognize God's existence. In this sense, the universe is one gigantic Petri dish full of possibility for consciousness. In the early stages of the evolutionary process (where we are presently), these conscious beings are more often a reflection of the evolutionary pressures that created them—selfish and focused on survival. However, since the fabric of the universe is infused with love and redemption, given enough time, all beings will trend towards the redemptive. In my opinion, we are best served by the understanding that God has created a universe in which love is designed to thrive. Therefore, if we choose to engage with that love, we will reap the benefits of our decisions.

INTERPRETATIVE INTERLUDE: WILL THE REAL JESUS PLEASE STAND UP?

A.1 Flavius Josephus, *The Antiquities of the Jews* (Brookfield: First Rate Publishers, 2013) Book 18, Section 4, Chapters 1-2.

A.2 Tibor Grull, "The Legendary Fate of Pontius Pilate," *Classica et Mediaevalia, Danish Journal of Philology and History* 61, no. 4 (2010): 151-54.

CHAPTER 5: BREAKING DOWN THE JESUS OF RELIGION

THE CHERRY TREE

5.1 Jonathan Fraser Light, "Longest Throws" in *The Cultural Encyclopedia of Baseball* (Jefferson: McFarland & Company Inc., 2005), 225.

5.2 Mason Locke Weems, *The Life of Washington the Great,* (Augusta: George P. Randolph, 1806), 8-9.

5.3 Mason Locke Weems to Mathew Carey, January 12, 1800, in Paul Leicester Ford, *Mason Locke Weems: His Works, His Ways: A Bibliography Left Unfinished*, 3 vols. (New York: Plimpton Press, 1929), 2: 8-9.

5.4 Raymond E. Brown, *An Introduction to the New Testament* (New York: Doubleday, 1997).

The list providing dates of the composition of the documents in the New Testament is primarily derived from Brown's book. Scholars determine dates of composition based on a number of different factors, the most important one being the events referred to in each document. We know from other historical sources when these events occurred. The order can also be determined by the authors' treatment of Jesus. The earlier the document, the less Jesus is considered divine. The later the document, the more Jesus is associated with God.

5.5 James D. G. Dunn, *Christology in the Making: A New Testament Inquiry into the Origins of the Doctrine of the Incarnation.*, 2nd *ed.* (Grand Rapids: Eerdman's Publishing Co., 1989), 98-128.

Conservative Christians will challenge my assertion by pointing out that Paul's letter to the church in Philippi contains a direct reference to Jesus having equality with God: "Let the same mind be in you that was in Christ Jesus, who, though he was in the form of God, did not regard equality with God as something to be exploited, but emptied himself, taking the form of a slave, being born in human likeness." *(Pp. 2:5-11).* I am in agreement with James D. G. Dunn that this text has been wrongly conflated with the Johannine tradition of Jesus being preexistent with God. I follow Dunn's argument that Paul's use of this hymn is consistent with his Adamic Christology found in Romans. In other words, Jesus was not born God *(Ga. 4:4),* but acquired divine attributes after his resurrection as a result of his glorification as the second Adam. Paul clearly believed Jesus was with God in heaven and would return to earth to establish God's kingdom and fully inaugurate his messiahship.

5.6 F. Brown, S. Driver, and C. Briggs *The Brown-Driver-Briggs Hebrew and English Lexicon* (Peabody: Hendrickson Publishers, Inc., 2001), 603.

5.7 Raymond E. Brown, *An Introduction to the New Testament* (New York: Doubleday, 1997), 766-67.

Even though the authorship is attributed to Peter, the man who walked the earth with Jesus, this is highly unlikely. It was very common during this period in history for individuals within a specific community to write letters as being from their leader, even if that leader had long since died. If you, as the writer, were steeped in that leader's teachings, then it was a sign of respect that you could write from that leader's perspective. The readers were under no illusion that Peter was the author. Using the name of the leader also gave the writing authority and was considered to be an extension of the author's thoughts. This letter was probably composed by one or more individuals associated with Peter's early churches.

THE LOOP

5.8   Mark P.O. Morford and Robert J. Lenardon, *Classical Mythology Sixth.*, 6th ed. (New York: Longman, 1999), 228-232.

5.9   Augustine, *Confessions,* trans. R. S. Pine-Coffin (New York: Penguin Books, 1961).
See 2.1, 2.2, 2.3, 3.1, 4.15, 6.16, 8.5, 10.34 for evidence of how Augustine keeps circling back to how his sexual impulses made him impure.

5.10 If you are interested in the subject of how Augustine's view of sex influenced the creation of his Doctrine of Original Sin, one of the best analyses is Stephen Greenblatt's book *The Rise and Fall of Adam and Eve* (New York: W. W. Norton & Company, 2017).

5.11 Matthew Cobb, *Generation: The Seventeenth Century Scientists Who Unlocked the Secrets of Sex and Growth* (London: Simon & Schuster, 2006), 202-203, 228-229.
This concept persisted into the 17th century. The first person to observe sperm under a microscope was Antonie van Leeuwenhoek in 1677. A student of Leeuwenhoek, Nicolaas Hartsoeker, believed that within the sperm was a tiny, but fully formed, human being, known as a Homunculus.

5.12 Elaine Pagels, *Adam, Eve, and the Serpent* (New York: First Vintage Editions, 1989) 105-126, 130-153.

THE FLAW IN THE DESIGN

5.13   F. Brown, S. Driver, and C. Briggs *The Brown-Driver-Briggs Hebrew and English Lexicon* (Peabody: Hendrickson Publishers, Inc., 2001), 9.

5.14   Ibid. 966. The Hebrew word שָׂטָן (satan) appears in the Old Testament in a number of different places. What most people don't realize is that the word *satan* in Hebrew was originally a verb that means to persecute, to be hostile towards or to accuse. The noun *satan* is derived from the verb and has two meanings: 1) adversary and 2) legal accuser. The verb predates the noun and there is only one instance of the noun Satan being paired with an angel in the Old Testament, found in the story of Job. This depiction was surely influenced by the cosmology of Zoroastrianism, which became intertwined with Judaism during the Babylonian Exile, well after the initial composition of Genesis. For more about this, read T. J. Wray and Gregory Mobley's *The Birth of Satan: Tracing the Devil's Biblical Roots* (New York: Palgrave Macmillan, 2005). Also, read Rivkah Schärf Kluger's *Satan in the Old Testament* (Evanston, IL: Northwestern University Press, 1967) for more information on Satan's evolution from a verb to a proper noun.

THE NEW ADAM

5.15   Bart D. Ehrman, *How Jesus Became God: The Exaltation of a Jewish Preacher from Galilee* (New York: HarperOne, 2014) 30-34.
I would recommend Ehrman's book as one of the best expositions on how the Christian perspective on Jesus evolved from a traditional Jewish messiah into God in the flesh. Ehrman covers all the angles that I cannot address in this book.

5.16   Nachum Amsel *The Jewish Encyclopedia of Moral and Ethical Issues* (Northvale, NJ: Jason Aronson Inc., 1994), 205-208.
For more context on the relationship between Jewish parents and their children before and after bar/bat mitzvah, read the

section entitled "The Difference in Sin Before and After *Bar Mitzvah*" on 207-208.

5.17 Friedrich Schleiermacher *The Christian Faith* Ed. H.R. MacKintosh and J.S. Stewart (Philadelphia: Fortress Press, 1976), 132.

The term *God consciousness* is not original to me, but comes from Schleiermacher. He defines God consciousness as the feeling of absolute dependence upon God: "The feeling of absolute dependence, accordingly, is not to be explained as an awareness of the world's existence, but only as an awareness of the existence of God, as the absolute undivided unity." My theology of Jesus is heavily grounded in Schleiermacher, who was influenced by the 2nd century theologian Irenaeus, Bishop of Lyon. Irenaeus' theory of recapitulation is the foundation from which I derived my perspective concerning Jesus' importance to our lives (for more on recapitulation see Notes on Chapter 10: Any Day Now).

5.18 Expansion on the statement: "Jesus is the first person to achieve a direct, fully formed connection with God." My reason for believing Jesus to be the first person to possess a fully formed God consciousness is based on two factors: 1) Jesus' teachings and characterization of God and 2) the characterization of individuals who have encountered God during Near-Death Experiences (NDEs) see Ed. Janice Holden, Bruce Greyson and Debbie James *The Handbook of Near-Death Experiences: Thirty Years of Investigation* (Santa Barbara, CA: Praeger Publishers, 2009), 18-27, 41-62. Jesus teaches his followers that God is a being of unconditional love. According to Jesus, there is nothing we can do that will separate us from God because God's love for humanity is unending. This characterization of God is unique among the religions of the world at the time. Many tribal religions portrayed the gods as angry, vengeful and judgmental. Even when a god was portrayed as loving, that love was often temporary and usually constrained by specific conditions. The fact that Jesus veers so dramatically from the normative religious traditions of his time tells me that there is something distinctive about the way he understands God, which leads me to the NDEs (see

The Handbook of Near-Death Experiences for the most complete compilation of NDE research to date). In our modern world, NDEs are more common thanks to improved medical technology that allows for resuscitation. What makes NDEs so compelling is that the experience has certain characteristics that tend to be similar regardless of the person's ethnic or cultural background. For those who enter into the heavenly realm (which represents only 10% of the people who have a NDE), many will interact with a powerful light, which is often referred to as a "Being of Light." This light is often interpreted by the person experiencing the NDE to be God. While in the presence of God, most people describe an intense feeling of unconditional love and acceptance unlike anything they have ever known in their lives. What's more, it's not just Christians having this experience. This description of unconditional love bridges cultural and religious affiliation. People from all over the world, even those who have never been exposed to Christianity report similar experiences. Therefore, given the direct parallels between Jesus' description of God and those who claim to have had an actual experience of God in the afterlife, I am forced to ask how Jesus came to his particular understanding of God? Since I do not adhere to an incarnational theology, I consider it feasible that Jesus gained his perspective from his God consciousness. My assertion that Jesus' God consciousness is fully formed is the result of Jesus describing God in such perfect parallel detail with NDEs. I don't claim to know how Jesus acquired this fully formed God consciousness, but it seems to have occurred following his baptism.

CHAPTER 6: FINDING OUR WAY BACK TO EDEN

THE FORMULA

6.1   For more on the subject of Firestone and their role in the U.S. automobile markets, read Quentin R. Skrabec, Jr.'s book *Rubber: An American Industrial History* (Jefferson, NC: McFarland & Company, Inc., 2014).

6.2 Donald N. Sull, "The Dynamics of Standing Still: Firestone Tire & Rubber and the Radical Revolution," *Business History Review* 73, no. 3 (Autumn 1999): 430.

6.3 Vadim Erlikman, *Loss of Population in the 20th Century* (Moscow: Russian Panorama, 2004), 23-35.

BATHED IN BLOOD

6.4 Frederick William Danker, *The Concise Greek-English Lexicon of the New Testament* (Chicago: University of Chicago Press, 2009), 261.

6.5 Ibid. 19. Reference for the word *hamaratia* being translated as *mistakes*.

6.6 Sidney Homer, *A History of Interest Rates* (New Brunswick: Rutgers University Press, 1963), 56-63.
The legal limit for interest on debt in the Roman Empire was generally capped at 12%. However, given that peasants had very little coinage at their disposal, they often bartered for loans with grain. The percentage of interest on grain loans could be as high as 50%.

6.7 Maria-Zoe Petropoulou, *Animal Sacrifice in Ancient Greek Religion, Judaism, and Christianity, 100 BC-AD 200* (New York: Oxford University Press, 2008), 161-163.

6.8 Ed. S. Hensrickx, R.F. Friedman, K.M. Cialowicz and M. Chlodnicki. *Egypt At Its Origins: Studies in Memory of Barbara Adams: Proceedings of the International Conference "Origin of the State. Predynastic and Early Dynastic Egypt", Krakow, 28th August -1st September 2002.* Belgium: Peeters Publishers & Department of Oriental Studies, 2004, 733-37. Diane Victoria Flores discusses how excavations of the oldest Egyptian burial sites from the Badari culture of Upper Egypt (4400-4000 BCE) contained animal remains. One grave contained sheep and goats and another contained gazelles that were placed at the feet of several human graves. These animals were killed in a sacrificial manner, a practice that would become normalized over the next several thousand years.

CHAPTER 7:
RETHINKING HEAVEN, HELL AND THE AFTERLIFE

THE GOLDEN TICKET

7.1 Isidore Singer and Cyrus Adler, *The Jewish Encyclopedia: A Descriptive Record of the History, Religion, Literature, and Customs of the Jewish People from the Earliest Times to the Present Day, Vol. 5* (London: Funk and Wagnalls Company, 1901), 582.

7.2 Ibid. 583.

7.3 Isidore Singer and Cyrus Adler, *The Jewish Encyclopedia: A Descriptive Record of the History, Religion, Literature, and Customs of the Jewish People from the Earliest Times to the Present Day, Vol. 11* (London: Funk and Wagnalls Company, 1901), 282-83.

IT'S ELECTION TIME!

7.4 Expansion on the statement: "…the first born male inherited the father's legacy and a double portion of everything the father owned." The double portion concept comes from Deuteronomy 21:17 and means that the firstborn son receives double what his brother(s) would receive. For instance, if a father has two sons, the firstborn receives two-thirds of the estate and the second son receives the remaining third. If the father has three sons, the first born receives half, while the next two sons receive a quarter of the estate.

7.5 John Calvin, *Institutes of the Christian Religion*, Trans. Henry Beveridge (Grand Rapids: W. B. Eerdmans Publishing Co., 1998), III xxi. 5.
"By predestination we mean the eternal decree of God by which…All are not created on equal terms, but some are preordained to eternal life, others to eternal damnation; and, accordingly, as each has been created for one or the other of these ends, we say that he has been predestined to life or death."

7.6 Origen, *On First Principles*, trans. George William Butterworth (London: SPCK Publishing, 1936), 1.8.4l; 2.1; 2.3; 3.1.

CHAPTER 8: BUILDING UP THE JESUS OF HISTORY

THE BLACK SWAN

8.1   Juvenal, *Satires of Juvenal*, Trans. by Thomas B. Lindsay (New York: American Book Company, 1890), Book I.
Black swans are native to Australia, so when the British started using Australia as a penal colony and discovered black swans, the phrase fell out of use.

8.2   Nassim Nicholas Taleb, *The Black Swan: The Impact of the Highly Improbable* (New York: Random House, 2007), xxii-xxiv.

8.3   Flavius Josephus, *The Wars of the Jews* (Charlotte: Information Age Publishing, 2009), Book 2, Chapter 9, Section 5.
In this section, Josephus lists the incomes of Galilee, Perea and other regions. When Josephus describes Galilee from his time serving as a military commander, he never mentions Nazareth. He clearly knew nothing about Nazareth even though it was located a mere five miles from Sepphoris, the largest city in the region.

8.4   For more information on the conditions of Nazareth during Jesus' lifetime see Scott Korb's *Life in Year One: What the World Was Like in First Century Palestine* (New York: Riverhead, 2011).

IT'S THE ECONOMY, STUPID!

8.5   Richard L. Niswonger, *New Testament History* (Grand Rapids: Zondervan Publishing, 1992), 121-24.
This discrepancy is the reason why scholars began using B.C.E. (Before the Common Era) and C.E. (Common Era) in lieu of B.C. (Before Christ) and A.D. (anno domini—the year of our Lord). It makes no sense to say that Jesus was born in 4 B.C. or 4 years before Christ.

8.6   Sidney Homer, *A History of Interest Rates* (New Brunswick: Rutgers University Press, 1963), 48.

8.7 David A. Fiensy and Ralph K. Hawkins, *The Galilean Economy in the Time of Jesus* (Atlanta: Society of Biblical Literature, 2013) 20.

"Our historical survey demonstrates that when the Jewish leaders of Galilee began to rule (with the exception of Herod the Great) they made significant financial investments in the region. These building projects provided employment, stimulated trade, and in general raised the level of prosperity."

8.8 Ibid. 171. David Fiensy notes that although Sepphoris and Tiberias housed the wealthiest citizens of Galilee, based on the excavations of the homes in these cities, "the extreme distance between the elites and the lower class, found elsewhere in the Roman Empire and evidently in Judea, was diminished in Galilee."

8.9 Sidney Homer, *A History of Interest Rates* (New Brunswick: Rutgers University Press, 1963), 48.

8.10 David A. Fiensy and Ralph K. Hawkins, *The Galilean Economy in the Time of Jesus* (Atlanta: Society of Biblical Literature, 2013), 168-69.

Judea, having become an official Roman territory in 6 C.E. felt the hit of this credit crisis early causing them to appeal to Tiberius for tax relief in 17 C.E. "Thus, the direct taxation from Rome seems to have contributed to a lower standard of living," which would have had a peripheral impact on the Galilean economy.

8.11 Sidney Homer, *A History of Interest Rates* (New Brunswick: Rutgers University Press, 1963), 48-51, 54.

What should be noted is that Egypt was considered a province of the Roman Empire. Because of the role Egypt played in the civil war, Augustus sought to make them pay by isolating their economy with fiat currency. Therefore, the Egyptian economy did not experience the same level of stabilization as the rest of the empire in the early years of Augustus' reign, which impacted Judea (and by extension, Galilee) when the credit crisis came to a head. The wealthy would survive, but peasants who had always struggled, would find themselves facing diminishing returns where interest rates could be as high as 50% on grain loans. This may be a a reason to why Jesus talks extensively about issues surrounding financial debts in the gospels.

8.12 David A. Fiensy and Ralph K. Hawkins, *The Galilean Economy in the Time of Jesus* (Atlanta: Society of Biblical Literature, 2013), 165-66, 171-72.
David Fiensy argues that the lower Galilean economy was still "young" at the time of Jesus' ministry. Unlike Judea, where the gap between the wealthy and the poor was wider, Galilee "had not yet developed into an oppressive society, but was perhaps moving in that direction." Thus, when I state that the credit crisis was causing peasants to forfeit their land, this was not ubiquitous. Clearly, this was an issue for the peasants drawn to Jesus' movement, but not yet at the level of what we see in 66 C.E. when the Sicarii burned the debt records in Jerusalem.

8.13 Sidney Homer, *A History of Interest Rates* (New Brunswick: Rutgers University Press, 1963), 48.
The credit crisis would be alleviated shortly after Jesus' death in 33 C.E. with the heavy distribution of coinage and no interest loans.

8.14 David A. Fiensy and Ralph K. Hawkins, *The Galilean Economy in the Time of Jesus* (Atlanta: Society of Biblical Literature, 2013), 92-95.
Contrary to what has been conveyed by Jonathan L. Reed, Dominic Crossan and other New Testament scholars, the archaeological record of Capernaum from the first century does not indicate that most of the villagers were living in abject poverty. In fact, excavations have proven the opposite to be the case. Stanisalo Loffreda, who is responsible for the excavation of numerous sites at ancient Capernaum, has found an abundance of early fine glass ware. Indeed, so much has been found at various locations around Capernaum that the village seems to have been home to people from all levels of economic strata. Such a quantity of fine ware would not be present in the archaeological record if everyone in Capernaum was living at subsistence level.

8.15 K.C. Hanson, "The Galilean Fishing Economy and the Jesus Tradition," *Biblical Theology Bulletin* 27 (1997): 99-111. Hanson makes clear the political reality that Herod the Great and his son, Herod Antipas, viewed the Lake of Galilee as a royal monopoly. Fishing was a highly regulated industry in which fishermen were not allowed to fish the lake without fishing contracts or leases that specified exactly how many fish they were allowed to catch at any given time. The catch of a fishing cooperative would be counted by a broker tax collector with any surplus being immediately seized. Furthermore, the terms of these contracts or leases could be adjusted for the benefit of the royal family depending on the economic circumstances. One can imagine how, as the credit crisis of the 20s started to accelerate, the amount of fish these fishing cooperatives were allowed to retain for sale at market slowed to a trickle.

ONLY THE FACTS, MA'AM

8.16 Flavius Josephus, *The Antiquities of the Jews* (Brookfield: First Rate Publishers, 2013), Book 17, Chapter 10, Section 5.

8.17 Flavius Josephus, *The Wars of the Jews* (Charlotte: Information Age Publishing, 2009), Book 2, Chapter 5, Section 1.

8.18 Frederick William Danker, *The Concise Greek-English Lexicon of the New Testament* (Chicago: University of Chicago Press, 2009), 349.

8.19 Max Alpine, *Was Jesus Ever a Disciple of John? A Historical Study* (Edinburgh: University of Edinburgh Publishing, 2011), 40-41. https://www.era.lib.ed.ac.uk/bitstream/handle/1842/5467/Aplin2011.pdf;sequence=2

8.20 Frederick William Danker, *The Concise Greek-English Lexicon of the New Testament* (Chicago: University of Chicago Press, 2009), 67.

8.21 David A. Fiensy and Ralph K. Hawkins, *The Galilean Economy in the Time of Jesus* (Atlanta: Society of Biblical Literature, 2013), 32.

8.22 For more on the Mandaeans see Jorunn Jacobsen Buckley's book *The Mandaeans: Ancient Texts and Modern People* (Oxford: Oxford University Press, 2002).

8.23 Flavius Josephus, *The Antiquities of the Jews* (Brookfield: First Rate Publishers, 2013), Book 18, Chapter 5, Sections 1-4.

8.24 Ibid. Book 18, Chapter 3, Section 3; Book 20, Chapter 9, Section 1.

For a good overview of the history of the controversy surrounding these two passages, see Alice Whealey's, *Josephus on Jesus: The Testimonium Flavianum Controversy from Late Antiquity to Modern Times,* (New York: Peter Lang Publishing, 2003). Book 18 contains the larger of the two passages, better known as the "Testimonium Flavianum", which is widely considered by scholars to be a later Christian insertion. Since the first person to reference the Testimonium was the church historian Eusebius in his works Demonstratio Evangelica, Theophania, and Historia Ecclesiastica, some scholars have speculated that Eusebius may be the interpolator. The second reference is found in Book 20 where Josephus describes James, Jesus' brother, being executed by the high priest Ananus. Although most scholars believe this particular passage is original to Josephus, there are a handful of scholars who speculate that the text may have been altered. One of the more compelling arguments comes from Richard Carrier in his article "Origen, Eusebius, and the Accidental Interpolation in Josephus, *Jewish Antiquities* 20.200." *Journal of Early Christian Studies* 20, no. 4 (2012): 489-514. Carrier believes that Josephus was referring to a different James, possibly the brother of the Jewish high priest Jesus ben Damneus. Carrier asserts that the insertion of Jesus as the "Christ" was the result of "an accidental interpolation or scribal emendation" at a later time.

TOPSY-TURVY

8.25 For more on the scholarly views concerning the length of Jesus' ministry see George Ogg's *The Chronology of the Public Ministry of Jesus* (Cambridge: Cambridge University Press, 1940).

8.26 Expansion on the statement: "The concept of God's kingdom is an amalgamation of a lot of different ideas from various religious traditions. The basis for the concept begins in Zoroastrianism…" Zoroastrianism is a monotheistic faith founded in ancient Iran by the prophet Zoroaster around the early 2nd millennium B.C.E. Zoroaster was one of the earliest monotheists. Scholars speculate that the Jews inherited their cosmology (a hierarchy of spiritual beings) and eschatology (thinking about the end of the world) from the Persians, whose leader, King Cyrus II, adhered to Zoroastrianism. Within Zoroastrianism are the seeds of all the language that would become important in Christianity—messiah, God's kingdom, angels, demons, etc. For a cursory introduction to Zoroastrianism, read Jenny Rose's *Zoroastrianism: An Introduction* (London: I.B. Tauris, 2010). If you desire a more thorough review of Zoroastrianism, see Mary Boyce's three volume opus *A History of Zoroastrianism* (Leiden: Brill; Repr. 1996).

8.27 Expansion on the statement: "For instance, if you had a child with a physical or mental handicap, the Jews believed that such maladies were the result of God punishing your family for their sins." It should be noted that in Makkot (24a) of the Babylonian Talmud there are four cases where the prophets overruled a law dictated by Moses in the Torah. The third case is the decree that God will punish children for the sins of the parents *(Ex. 20:5, 34:6; Dt. 5:9)*. This decree was revoked by the prophet Ezekiel *(Ez. 18:4)*. Thus, the Talmud suggests that this belief was no longer seen as valid among the Jewish community. However, in practice, this belief persisted well into the first century. This can be seen in writings of Rabbi Akiva (50-137 C.E.) when he speaks concerning the Jewish views on poverty. Akiva affirms that poverty is punishment from God for sins committed (Bava Batra 10a). That said, Akiva also affirms the responsibility of a Jew to serve those in poverty regardless of how they arrived there. Indeed, as Judaism evolves beyond the first century C.E., the notion that poverty is punishment for sin will be contradicted by other rabbinical sources in favor of the belief that poverty is often a result of chance, environment and personal choices rather than God.

For more on this, read chapters 1 and 4 of Jill Jacobs *There Shall Be No Needy: Pursuing Social Justice Through Jewish Law and Tradition* (Woodstock, Vermont: Jewish Lights Publishing, 2009).

8.28 Reza Aslan, *Zealot: The Life and Times of Jesus of Nazareth* (New York: Random House, 2013), 103-114.

JESUS' MASTER PLAN

8.29 For more on the Jewish Temple system, read S. Safrai and M. Stern, ed., *The Jewish People in the First Century: Historical Geography, Political History, Social, Cultural and Religious Life and Institutions, Vol. 2* (Philadelphia: Fortress Press 1987) 865-907, and the essays found in John Day, ed., *Temple and Worship in Biblical Israel* (New York: T&T Clark, 2005).

8.30 Hersh Goldwurm, *History of the Jewish People: The Second Temple Era* (New York: Mesorah Publications Ltd., 2003), 150.

8.31 Flavius Josephus, *The Wars of the Jews* (Charlotte: Information Age Publishing, 2009), Book 2, Chapter 9, Section 2-4.

CHAPTER 9: THE RESURRECTION

A SHADOW OF A DOUBT

9.1 "64% Believe Jesus Christ Rose From the Dead," The Rasmussen Report, last modified March 29, 2013, http://www.rasmussenreports.com/public_content/lifestyle/holidays/march_2013/64_believe_jesus_christ_rose_from_the_dead

NOT ALL RESURRECTION ACCOUNTS ARE CREATED EQUAL

9.2 Bart D. Ehrman *How Jesus Became God: The Exaltation of a Jewish Preacher from Galilee* (New York: HarperOne, 2014), 176-204.
Conservative Christians will disagree with my assertion that Paul witnessed Jesus' resurrection as a vision. Their argument

is primarily derived from chapter 15 of 1 Corinthians where Paul explicitly discusses the bodily resurrection of Jesus. Indeed, Paul goes into great detail about what our resurrected bodies will look like *(1 Co. 15:35-58)* and he writes the description in such a way that one assumes the details come directly from his encounter with Jesus. I would not dispute that when Paul encountered the resurrected Jesus, Paul observed a Jesus with physical, bodily features. However, as Ehrman suggests, even though Paul describes Jesus as possessing a spiritual body, what Paul experienced was akin to what we find in other well documented religious visions.

9.3 Raymond E. Brown, *An Introduction to the New Testament* (New York: Doubleday, 1997), 148-149.
Later editors did not like that Mark excluded an encounter with the resurrected Jesus, so two separate people added two different endings to Mark's gospel. However, we know from the earliest copies of Mark that those endings are not original to his gospel.

9.4 Flavius Josephus, *The Wars of the Jews*, Book 5, Chapter 1.

9.5 Flavius Josephus, *The Wars of the Jews*, Book 5, Chapter 12.

9.6 For more on Jewish burial practices, particularly those connected with bone collection in ossuaries read Eric M. Myers Jewish Ossuaries: Reburial and Rebirth (Rome: Biblical Institute Press, 1971).

9.7 Expansion on the statement: "John's gospel is partially written from a Gnostic Christian perspective." Rudolf Bultmann is the one who first posited the idea that John's gospel was influenced by Gnosticism in *The Gospel of John: A Commentary* (Eugene, OR: Wipf & Stock Publishers, 1971). Although scholars like Raymond E. Brown believe that Bultmann greatly overstates the degree to which John was a "gnostic" gospel, it is clear that John's gospel contains some proto-gnostic elements. This is supported by the fact that Irenaeus had to spend copious amounts of time in Book III of *Against the Heresies* defending John from being co-opted by Gnostic Christians, who found John's gospel had enough in common with their own view of Jesus that they wanted to claim it as a Gnostic scripture.

This is not to say, however, that John's gospel is even close to the fully developed Christian Gnosticism of the 2nd century, which diverged significantly from orthodox Christianity. If it had been, Irenaeus would not have been able to save John from becoming part of the New Testament apocrypha. For a good translation of *Against the Heresies* read Alexander Roberts *Saint Irenaeus of Lyons: Against Heresies* (Ex Fontibus Company, 2015).

9.8 Frederick William Danker, *The Concise Greek-English Lexicon of the New Testament* (Chicago: University of Chicago Press, 2009), 80.

9.9 Raymond E. Brown, *An Introduction to the New Testament* (New York: Doubleday, 1997), 360.
The idea that Jesus is purely spirit in this particular passage is often rejected because the reason for Jesus' appearance is directly related to Thomas' desire to place his hand in the physical wounds Jesus incurred from his crucifixion. However, even though Jesus appears to Thomas and offers him the opportunity to place his hands in the wounds, the text never describes Thomas as actually touching Jesus. Brown argues that "[t]o have done so would probably have signified that Thomas' disbelief remained." I would argue that this scene is intentionally ambiguous in terms of whether or not Jesus' resurrected form is strictly bodily. Three elements lead me to this conclusion: 1) the fact that Jesus is portrayed as walking through walls; 2) Thomas not taking advantage of the opportunity to actually touch Jesus; and 3) the later addition of Chapter 21 portraying Jesus consuming calories to confirm Jesus' resurrection was bodily (which bears a striking resemblance to the affirmation found in *Lk. 24:41-43*). Together these factors support a proto-gnostic or even Docetic view of Jesus where Jesus' spirit gave the appearance of being human by maintaining the wounds so there could be no confusion as to who he was or the wisdom he was there to impart.

9.10 Raymond E. Brown, *An Introduction to the New Testament* (New York: Doubleday, 1997), 366-368.

THE FLY IN THE OINTMENT

9.11 Reza Aslan, *Zealot: The Life and Times of Jesus of Nazareth* (New York: Random House, 2013), 154-155.

9.12 Katharina Galor, *Finding Jerusalem: Archaeology Between Science and Ideology* (Oakland, CA: University of California Press, 2017), 136-139.

Although no one actually knows where Jesus was crucified, one of the popular theories among modern Protestants is what has become known as Skull Hill, a rock face near the Garden Tomb that looks like a skull. This theory became popularized in 1883 by General Charles George Gordon after his visit to Jerusalem. Although the depressions of the rock face resemble a skull, Galor argues that the popularity of the site has more to do with being a Protestant alternative to the very Catholic site of the Church of Holy Sepulchre. Furthermore, Gordon made his assertion based on no archeological or scientific evidence that crucifixions were performed on the site. His assertion was based entirely on the fact that the rock face looked like a skull. Galor states that "the archeological evidence establishes unequivocally that area had not been used as a burial ground at the time of Jesus' death." If this rock face had been the location of Roman executions, then archeologists would have found some bone evidence from these executions. None exists and, therefore, Skull Hill should not be considered as a site for Jesus' execution.

9.13 Bart D. Ehrman, *How Jesus Became God: The Exaltation of a Jewish Preacher from Galilee* (New York: HarperOne, 2014), 156-164.

ANY DAY NOW

9.14 Guy G. Stroumsa, *The End of Sacrifice: Religious Transformations in Late Antiquity,* trans. Susan Emanuel (Chicago: Chicago University Press, 2009), 56-83.

This argument was not very successful at convincing the Jewish people of the need for Jesus. Prior to its destruction, the Jerusalem Temple was falling out of favor with the Jewish people as a means for obtaining forgiveness. The expense of the sacrifice on top of the fact that many Jews saw the Temple as corrupt led several Jewish sects to boycott the Temple. Indeed, many of the Pharisaic rabbis began promoting the idea that Jews could be forgiven by God without the need for sacrifice prior to the destruction of the Temple. Therefore, the destruction of the Temple only concretized a belief that was already present in parts of the Jewish populace.

9.15 Alexander Roberts, *Saint Irenaeus of Lyons: Against Heresies* (Ex Fontibus Company, 2015), 332-355, 419-30, 496-99. The church father Irenaeus (130-202 C.E.) was the first person to attempt to develop a consistent theology of Jesus' life. Interestingly, even though Irenaeus wrote his work *Against the Heresies* more than 100 years after the death of Jesus and Paul, he didn't know what Jesus' death on the cross meant. This in spite of the fact that he had read Paul's letters and knew Paul's theology. Instead, Irenaeus developed an atonement theory called recapitulation that suggests the reason why Jesus renders us forgiven by God is because Jesus relived every stage of Adam's life perfectly. For Irenaeus, Jesus' death on the cross was not a necessary part of God's requirement for forgiveness. This tells us that Paul's understanding of Jesus' death forgiving sins was not ubiquitous among early Christians.

9.16 Expansion on the statement: "Indeed, it seems that the earliest Christians were not entirely certain what Jesus' death on the cross meant for them." If you return to the timeline for the New Testament, you will see that the first gospel, Mark, was written around the same time as the destruction of the Temple in 70 C.E. Interestingly, if you scour Mark's gospel there is only one reference in Chapter 2 to Jesus' ability to forgive sins. Beyond that one reference, the idea is never mentioned throughout the entire gospel. The reason this new strategy for recruiting followers of Jesus is not found in Mark's gospel is because Christians had not yet fully developed the argument that one needs to believe in Jesus for their sins to be forgiven. Some scholars, like Hyam Maccoby in his book *The Mythmaker: Paul and the Invention of Christianity* (New York: Harper Collins, 1987), speculate that the idea of Jesus dying for our sins originated with Paul, since this concept is clearly present in Paul's letters (Galatians, 1 Corinthians, Romans), but had not yet found wide use in the larger church. However, by the time Matthew, Luke and John write their gospels, Paul's theology had become more dominant in the church, causing this idea to become more prevalent in Christian thinking.

CHAPTER 10: THE TEACHINGS OF JESUS

ALL YOU NEED IS LOVE

10.1 Louise Story, "Anywhere the Eye Can See, It's Likely to See an Ad" in *The New York Times,* last modified January 15, 2007, https://www.nytimes.com/2007/01/15/business/media/15everywhere.html?pagewanted=all&_r=0
"Yankelovich, a market research firm, estimates that a person living in a city 30 years ago saw up to 2,000 ad messages a day, compared with up to 5,000 today."

WINNING BY LOSING

10.2 Expansion on the statement: "If God's being is truly one of love, then I do not believe that God would desire for human beings to suffer." Given the fact that natural disasters, disease and cancer are a byproduct of living in the natural world, one might conclude that God *does* want us to suffer because God is responsible for the creation of the physical universe. Since God is responsible for the way the universe functions, doesn't that point to the reality that God desires the suffering that results from the natural phenomena of life? For instance, the process of evolution can result in a great deal of suffering for organisms that cannot adapt to a changing environment. If God is so against suffering, why not allow life to develop via a less abrasive process? In my opinion, the answer to this question is found in the mystery of consciousness. The universe can certainly be a very hostile place for life. Thankfully, the organisms that survive in the most extreme environments (like bacteria) have no conscious feelings of pain. Therefore, if our planet is an example of what happens in other parts of the universe, more complex life only tends to emerge when the planetary conditions are safer and more conducive to conscious life. Human consciousness emerged when the planetary environment had achieved an equilibrium with a stable atmosphere and normalized temperatures. Interestingly, even though consciousness makes us aware of our suffering, our consciousness also provides us with the ability to take steps to alleviate our suffering (e.g. medicine, food production, environmental controls). Thus, even though God brings about life through a process that can be brutal, God shields most organisms from an understanding of that reality until the circumstances are more favorable to their survival. In this way, when an organism does evolve the ability to be aware of its suffering, it can do something about it. This is why I believe God does not want us to unduly suffer from the natural forces that created us.

THE RESURRECTED LIFE

10.3 Expansion on the statement: "In this way, there was not a single moment of transformation where he was changed from a bad person to a good person." Although modern conservative Christianity places a heavy emphasis on the moment of conversion, this is not the norm for the vast majority of Christians throughout history. Many conservatives point to Paul's conversion in Acts 9:1-9 as the primary example of what a conversion should be—sudden and dramatic where one's whole character is transformed. Interestingly, Paul's own account of his conversion in Galatians 1:11-17 is nothing like what we find in Luke's Acts. It would seem that Paul himself may have come to his belief in Jesus over a long period of time.

THE KINGDOM OF GOD IS AT HAND

10.4 For more on the relationship between Suzanne Massie and Ronald Reagan see Massie's book *Trust but Verify: Reagan, Russia and Me* (Blue Hill, Maine: Hearttree Press, 2013).

CONCLUSION: THE NEW GOSPEL

B.1 "America's Changing Religious Landscape," Pew Research Center: Religious and Public Life, last modified May 12, 2015, http://www.pewforum.org/2015/05/12/americas-changing-religious-landscape/

B.2 Ernst Jenni and Claus Westermann, *Theological Lexicon of the Old Testament*, Vol. 2 and 3, trans. Mark E. Biddle (Peabody: Hendrickson Publishers, 1997), 852-862 and 1422-1424.

TOPICAL INDEX

conservative Christians   *xiii-xv, 5, 26, 108, 123, 131, 143, 156, 211, 239*
creation myths   *31-33*
crucifixion, general references to   *167, 170, 193-195, 220*

D

David, king   *21, 23, 172*
debts (financial and sin)   *123, 128-130, 164, 176,*
denial of self   *153, 220-222*
denominations (of Christianity)   *11, 108, 189, 208*
diplomacy   *228-230*
doctrine
  Original Sin   *105-107, 119, 235*
  Predestination   *150-153*
dojo   *225-226*

E

Earth, age of   *xviii*
Easter   *185-186*
elect, the   *150-152*
Elijah   *101, 148, 181*
Emperor, Roman
  Augustus   *162*
  Tiberius   *163*
Enoch   *148*
Epic of Atrahasis   *32*
Epic of Gilgamesh   *32*
Esau   *150-151*
Eve   *105-106, 109-114, 119*
evil inclination   *36-38*
evolution   *xviii, 83, 109, 116, 233*
execution   *74, 85, 93, 100-101, 166, 170, 177-178, 181, 185-186, 194-195, 199, 216*

F

Firestone, Harvey Samuel   *121, 123*
Firestone Tire and Rubber Company   *121-123*
fisherman   *164-165*
flood, the   *21, 31-36, 38*

Flynn, Ed *81*
Ford, Henry *121*
Fredericksburg, Virginia *21, 97*
free will *37, 58-62, 75, 79, 117, 180, 238*

G

Galilee *28, 160, 162, 164-166, 168-170, 183*
Gandhi *78*
Gehenna *145-147, 149, 156*
Gentile *113, 154, 191, 199-200*
gluttony *36*
Gnostic Christianity *191-193, 199*
God consciousness *109, 116, 119, 171, 180, 209, 218, 220, 225-226, 238-239*
gods
  Ea *32*
  Enki *32*
  Enlil *32*
  Mami *32*
Gorbachev, Mikhail *230*
Golgotha *195*
Gorbous, Glenn *98*
gospels, the
  names not original *25-26*
  accuracy of the oral tradition *27-30*
Greatest Commandment, the *208-215*
Greek language *24, 36, 51, 109, 128-129, 145, 159, 169, 179, 191*
Greeks, the *48-49, 64, 191-192, 194, 217*

H

heaven *xviii, xix, 6, 8, 68, 76, 101, 123-125, 128, 132, 136, 143-147, 148-154, 156, 171, 188, 197-198, 200, 202, 205, 222, 239*
Hebrew language *36-38, 61, 65, 100, 109, 179, 208, 239-240*
Hebrews, the *49-50, 61-62, 68, 198, 230*
hell *xiii, xiv, xviii, 6, 11, 68, 107, 124-125, 132, 136, 139, 143-147, 149-153, 155-156, 221, 235*
Herod Antipas *162, 165, 168, 170-171*
heroin *37*
Hindu *4, 145*

holy   *49, 61-62, 64*
Holy Spirit   *107, 200-203, 205*

Jews *15-16, 57, 100-101, 109, 114, 125, 130-131, 133, 147-149, 154, 160-162, 164-165, 172-174, 179, 188-189, 191, 198-200, 217, 238*

John, Gospel of *5, 15-17, 25, 99, 102, 160-161, 186, 191-192, 201*

John the Baptist *94, 166, 169-171, 183*

Joseph *63, 65-70, 73-74, 179*

Josephus, Flavius *170*

Judaism *7, 16-17, 24, 62, 95, 110, 113-115, 125, 147, 169, 177, 190-191, 201*

Judas
    the Galilean *167*
    the brother of Jesus *102*
    the disciple of Jesus *179-180*

justice *71, 73-75, 81, 87, 135-136, 150*

Juvenal *158*

K

King, Jr., Martin Luther *71-72, 78*

kingdom of God *27, 79, 92, 101, 114, 129-130, 148-149, 152, 154, 156, 166, 169, 171-174, 177-178, 181-183, 196-197, 200-205, 225-227, 230-236, 239*

kingdom thinking *231-232, 234, 236*

Klu Klux Klan *71-74*

L

Lake of Galilee *162-165, 167*

Lanza, Adam *43-46*

Leo X, Pope *9*

literalism *5, 25*

loans *129*

Lord *100-101, 114, 124*

Lord's Prayer *128-129*

love
    of enemy *78, 224-225, 227*
    of God *208-211, 214-215*
    of neighbor *78, 208, 211-215, 232, 236*
    of self *208, 211-215*

Luke, Gospel of *25, 27, 95, 99, 107, 128-129, 181, 186, 188, 191, 193-194, 200, 203, 205*

lust   *36, 105, 133*
Luther, Martin   *6-12, 18, 20*

M

Mandaeans   *170*
Mark, Gospel of   *25-27, 29-30, 93-95, 99, 102, 171, 179, 181,*
   188, 194, 201
Massie, Suzanne   *229-230*
Matthew, Gospel of   *25, 27, 78, 99-100, 102, 107, 127-129, 181,*
   186, 188, 191, 193-194, 202-203, 205, 224
McKinstry, Carolyn   *73*
McNair, Denise   *72-73*
Mediterranean Sea   *33-34*
messiah   *16, 26, 100-102, 114, 154, 161, 165, 170-171, 174, 177,*
   181-183, 189, 193-194, 197-203, 216
Michelin   *122-123*
Milwaukee Police Department   *81-82*
miracle   *53-54, 57, 238*
monks
   Augustinian   *7-8*
   Benedictine   *78, 222-224*
Mueller, Kayla   *52-53, 55-56, 63, 85, 219*
mythology   *xix, 12, 103-104, 114, 147, 238*

N

Nathaniel   *161*
Narcissus   *103-105*
Nazareth   *102, 160-162, 166, 168, 174, 183, 195*
Noah   *21-23, 30-31, 35-40, 67*

O

omnibenevolent   *48-49, 63-64*
omnipotent   *48-49, 57-58, 62, 64*
omnipresent   *48-49, 51, 64*
omniscient   *48-49, 64, 75*
oral tradition   *28-30, 35, 40, 181*
Origen   *154*
Oxford University   *78, 157, 222*

P

Q

R

T

U

V

W

Y

Z

BIBLE VERSES MENTIONED

OLD TESTAMENT

GENESIS (GN.)
Gn. 1   *50*
Gn. 1:26   *45*
Gn. 2:7   *109*
Gn. 3:5   *111*
Gn. 4:14   *110*
Gn. 6:5   *36*
Gn. 6:5-8   *31*
Gn. 15:18-21   *154*
Gn. 17:1-8   *154*
Gn. 24:35   *173*
Gn. 25-27   *150*
Gn. 26:12-13   *173*
Gn. 32:13-15   *173*
Gn. 37   *65*
Gn. 37:25-28   *179*
Gn. 37:35   *147*
Gn. 39-50   *65*
Gn. 50:19-20   *68*

EXODUS (EX.)
Ex. 3:13-14   *50*
Ex. 20:5   *267*
Ex. 34:6   *267*

LEVITICUS (LV.)
Lv. 4:27-31   *130*
Lv. 19:8   *208, 211-212*

NUMBERS (NU.)
Nu. 19:1-9   *169*

DEUTERONOMY (DT.)
Dt. 5:9   *267*
Dt. 6:4-5   *208*
Dt. 6:7   *62*
Dt. 21:17   *261*

2 SAMUEL (2 SA.)
2 Sa. 12:13-14   *172*

1 CHRONICLES (1 CH.)
1 Ch. 20:1   *230*

JOB (JB.)
Jb. 1:1-8   *173*

PSALMS (PS.)
Ps. 6:5   *147*
Ps. 30:3   *147*
Ps. 88:3   *147*
Ps. 139:8   *147*
Ps. 33:6-9   *50*
Ps. 91:11-12   *180*

PROVERBS (PR.)
Pr. 8:22-36   *50*

ECCLESIASTES (EC.)
Ec. 3:19-22   *147*
Ec. 9:5   *147*

ISAIAH (IS.)
Is. 11:1-8   *172*
Is. 14:9   *147*
Is. 45:6-7   *61*
Is. 58:6-11   *172*
Is. 65:17-25   *172*

JEREMIAH (JE.)
Je. 18:6   *80*

EZEKIEL (EZ.)
Ez. 18:4   *267*

MICAH (MC.)
Mc. 4:1-3   *172*

MALACHI (ML.)
Ml. 1:2-3   *150*

NEW TESTAMENT

MATTHEW (MT.)

Mt. 1:18-25 *102*

Mt. 5-7 *224*

Mt. 5:17, 19 *128*

Mt. 5:27-28 *133*

Mt. 5:43-44 *78*

Mt. 6:9-23 *128*

Mt. 6:24 *169, 176*

Mt. 12:13-14 *177*

Mt. 13:50 *146*

Mt. 16:28 *200*

Mt. 18:7 *112*

Mt. 21:22 *54*

Mt. 25:34-40 *152*

Mt. 25:35-36, 40 *203*

Mt. 26:29 *178*

Mt. 26:52-53 *181*

Mt. 27:47-50 *181*

MARK (MK.)

Mk. 1:9-11, 6:1-3 *171*

Mk. 3:6, 14:1 *177*

Mk. 3:19b-21 *102*

Mk. 6:2 *95*

Mk. 6:3 *102*

Mk. 8:34 *218*

Mk. 8:34-37 *216*

Mk. 8:34-38 *153*

Mk. 9:1 *200*

Mk. 9:32 *178*

Mk. 10:18 *116*

Mk. 10:23 *169*

Mk. 10:23-27 *173*

Mk. 10:24 *172*

Mk. 10:43 *92*

Mk. 12:29-31 *208*

Mk. 14:25 *178*

Mk. 15:34 *180, 194*

Mk. 15:35-36 *181*

Mk. 16:8 *188*

LUKE (LK.)

Lk. 1:26-38 *102*

Lk. 2:43, 46-47 *95*

Lk. 3:15 *170*

Lk. 9:45 *178*

Lk. 11:2-4 *128*

Lk. 12:13-21 *169*

Lk. 14:25-33 *169*

Lk. 15:24 *140*

Lk. 15:32 *141*

Lk. 16:19-31 *169*

Lk. 17:20-21 *200*

Lk. 18:19 *116*

Lk. 18:34 *178*

Lk. 22:2 *177*

Lk. 22:18 *178*

Lk. 23:42-43 *181*

Lk. 24:41-43 *270*

JOHN (JN.)

Jn. 1:1-4 *102*

Jn. 1:46 *161*

Jn. 11:53 *177*

Jn. 14:6 *5, 18*

Jn. 14:26 *201*

Jn. 20:26 *192*

ACTS (AC.)

Ac. 9:1-9 *274*

ROMANS (RM.)

Rm. 3:22-24 *8*

Rm. 5:12-21 *114*

Rm. 11:26 *154*

Rm. 11:32 *154*

ABOUT THE AUTHOR

Rev. Alexander Lang is a Presbyterian pastor in the northwest suburbs of Chicago. Known for his distinctive preaching style, Alex blends history, science, culture and scripture into spiritually relevant messages for his congregation. Alex's interests include independent film, electronic music (this book is best enjoyed while listening to atmospheric and progressive breaks) and deep conversation with people who question, doubt and want to dig into the most complex issues we face as humans. When he's not working on books, sermons or scripts, Alex enjoys spending time with his family by reading books aloud with his wife and playing crazy games invented by his two sons.

Printed in Great Britain
by Amazon